Essential Skills in Organic Modeling

T0143603

Essential Skills in Organic Modeling

NICHOLAS B. ZEMAN

CRC Press
Taylor & Francis Group
Boca Raton London New York

CRC Press is an imprint of the
Taylor & Francis Group, an **informa** business

AN A K PETERS BOOK

CRC Press
Taylor & Francis Group
6000 Broken Sound Parkway NW, Suite 300
Boca Raton, FL 33487-2742

© 2018 by Taylor & Francis Group, LLC
CRC Press is an imprint of Taylor & Francis Group, an Informa business

No claim to original U.S. Government works

Printed on acid-free paper

International Standard Book Number-13: 978-1-4987-5449-1 (Paperback)
978-1-138-50376-2 (Hardback)

Visit the Taylor & Francis Web site at
http://www.taylorandfrancis.com

and the CRC Press Web site at
http://www.crcpress.com

Printed and bound in the United States of America by
Edwards Brothers Malloy on sustainably sourced paper

Contents

Author

Professor Nicholas B. Zeman is a 16-year veteran of the game industry, first getting a job at Red Zone Interactive in 1998, which was purchased shortly after by SCEA, where he worked on several top-selling NFL titles pioneering rigging methods and facial animation in real-time environments. His next career move took him to TakeTwo Interactive at 2K Sports, where he continued his work as a character rigger and face animation specialist on such titles as *NBA 2K* and *MLB 2K*. He then left the industry to teach full time at Northern Kentucky University and pass on his knowledge by building a curriculum for aspiring game developers everywhere. He is now a learning designer and academic web developer for Saint Leo University, Tampa, Florida, where he has taken on a new venture to bring interactive learning and gamification to the next level for the purpose of modern education through dynamic technology.

Introduction

WHAT IS ORGANIC MODELING?

The term *organic modeling* can be difficult to interpret in terms of 3D geometry and content development. Why? Because the term itself has a double meaning. On the one hand, it can refer to the modeling of organic shapes, creatures, objects, and life-forms. On the other hand, it also refers to a technique or set of techniques used in modeling an object with 3D content development software. So when somebody uses the term *organic modeling*, they can be referring to either the type of object modeled or the technique used in modeling. It's possible, therefore, to model an organic shape in a nonorganic way, just as it is to model a nonorganic object in a totally organic method! Does this sound confusing? If it does, don't worry. You're not alone. The important thing is to know that this book is intended to teach you all about organic shapes and structures as well as organic modeling techniques. So you'll get the full spectrum of comprehensive and functional understanding of organic modeling in 3D. By the end of this book you should have a solid grasp on the fundamentals of organic shapes, structures, and forms as well as how to approach modeling them in a fast, easy, and flexible way! The function of this book is to demystify the top-level modeling techniques of difficult geometry and begin to crack the code of creating high-quality, efficient polygon structures in 3D that will be serviceable in any game engine or film.

WHAT QUALIFIES AS ORGANIC?

Organic is a pretty simple term to define when it comes to items or objects. The most important definition of an organic object is that it is alive, or was once a living creature (it could be fossilized or a seashell). What does that leave out? A lot of thing. Man-made items, such as a telephone, a building, or a computer monitor, would generally not be considered organic, because they were all created and built by a human.

They tend to have structures that are far different than organic items would have. This is not to say that a human can't create an organic structure; in fact many science fiction movies have used artists with highly "organic" styles of artwork (H.H. Giger is the most famous example; he designed the original creatures and set of *Alien* and creates eerie furniture and gigantic murals). Organic structures are generally natural, or derived from natural forms in some way (such as Giger's artwork). Not all natural forms are organic in terms of structure, however! The notable exceptions are things like crystals, which have a much more regular and angular structure than something we would consider "organic" (more on this later). Things like animals, plants, and single-celled organisms are all examples of what we would consider organic. There are certain features of organic life-forms in terms of structure that would qualify it as such.

1. Branching

2. Symmetry

3. Asymmetry

4. Curves

5. Mathematical relationships

These are features that are vital in recognizing the aspects of the organic shape we want to model, because they will in turn shape the techniques we use to create the geometry.

WHAT IS AN ORGANIC TECHNIQUE OF MODELING VERSUS A NONORGANIC TECHNIQUE?

It's an excellent question, and something we will strive to determine in the second half of this book. What constitutes an "organic" technique? What are the advantages and disadvantages of organic techniques versus nonorganic techniques? In this book, we will explore both organic and nonorganic methods of modeling similar objects so that we may understand what the advantages and disadvantages are of multiple approaches, as well as how the desired output will shape the technique the modeler will choose. Often there are multiple platforms and output necessities that drive a modeler's choice in the toolbox they use to create content, and those output needs are what determine how they approach the modeling task. Nonorganic modeling techniques are much more like planning and laying out a building as an architect than sculpting a piece of clay. Sometimes the topology of a character or creature must be carefully considered before construction, and sometimes the "sculpted version" can be used as a 3D guideline for the final result, which will be more useful when rigged and animated. There are several organic sculpting software packages out there, the most prominent being ZBrush and Mudbox (Autodesk), which allow the artist a wide range of 3D brush-like interfaces to sculpt a high-resolution model like a piece of clay. The pipelines for all of these techniques can be deconstructed and explained to the beginner modeler.

1. Curve-based modeling (Bezier and NURBS)

2. Procedural modeling with math

3. Fractals and branching geometry

4. Symmetrical modeling workflow

5. Standard organic structures

6. Edge-loop modeling

7. Radial edge looping

8. Surface sculpting tools

9. Global deformer-based modeling

WHAT WILL I LEARN IN THIS BOOK?

This book is designed to teach you the very basics of organic structures, organic shapes and how they operate in physical and mathematical terms, as well as how to approach modeling and exporting them for use in real-time applications or film/video. There will be ample exercises and step-by-step instructions with examples, and by the end of this book you should have a solid grasp on how to approach any organic model, from beginning to end. This book is *not* a step-by-step guide to modeling a human or humanoid creature in some specific software package. If you want something along those lines, there are literally hundreds of "How To Model a Human" books floating around, most of them very good step-by-step guides to modeling a human character, which is the bulk of most game-based characters.

This book, rather, is a comprehensive guide to the assessment, approach, and universal understanding of how shapes occur in nature and how to choose the best approach for creating them in 3D. In order to learn the basic tools of the organic modeler, you must first learn the basic structures of the organic creature, which will guide your work as a 3D modeler.

Organic structure, in terms of 3D modeling, is vital because most games and video content rely on moving, breathing, living creatures and characters to populate them. Many of these creatures are completely fantastical and don't exist anywhere in the real world! We can't really get detailed physical references and information about a character or creature that has no counterpart in the real, natural world. *Star Wars* has a litany of incredibly vivid and varied races of creatures, with alien physiology to match. Some are more or less bipedal humanoid, but some are extremely unique and fantastical. But if you look across the entirety of the franchise characters, they all seem to have certain common characteristics that match the organic structures in more mundane, Earth-based plants and animals. And that's the thing; you can always use the natural world we exist in to extrapolate what a new monster, creature, or alien character will look like and how it will be structured. So learning organic structures and modeling of things that already exist can give you an incredibly good grasp of how to create anatomical structures that don't exist. How do you make wings on a dragon? Well, you can look at the wings of birds, bats, dinosaurs, or insects to give you a good idea. You have natural structures to draw from that are easily recognizable. Using your knowledge of organic structures and organic modeling techniques can assist you in designing and creating anything you (or your concept artist) can imagine!

CHAPTER 1

Organic Structures

WHAT IS AN ORGANIC STRUCTURE?

As we learned in the Introduction, pinning down the definition of an organic structure can be tricky. There are multitudes of explanations of what it entails, from mathematical formulae to religious connotation. But ultimately, it's a subjective definition. Is something an organic shape? Are all natural (non–man-made) objects organic by nature? Are all man-made objects nonorganic? There are a lot of questions. Defining something as "organic" can be better understood by paying attention to things that are decidedly in the category of "totally nonorganic" or "very organic," so that we can find the middle area, where things get less decisive. So let's look below at a few basic objects and things that we might recognize as absolutely in one category or another.

An iPhone

This is definitely not an organic shape. It's very square with hard, angled edges, a shape that does not occur very commonly in most natural settings. So we can say this object is definitely nonorganic, and definitely man-made (Figure 1.1)!

A French Bulldog

Isn't this little guy cute? I picked the Frenchie because they have such rippled facial features and jowls, which appear to only have the evolutionarily successful trait of making them way too cute for anybody to be mad at them for long. But the folds in the flesh of the face are very curved, soft, and somewhat meandering. These vaguely random curves are very good

FIGURE 1.1   An iPhone is an example of a man-made, nonorganic object, which we can clearly recognize as such. (Courtesy of Wikimedia Commons World Super Cars, CC BY-SA 3.0, https://commons.wikimedia.org/w/index. php?curid=43505849.)

examples of geometry and shapes that would appear to be considered "organic" (Figure 1.2).

A Weeping Willow Tree

This is a great example of a fully organic structure. The tree has a main trunk, but with multiple, branching structures that hang with a downward growth pattern. This is a very organic structure because it's something we find prominent in all areas of living creatures and is indicative of progressive growth, which tends to exhibit a very specific set of mathematical formulae (Figure 1.3).

A Skyscraper

Another man-made object, this building is very square and smooth. It has curves, but the curves are subtle and only noticeable at closer distances. It resembles very little from the natural world, and the structure is ordered very neatly (Figure 1.4).

FIGURE 1.2 (See color insert.) A French bulldog has a complex, folded, and adorable face that we cannot ever mistake for something made by a human. (Courtesy of Flickr, CC BY 2.0, https://commons.wikimedia.org/w/index. php?curid=1923093)

FIGURE 1.3 Another non–human-made object, this living tree is immediately recognizable as an organic structure. (Courtesy of Magdalena Šajinovićová, CC BY-SA 3.0, https://commons.wikimedia.org/w/index.php?curid=22693292)

A Volkswagen

Here is a conundrum. The VW Beetle, both modern and vintage, is a very curve-heavy car. It's even named after a bug! The car has very organic shapes and curves, deliberately inspired by what we would find in nature. So although this is a machine, made by a factory of people, it was designed by someone trying to mimic the natural forms found in nature (specifically the insect world) (Figure 1.5).

FIGURE 1.4 Tall buildings and architectural structures have straight and angled lines that we always know are created by human means. (Courtesy of Mushashugyo—Louisville from the Belvedere, CC BY 2.0, https://commons.wikimedia.org/w/index.php?curid=6868591)

FIGURE 1.5 (See color insert.) The VW beetle is a great example of something created by man in order to resemble something already present in nature. For that reason it has some organic features. (Courtesy of Spurzem—Lothar Spurzem, CC BY-SA 2.0 de, https://commons.wikimedia.org/w/index.php?curid=8360265)

Quartz Crystal

Crystal structures represent the most angular and ordered natural structures known to man. All of the molecules and atoms of a crystal line up in an orderly fashion, creating amazingly sharp angles, edges, and geometrically symmetrical patterns. So although this is a natural object, we would consider it a nonorganic shape (Figure 1.6).

Out of all of these objects, the VW is the one that presents us with the biggest conundrum. Although it is man-made, it has a very organic shape. So there are many things that will fall into one category or another absolutely, there are many things that will be somewhere in the middle. This idea of the organic shape is much more than just being alive or not, or being made by nature or not; rather it's the way it is structured in three dimensions that really determines whether we can consider it "organic" or not.

All organic structures have commonalities. These commonalities are iterated through all forms of life on Earth, from microscopic bacteria to dinosaurs. These common structures and shapes are a vital tool for the

FIGURE 1.6 A quartz crystal is an example of an angular structure in nature, which is organic but has elements that you could imagine were made by a human. (Courtesy of JJ Harrison, CC BY-SA 2.5, https://commons.wikimedia.org/w/index.php?curid=6023737)

organic modeler to unlock the ability to see, conceive, plan, and execute an organic model of any kind. These basic structures will present themselves again and again, in every aspect of the living world. Some of them, like the golden ratio spiral of a nautilus shell, are beautifully mysterious. Some of these structures, such as the simple tapered tube of a blood vessel, are highly functional for their specific purpose.

1. *The curve*: All organic structures are built upon simple curves. A curve will determine the shape of everything in an organism, both minor and major. Understanding the basics of the parabolic and hyperbolic curve is almost absolutely essential in becoming a successful organic modeler. In 3D modeling content creation packages, there are multiple tools to generate and edit curves for the purpose of generating geometry.

    a. *Two-point arc*: Two Bezier points, at either end of the curve, with the lengths and angles of the handle creating the weight and the angle of the curve. This simple representation can be seen to underlie almost every single organic shape known to man (including himself).

    b. *Spirals*: Spirals are an extended and specialized form of arc curve, in which the angle of the curve path increments exponentially or logarithmically as it grows, resulting in the swirl shape that we are so familiar with through organic structure such as goat horns, flowers, tornadoes, and certain types of sea creature, like the nautilus.

    c. *Circle/ellipse*: The representation of the never-ending curve, which connects the end to the beginning.

    d. *Horseshoe*: An upside-down U with wings, this is the shape that the vertebrae have taken and therefore has relevance to every single animal with a spine that exists.

2. *Tapered tubes*: Tubes are circular structures that taper in diameter from base to end. The shape of the curve and the path can vary wildly (and even animate or undulate). They are almost universal in organic structures of all species.

3. *Growth*: Most organic things and objects that aren't man-made will exhibit growth patterns. They will have larger and larger layers of some kind extending in a pattern, like a seashell or a coral reef.

4. *Branching*: Branching geometry, whether it be a tree or the fingers of your hand, is a hallmark of organic shapes. Branching is often a form of growth that creates self-similar appendages from bigger appendages, such as a tree.

5. *Folds*: Organic objects often have folds (just like our squishy Frenchie in Figure 1.2). These folds often appear wavy or rippled with random variations.

6. *Segmentation*: Found in both the plant and animal world, segmentation is a way to create more complex forms from simpler ones. Independent, self-similar segments are very common in the forms of animals such as worms, in which each segment can grow into the entire animal over again. Insects and crustaceans commonly have segmentation as a form of structure caused by repetitive growth, much like the branching patterns previously mentioned.

7. *Bulbous shapes*: The shape of a pear, apple, womb, and bladder all have similarities that can be easily seen at first glance. These bulbous shapes, including the one of your own head, are found everywhere in nature. Circular, round, and sometimes even uneven, they are one of the recurring shapes that nature uses to create its many forms. Often you will see these forms in the process or use of procreation and reproduction, from the baby in the mother's womb to a ripe piece of fruit.

8. *Ridges and hard edges*: Ridges are formed in regular growth patterns in both plant and animal structures. These ridges, like the plates of a mollusk, are quite common in the natural organic structure of plants and animals.

9. *Radial*: Many plants and some primitive types of animals, like the sea urchin or starfish, have limbs or appendages extruding from a central core in a radial manner. This radial geometry can be seen in many plant forms, such as the center of a sunflower.

10. *Regularity and symmetry*: Symmetry is a feature of both organic and nonorganic shapes. There is often symmetry in branching (like our own bodies) or asymmetry in organ structure. Symmetry does not make an organic shape, but most organic objects display some symmetry of a kind. Inorganic objects can have built-in geometrical

symmetry (like a cube or a pyramid) or be entirely asymmetrical. Symmetry is more often seen in higher level complex animals with fixed structures, like an insect with six limbs and two wings, equal on both sides, or even our own species, with two arms and five fingers on each hand.

Curved Shapes

Organic shapes generally have curved structures. The curves can present themselves in varying patterns, but most often they will be logarithmic or exponential in more than one dimension. That is to say, the *amount* of curvature will increase or decrease in degree as the curve reaches the end. The level of curvature will rarely be even all the way through. Look at the two examples in Figures 1.5 and 1.6. Figure 1.6 shows a traffic cone, like the ones we all see every day driving to work. The curve of the cone is a tapered shape, but the taper is very even. The amount of taper stays the same from beginning to end, providing a nice, even appearance. In Figure 1.6, you can see a goat's horn. Notice that the shape is not so different from a traffic cone. It tapers from top to bottom. The goat horn, however, has an exponential taper. It tapers *more* as it goes from the base to the tip. Therefore it has a sloping appearance and not a conical one. This sloping, exponential growth structure is very prominent and common in organic structures and is absolutely necessary to getting the shape correct, whether you're modeling a goat or some devil-like creature with horns on his head! Without understanding the curvature of the horn, you wouldn't be able to model it properly.

Two-Point Arc

The simple two-point arc curve illustrated in Figure 1.7 uses two Bezier handles, a mathematical method of defining a curve with single points. A simple, two-point Bezier curve is a staple element of a modeler's toolset. The arc of this curve will be seen across the wide spectrum of organic structures.

The Spiral

The spiral can be even, as in Figure 1.8, or logarithmic/exponential, as in Figure 1.9. There are plenty of spirals in organic structures, especially mollusks and flowering plants (Figure 1.10)!

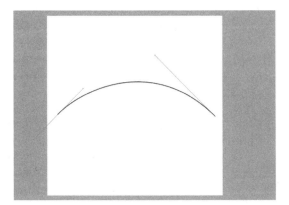

FIGURE 1.7   The simple ellipse or curve, here constructed with two Bezier points. This curve can be used to define almost anything organic. You will see it repeated over and over.

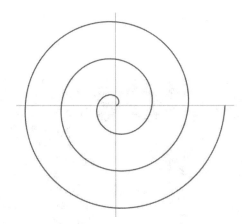

FIGURE 1.8   The traditional, evenly spaced, spiral. (Courtesy of AdiJapan, CC BY-SA 2.5, https://commons.wikimedia.org/w/index.php?curid=849746)

The Ellipse

An ellipse is a circle, but not necessarily perfectly round. It has so many examples in nature that it would be hard to list them all! The curvature of many naturally occurring objects requires a circular or elliptical shape that should be easy to recognize—the curvature of the ribcage or hipbone, for example, of a wooly mammoth, as seen in Figure 1.11. The ellipse in vertebrates is often found in the cross-section shape of their bodies.

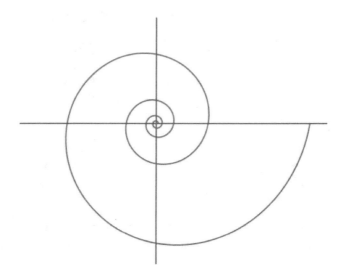

FIGURE 1.9 The exponential, or Fibonacci, spiral. (Courtesy of Leafnode, https://commons.wikimedia.org/w/index.php?curid=3995383)

FIGURE 1.10 (See color insert.) A snail shell, an example of growth through a spiral. (Courtesy of H. Zell, CC BY-SA 3.0, https://commons.wikimedia.org/w/index.php?curid=24621809)

FIGURE 1.11 (See color insert.)   Multiple examples of our elliptical curve across a single skeleton. (Courtesy of Colts12871, CC BY-SA 3.0, https://commons. wikimedia.org/w/index.php?curid=33843793)

The Horseshoe

This outline shape is nearly universal among animals with a backbone and mostly absent in those that do not (Figures 1.12 and 1.13). It's important, however, because it clearly defines the entire length of the body with its structure, which is definitively horseshoe-shaped. As you will see when we begin to model the vertebrates in Chapter 7, the length of the spine is one of the most important vectors to the initialization of the structure.

Tapered Tubes

Tubes are very common organic structures. But they can also be very common nonorganic structures, like in packaging materials or pipes. Although piping has a round shape, man-made pipes (by their design) always have straight and even curves. A lot of plants, fungi, and other organisms have tubelike structures, which are incredibly convenient for pumping action, holding water, or drawing up nutrients from the soil. Our own bodies rely heavily on tubes for pumping fluids like blood, bile, and nutrients from food. You could say that the tube is the primary

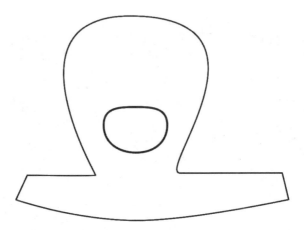

FIGURE 1.12 This is a horseshoe shape, which is extant in the spinal columns of all vertebrates.

FIGURE 1.13 A whale vertebrae with the horseshoe shape. (Courtesy of Gailhampshire from Cradley, Malvern, U.K., CC BY 2.0, https://commons. wikimedia.org/w/index.php?curid=49993421)

source of movement for life! Therefore, it's obvious that we would create man-made tubes for the same purpose (it's just a matter of physics). The difference would be that if we wanted to model a system of piping for an industrial environment for a game (like, say, *BioShock*), we would use a much different methodology than if we were modeling the ventricles of a heart muscle. One of the things about tubing that is very indicative of the nonorganic is the *regularity* of the structure. The more regular and identical one piece of the tube is to another, the more likely we are to say that it's not an organic structure and therefore we can find a normalized, or regulated, method of creating the geometry (Figures 1.14 through 1.16).

Growth

Growth patterns are a prominent feature of almost all complex life. As the life-form grows, it changes. It gets bigger. It grows layers, channels, and chambers. It branches into more, smaller versions of itself. The traces of growth patterns are usually a good way to indicate that some form of organic pattern is emerging. Some life-forms, such as plants, show evidence of growth because the old growth is still there, like the trunk of a tree. The new growth branches off of the original, but leaving it to grow as well. So you have the main trunk of a tree (Figure 1.3), with more and more branches, which in turn branch (more on this later). Seashells, crustaceans, and mollusks present growth patterns as well, with very dramatic

FIGURE 1.14 Roots of a tree curling around one another. (Courtesy of Roots.jpg: Bill, CC BY-SA 3.0, https://commons.wikimedia.org/w/index.php?curid=16234108)

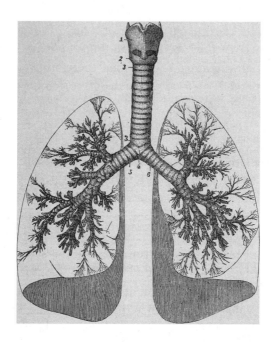

FIGURE 1.15   Bronchial tubes, similar in structure to a tree branching; these tubes taper from larger to smaller. (Courtesy of Internet Archive Book Images, https://archive.org/stream/anatomyphysiolog00walk/anatomyphysiolog00walk#page/n242/mode/1up)

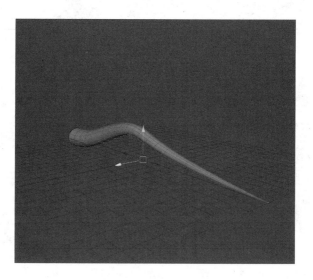

FIGURE 1.16   A simple 3D tapered tube, which is a fundamental structure in natural objects.

and beautiful curvature. The nautilus shell, thought to be one of the most intricate of seashells, is a classic example of intricate organic geometry at work through growth patterns. The nautilus creature secretes chitin to build a chambered shell outward in a spiral pattern as it grows (see Figure 1.8), making each chamber successively larger as the soft-tissued creature in the shell grows larger. The interesting aspect of this outward growth is the tendency to create mathematically reproducible formulae in regard to the dimensions of the chambers. This is very nice for 3D modelers, who can use procedural modeling techniques to build the geometry. Growth patterns are great because they generally allow the artist to reproduce the shapes in a procedural manner, which is basically using math to model. This is what we would refer to as a *nonorganic method of modeling*, but it is a great way to model organic shapes that are constructed with regular growth patterns. Here would be a great example of a place where an organic modeling technique would be less effective than another, more mathematical method.

Branching, of course, is a form of growth pattern but it differs in higher-level organisms because it has a set pattern of growth in the sense that the number and permanence of the branches are fixed. Growth patterns like the one depicted in Figure 1.17 continue until the animal's death,

FIGURE 1.17   A nautilus shell, illustrating once again the growth pattern of spirals. (Courtesy of Chris 73/Wikimedia Commons, CC BY-SA 3.0, https://commons. wikimedia.org/w/index.php?curid=19711)

getting larger each time. The nautilus shell depicted in Figure 1.17 has a spiral growth pattern, exhibiting a nearly perfect example of the golden ratio of phi, or 1.618.

Branching

Branching, or the extrusion of limbs and organs, is a foundational hallmark of all life-forms (with the exception of some microorganisms like the amoeba). A branch consists of a trunk, or base object, with smaller objects sticking out from it. Your fingers and toes are great examples of branching. You have five fingers, sticking out of your handlike structure. A spider has six appendages, sticking out of its torso. A tree has multiple branches, which in turn branch as it grows, displaying both a growth pattern and a type of mathematical relationship known as a *fractal*. All of these things are related to living structures because they are both types of growth patterns and appendages, which are near-universal in the formations of life and organic structures.

Appendages are incredibly important structures for multiple reasons (and we will be spending a lot of time on their structure and architecture in both biological and geometric perspectives). Appendages are an essential function of locomotion and manipulation of the environment, such as grabbing food or bringing it to your mouth to consume. You can look down at your hand and see a very well-structured branching geometry that allows for complex manipulation of the environment through a beautifully constructed series of bendable joints and hierarchical relationships.

Branching can occur in three organic forms: self-replicating, radial, and bilateral. *Self-replicating* is when each branch comes off of the object as an exact duplicate of its parents, however with a slightly smaller and tapering scale. We see this all the time in trees and plants, where each branch extends from a larger branch, and it contains the exact same structure as the parent limb, until it terminates in a leaf. There is usually not total symmetry to this branching, but there is a pattern. *Radial branching* is done in a circular pattern, and we can see perfect examples of this in the microscopic world (where it is most prevalent) as well as the macroscopic world in cephalopods such as an octopus. The radial nature of the branching creates branches in a circular pattern around a central hub. *Bilateral branching* is what we possess, where the branches are not duplicates of the parents, but they match on opposite sides of a central axis (depending on the direction of the spine) (Figures 1.18 through 1.21).

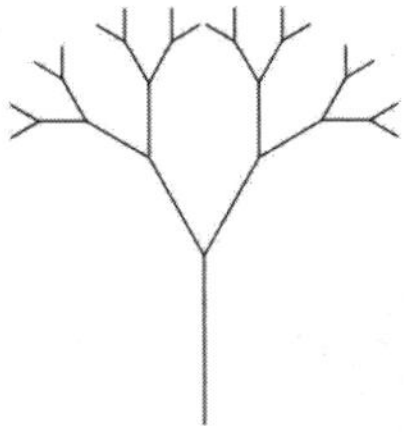

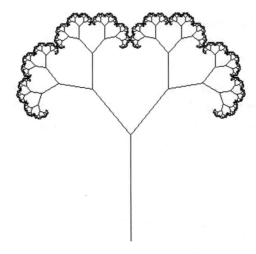

FIGURE 1.18 A simple, self-replicating branching pattern.

FIGURE 1.19 The same pattern as Figure 1.18 but now with multiple iterations.

FIGURE 1.20 A more plant-like branching pattern, in which the branches alternate and only some sprout subbranches.

FIGURE 1.21   An example of radial branching.

Folds

Folds are a key part of organic structures because they occur so frequently in nature and with some level of complex mathematics that is still being researched today by biologists. The structure of a fold is seemingly random, like the lip of the clam in Figure 1.12. If you look back at Figure 1.2 of our Frenchie, you can clearly see the natural folds in the jowls vaguely resemble the same structures in the clam lips. Humans have folds in various places, including the internal organs (most prominently the large intestines). Folds occur frequently in the plant world, in the edges of flowers and the internal structures of seed pods. Insect often employ complex folds for wing structures and cocoons. The butterfly emerging from a cocoon in Figure 1.13 has an incredibly complexly folded body when compressed into the cocoon, which rapidly unfurls to reveal the entire wing structure like a piece of origami.

Figures 1.22 and 1.23 show a great example of folding patterns on the lip of a giant clam shell. The folds are wavy, sine-curve structures that, if broken apart, end up being representative of our simple arc! These ripples, or folding structures, can be found in the natural world in many places. These "rippling" structures have an element of randomness that is just as common as symmetry in organic shapes! The intestines in your own body exhibit these irregular features that happen with regularity (Figure 1.24).

Segmentation

Segmentation can happen in many forms. In some organisms, such as a tapeworm or flatworm, each segment is a perfect replica of the previous one, with the exception of the head. This allows the creature to grow as

FIGURE 1.22   Ripples in the giant clam lips. (Courtesy of Nhobgood Nick Hobgood, CC BY-SA 3.0, https://commons.wikimedia.org/w/index.php?curid=5633926)

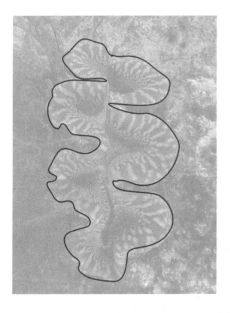

FIGURE 1.23   The rippled curve revealed in the outer rim of the giant clam.

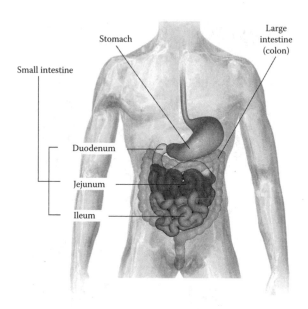

FIGURE 1.24   Intestines in the human body exhibit the same rippling, folding pattern. (Courtesy of BruceBlaus, CC BY-SA 4.0, https://commons.wikimedia.org/wiki/File:Blausen_0817_SmallIntestine_Anatomy.png)

big as it wants for as long as it wants and assists in replication and reproduction by allowing the segments to grow into full replicas of the parent creature using asexual reproduction (Figure 1.25).

Another form of segmentation is found in the exoskeleton of an arachnid or insect class, in which each part of the body is like an armored segment, slightly overlapping the preceding section. These hard, overlapping segments provide mobility and protection for the softer organs underneath. The muscles of the creature flex and pull the segments together or push them apart, creating the ambulatory action of the creature.

Spherical and Ovoid Shapes

Ovoid shapes are interesting natural structures because they are often seen in reproductive parts of the organism, as well as areas that need to contain a large volume of space. You can divide this category into a few subcategories that have individual characteristics.

Ovoid

Ovoid shapes, like eggs, are 3D representations of an ellipse. You will see this in eggs, fruits, and internal organ structures.

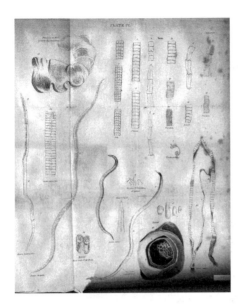

FIGURE 1.25 A tapeworm, with a classically segmented form. (Courtesy of William Miller, https://commons.wikimedia.org/w/index.php?curid=2129982)

Spherical

Many fish eggs and fruits (such as grapes, berries, etc.) have this perfect spherical shape.

Bulbous

Bulbous shapes are often the intersection of two spheres, or an ovoid and a sphere. Often things that need to contain a volume of fluid or soft organs, like the brain, are shaped in a bulbous manner. This shape includes the skull and many fruits.

Bolus

A bolus is a tube slightly pinched at the ends and is often the result of organic material being shaped by the tube in which it is being processed (like the intestines); this is actually a very common structure seen in waste or feces (Figures 1.26 and 1.27).

Bulbous shapes can be subdivided.

Angles, Ridges, and Hard Edges

One feature that is noticeably lacking in most organic shapes is the hard angle. In living biology, there are very few hard, right-angular shapes.

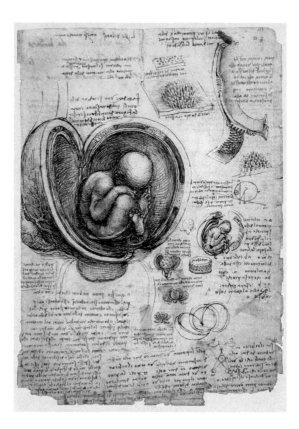

FIGURE 1.26   Ovoid, bulbous, and spherical shapes as they appear in the human womb. Notice the similarity here to the pear or melon. (Courtesy of Wikimedia Commons, https://commons.wikimedia.org/w/index.php?curid=1724977)

FIGURE 1.27   Pears and apples, which are of similar shape to the animal womb. (Courtesy of Rhododendrites, CC BY-SA 4.0, https://commons.wikimedia.org/w/index.php?curid=54290715)

Consider the picture of a simple box from a packing company in Figure 1.9. It has multiple surfaces, but it has very regular, hard angles. Those angles should make you feel it is not an organic structure which *grew* that way but a man-made item which was *constructed* that way. The same would go for a picture of the Great Pyramid of Giza! The pyramid is a regular, symmetrical, hard-angled object. There is very little doubt that this object was constructed and not grown. Angles can exist in nature, most often in the form of minerals, crystals, and erosion features in topography and geology. Also, organic creatures can often produce hard angles in their construction. If anybody is familiar with the shapes of the spider's web, as in Figure 1.11, you can appreciate the regularity and hard angles produced by the spider as it builds a web. So there are hard angles, but interestingly enough those hard angles are structured in a somewhat "rounded" or radial pattern. Radial edge looping, which will be covered later, is an absolutely essential part of modeling organic shapes properly!

Most of the structures we see as heavily angled can be approached in a nonorganic manner of modeling, so it's important to identify that which can be constructed with angled geometry. It's far easier and quicker to put together a series of straight lines and convert these into structural geometry than it is to construct them with organic methods. Therefore, the identification of when to use these nonorganic modeling techniques is a particularly important aspect of modeling.

But if only it were that easy! We *do* have several instances in which ridges, or hard-angled edges, are found in nature. Generally, when two curves that make up the structure of some organic shape come together at a sharp angle, they will form a ridge. This creates quite a thin, sharp surface, which is why fish are hard to keep hold of (if you've ever tried to take a fish off of a line, you can easily slash your hand on its dorsal ridge as it thrashes around), plants can cause scratches, and your cat's claws tear up the furniture! Hard ridges are all over nature, hiding in the most obvious of places. In fact, right now you have them all over your own organic structure in your teeth and nails (Figure 1.28).

The basic shape of an organically produced wedge forms a ridge. This could be from a crab claw, a fish spine, or your canine incisor tooth! When two curves come together at a sharp angle, it will form a sharp ridge (Figure 1.29).

Hard substances are generally what form ridges and ridge shapes in organic structures; therefore, you will see a lot more of them in animals that are protected by a shell or have an exoskeleton. Insects, crustaceans,

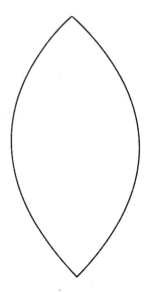

FIGURE 1.28   A seed, claw, or other ridged, angular edge. This shape appears all over nature and is just two ellipse curves joined together.

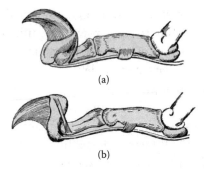

(a)

(b)

FIGURE 1.29   The wedge shape of the bird talon, both in (a) and (b) above, is just like the edge of a seed (but sharper and harder). (Courtesy of Wikimedia Commons, https://commons.wikimedia.org/w/index.php?curid=26051707)

and mollusks all have spiny protrusions that have ridges inherent in the geometry. The hard material, such as chitin, works well for creating hard ridges because it provides the necessary structure to maintain a hard edge (Figures 1.30 and 1.31).

Radial

Radial structures are structures and shapes that occur in a circle. Some entire organisms are radial, while others are muscular structures that are constructed in a radial manner. The eye and mouth muscles of any mammal are a great example of radial structure in the natural world. The rounding allows the eyeball great control and flexibility, something that a creature would need to make quick changes in its perspective and see in a greater range for the purpose of hunting. Plants have highly

FIGURE 1.30 The spiny crab, with extrusions that exhibit the wedge shape. (Courtesy of Neal Ziring, http://www.public-domain-image.com/public-domain-images-pictures-free-stock-photos/fauna-animals-public-domain-images-pictures/crabs-and-lobsters-public-domain-images-pictures/spiny-crab.jpg)

(a)

FIGURE 1.31 (a) Ridges in a simple seashell bivalve. (Courtesy of The Photographer, CC0, https://commons.wikimedia.org/w/index.php?curid=24418151) *(Continued)*

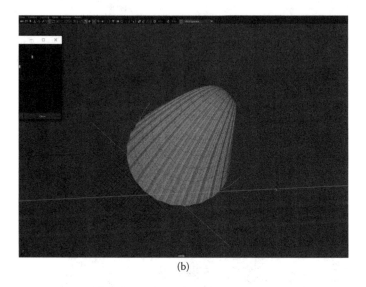

(b)

FIGURE 1.31 (Continued) (b) A 3D representation of ridged geometry.

radial structures evident in their flowers and fruits, as you can see in the magnolia flower in Figure 1.32.

Radial geometry is a staple for generating eye sockets and primate-like mouths, and it is a very tricky thing to set up properly in 3D geometry.

FIGURE 1.32 (See color insert.) Radial floral structure of a magnolia flower. Note the petals with the cup (half-bulbous) shape surrounding the central bolus of the stamen. (Courtesy of Derek Ramsey (Ram-Man), CC BY-SA 3.0, https://commons.wikimedia.org/w/index.php?curid=11814157)

Regularity and Symmetry

In the natural world, symmetry and regularity are just as common as non-regularity and asymmetry! It's more complex than just *being* symmetrical or nonsymmetrical, or having the appearance of regularity. It's more about the method of regularity and growth pattern mathematics, or the type of symmetry. For instance, if we look at an outline of the human body, such as in Figure 1.12, we can see complete symmetry of the structure. We have two hands, two legs, two eyes, and our body can be split down the middle, resulting in two equal halves! This is called *bilateral symmetry.* So you would assume that we are completely symmetrical, correct? On the outside, this may be true, but our internal organs are all over the place! Look at the inside schematic of the human body in Figure 1.13. You can clearly see that our internal organs are in asymmetrical parts of our body, squeezed into the frame, which is technically bilaterally symmetrical. So if you cut us in half, we really aren't bilaterally symmetrical. The outside and the skeleton, however, are symmetrical.

Taking this same idea into account, we can also look at the regularity of a structure. This is a feature we can see prominently with growth patterns. An organic object, plant or animal, has a clear set of patterns when growing or building new structures. Defining or deriving that natural growth pattern is a delicate mathematical procedure, still subject to some amount of mystery. Let's take our weeping willow, from Figure 1.3. It has a growth pattern, in that it creates new branches, which in turn grow new subbranches. This is a very important type of math, which is often used in computer graphics, known as *fractal* equations, which involve branching features of geometry. You can construct an entire piece of geometry using fractal calculations to create geometric features, and indeed it is most often used for the procedural creation of plants in scenery for games and film. Most game development solutions and content creation software packages come with a landscape designer and tree creator that uses fractal-based equations to produce branching geometry based on input parameters, rather than hand-model every branch.

In Figure 1.33, we can clearly see the vertebrate symmetry that is symmetrical along the length of the spine with equal geometry on either side. As a modeler we can leverage this phenomenon by using symmetrical modeling techniques, speeding up the process of modeling a creature by only working on half of the structure at once while mirroring the other half automatically (see Chapter 4, "Organic Modeling Techniques") (Figure 1.34).

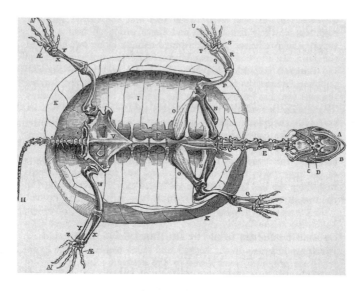

FIGURE 1.33 Bilateral symmetry in a biped—a feature that is universal in vertebrates. (Courtesy of Internet Archive Book Images, https://archive.org/stream/b20416039_001/b20416039_001#page/n105/mode/1up)

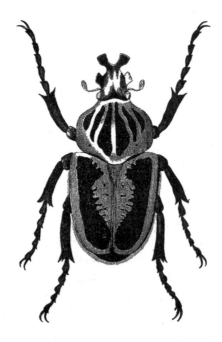

FIGURE 1.34 More bilateral symmetry, which is also near-universal in the invertebrates! (Courtesy of Encyclopedia Britannica, https://commons.wikimedia.org/w/index.php?curid=5939861)

FIGURE 1.35 Bilateral symmetry in the plant world! Plants have bilateral areas and nonbilateral areas. (Courtesy of Flickr, CC BY 2.0, https://commons.wikimedia.org/w/index.php?curid=1123806)

Plants can exhibit symmetry in some places and not others. For instance, the palm frond exhibits symmetry along the central shaft, where the leaves branch off of the central stem, as you can see in Figure 1.35. The tree itself, however, does not have perfect symmetry in its growth. So the structures of symmetry and regularity can exist in different patterns and in different combinations.

CONCLUSION

By learning these vital structures and shapes as they appear in the natural world repetitively, the 3D modeler can create a mental library of forms and learn to combine them or construct them. 3D organic modeling is a skill set that requires both an artistic eye and technical expertise, which when combined with a solid knowledge of basic anatomy can make them versatile and able to construct anything alive that vaguely resembles organic life-forms as we know them. Many games and films require fantastical creatures or beasts to walk and talk as if they were real, and now more than ever there is both an interest and a market for high-quality organic modeling. Becoming a good organic modeler requires physiology, creativity, and efficient engineering. The structures presented here can be built in certain ways (which you will learn in Chapters 5 through 7 in the second half of this book) that will work for the endeavor of breathing life into them through skinning, deformation, and rigging.

Learning how to see the similarities in all organic shapes and forms will make it easier and more efficient to model them, because you will be able to draw upon a robust, internal library of techniques and methods for building those shapes. If somebody wants you to model a dragon that only has four limbs (meaning the arms are the wings) for an upcoming game title, you can use all of your structural knowledge of anatomy and physiology to study and build a seamless, polygonal mesh that is both efficient and suited for rigging and modeling, based upon the common anatomical structures of the creatures it most resembles.

Although these are the most common structures in nature that I have been able to identify, they certainly aren't the only ones! I highly suggest going on a walk outside and really examining everything in the natural world that you can see. Make careful note of the shapes in 3D and how they form repetitive patterns. See if you can relate one shape to another, and you will eventually find that the shapes in nature are very often constructed of smaller structures that mirror the bigger ones and vice versa. The more complex life-forms often have multiple hierarchies of structures that can be separated into the basic structures outlined in this chapter.

CHAPTER 2

Plant Physiology and Construction

INTRODUCTION

Let us first consider the plant world, since it is possessed of a very wide range of shapes and structures that are intended for passive use—that is to say that they do not directly move in any way. Plants are far from stationary, however; it's just that they do not move without some external stimuli (the sun or nutrients in the soil), and most of their movement is strictly through growth patterns or indirect chemical reactions, such as the leaves turning to catch the sunlight.

What is the purpose of the organic structure of the plant? This is a really good question, because we can begin to see how the intention of the structure is pertinent to our construction of it as a model. Plants have structures that are deliberately designed to function as their intended purpose. That purpose is to draw nutrients and water from the soil (root structures), to gather light from the sun (leaves), and then reproduce in an asexual or sexual manner, which involves the creation of structures like flowers for attracting bees, fruits for attracting herbivores, or seeds for scattering into the local area. Figure 2.1 shows a flowering magnolia tree, which possesses every common plantlike structure for us to deconstruct and analyze.

FIGURE 2.1 A flowering magnolia tree. (Courtesy of maz84, CC BY-SA 2.5, https://commons.wikimedia.org/w/index.php?curid=1893571)

ROOTS

The roots of the tree (Figure 2.2) are curve-based growth patterns, displaying the distal taper with irregularities of growth (which was influenced by external stimuli) and the regularity of the taper. So there are examples here of both regularity and irregularity. Regularity is demonstrated by the constant value of the taper as the root grows from the tree base to the tip. You will see this pattern repeat itself in many organic objects, because it is a result of growth. The tree root, trunk, and branch, from sapling to fully grown adult, slowly expands its circumference year after year as it grows, which leaves the oldest part of the tree the thickest (or widest in circumference) and the youngest part of the tree the thinnest. Although the change in external conditions year after year can have significant effect on the root shape, the constant of time allows for some regularity to be determined and recreated in 3D modeling.

Depending on the type of tree, the roots can create branches and sub-branching structures of their own. Roots will almost universally be more chaotic and crooked than the upward branches, due to the fact that the

FIGURE 2.2 (See color insert.) Growth causes random or seemingly random shapes to occur in the downward-growing roots of this tree. The shapes are developed over many years by multiple factors. (Courtesy of Wikimedia Commons, CC BY-SA 3.0, https://commons.wikimedia.org/w/index.php?curid=127103)

stimuli that drives their growth doesn't come from directly overhead, like the sun! So instead of reaching upward they burrow downward into the ground, creating a strong support network for the tree and seeking chemical nutrients from the soil. The good news is that, since they are mostly hidden, you won't often have to model them in any great detail. But if you are called to do this, they are simply crooked paths with tapered tubes extruded along them. One aspect of roots that is noticeably absent from the trunk branches is the possibility that they could grow together, creating large lumpy shapes like the one in Figure 2.2. In this case, modeling them becomes much more difficult because you have to create a method to merge shapes together. Merging geometry together in a "blobby" manner is a trick that is usually relegated to "metaballs," or geometry that melts together based upon proximity. There are several metaballs and squishy geometry plugins out there for most 3D content-creation software to choose from.

BRANCHES

Branching structures, as described in Chapter 1, are places where a main structure has one or more extruding structures emerging from it. The structure of branching is one of the most universal, prominent, and common organic forms. From yeast cultures to trees to the human circulatory system, the branching structure can be seen through a myriad of examples in the organic world.

The structure of branching can be placed into two categories, *lateral* (or axillary) and *dichotomous*. They sound like fancy terms, but they accurately describe the two main ways a branch can occur, based upon the pattern structure.

Dichotomous Branching

Dichotomous branching occurs when the main shoot branches out to two or more branches but ceases to maintain itself. This is much more common in simpler plant structures such as lichens, mosses, grasses, and similar plants. The termination of the original shoot occurs when the branching happens. There are three kinds of dichotomous branching patterns:

1. *Isotomous*: The branches are similar lengths and angles (Figure 2.3).

2. *Anisotomous*: The branches are unequal size and the branching angle is slightly away from the primary angle of growth (Figure 2.4).

3. *Pseudomonopodial*: The branches are different lengths and one of them can take on the primary angle of growth, making it appear like a monopodial branching pattern (Figure 2.5).

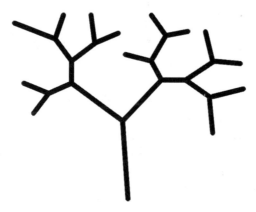

FIGURE 2.3   Isotomous branching example.

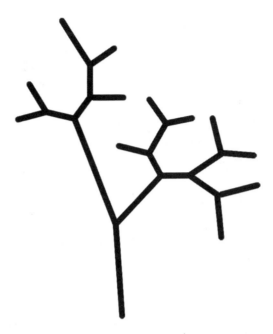

FIGURE 2.4   Anisotomous branching.

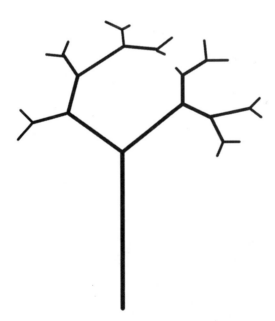

FIGURE 2.5   Pseudomonopodial branching, where a secondary branching is growing upward at an angle similar to the primary branch.

Lateral/Axillary Branching

This is how trees and treelike plants branch, and so it includes many more of the branching patterns we are familiar with. Lateral branching is where the main branch continues to grow, while branches extend from it with some regularity as it grows.

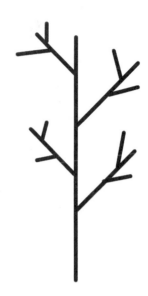

1. *Monopodial/racemose branching*: This is where the main branch continues to grow indefinitely upward, continuing to sprout branches from its base, somewhere above the previous branches. Some monopodial tree types are pines and redwoods, which grow very tall and have regularly sprouting branches as they grow (Figure 2.6).

FIGURE 2.6 Monopodial branching, where a single stem continues to grow and branch at upward angles.

2. *Cymose branching*: Less common than the monopodial in trees, cymose branching is when the main branch stops growing but the lateral branches continue to grow and branch. Oak trees are actually cymose plants, because the primary trunk node splits off into multiple branches, which continue to grow longer and thicker, sometimes competing in weight and dimension. This is actually why it's often necessary to trim these branches from the oak tree for landscaping, or they may crack and fall off as the tree struggles to find equilibrium.

   a. *Scorpioid cymose*: This is where the lateral branches zigzag, creating an elevation in height based on the structure of the branching and not the continuing height of the main branch. Grape leaves follow this pattern (Figure 2.7).

FIGURE 2.7 Scorpioid cymose, where the branching zigzags.

b. *Helioid cymose*: Helioid branching is similar to scorpioid, with the exception that all the lateral branching occurs on one side, making a spiral pattern (Figure 2.8).

c. *Biparous cyme*: Almost the same as dichotomous branching, the biparous cyme sprouts multiple branches at every branch, but not at the termination point, as the branch continues until termination at the end (ostensibly at a flower or fruit) (Figure 2.9).

FIGURE 2.8 Helioid cymose, where all branching happens on a single side, giving it a spiral curl.

Branching, no matter what form it takes, always occurs in a hierarchy. The main, or *parent branch*, splits off into multiple *child branches*. Each child branch in turn branches off again into more child branches. This occurs for a set order of iterations, and the branches finally terminate in leaves, fruit/seed, or flowers. Depending on the plant species, this could be three to seven iterations. Those branching iterations follow several pattern types, often being determined by the species and the conditions of growth, such as climate and temperature. The next time you walk outside, take a look at the trees and foliage around you to see how the various plants fall into this morphology. I'm willing to bet you'll see a variety of patterns, and by recognizing the differences you will also be able to start identify trees from the same species! They all have very unique morphology between common species.

LEAVES

The leaf of the magnolia tree (Figure 2.10) is a parabolic curve. It is symmetrical in shape, having the same curvature on either side (more or less),

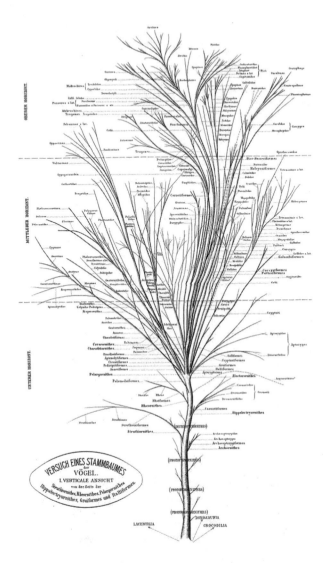

FIGURE 2.9 An example of biparous branching, with multiple branching from a single stem. (Courtesy of Max Fürbringer, https://commons.wikimedia.org/w/index.php?curid=49269123)

with a spine in between, which is characterized by a distinct round taper, which in turn resembles the taper of the roots. Leaves grow much faster than the roots of the tree, which would account for a much more uniform shape, since there is less random external influence. That means if every root were completely symmetrical and evenly distributed, the plant would

FIGURE 2.10 (See color insert.)   The magnolia leaf, which is basically two elliptical curves in a bilateral configuration.

not look very "natural" to the eye! A bunch of completely regularly shaped leaves, however, would appear far less unnatural but still a little too "fake" for the human eye. Since a leaf grows, like all other parts of the tree, it too is subject to some outside factors. If you look at the side of the leaf, you will notice a slight "wavy" pattern. You should make the connection here between the folds of a clam's lip to the folds in this leaf! They are both indications of a certain "randomness" inside of an ordered structure. The central spine and subsequent miniature veins sprouting from this leaf also show a magnificent form of symmetry, and one that is noticeably lacking in the branching of the main trunk. Although there is some randomness in the branching of the trunk into the secondary branches, there's still a certain order in which they are placed (otherwise the tree would probably fall down).

Other leaf types can exhibit multiple branching forms. The lobed (oak) leaf, for example, in Figure 2.11, you can see a multiple branching struc-ture. The secondary ribs branch off from the main rib, which in turn has branched off from the branch. Each secondary rib has tertiary veins,

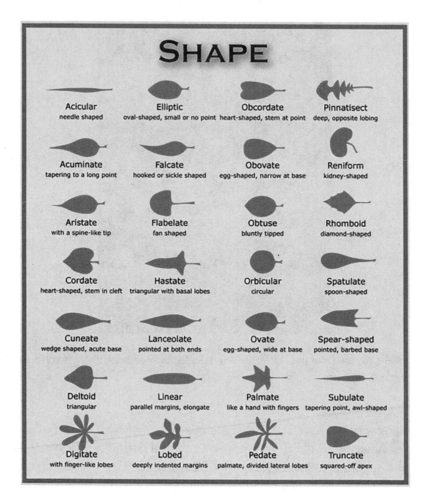

FIGURE 2.11 Multiple examples of leaf shapes.

which in turn branch out again to deliver water and nutrients to the entire surface of the leaf, as well as deliver energy to the rest of the plant through photosynthesis. There are far too many leaf shapes to go over individually, but they all present unique modeling challenges for the organic modeler. The basic method of generating leaf geometry is simple, however, and is based upon creating a half-curve shape, following the curvature of the leaf, then mirroring that curve and generating a loft between them. This loft creates a depthless, single-sided polygonal surface, which will be rendered in 3D. The leaf in real life is so thin that it essentially has no depth; there isn't enough of a thickness in the structure to require a

FIGURE 2.12 (See color insert.)   A 3D modeled version of the magnolia leaf.

full polygonal shell. Therefore we can easily pump out leaf shapes rather quickly, modeling them in two dimensions and then offsetting them slightly in order to generate the 3D appearance (Figure 2.12). The primary leaf vein can be modeled in 3D, or it could be simply a texture with a bump map, something that would vastly improve the efficiency of the scene if you intend to have full foliage!

FLOWERS

What else does a plant produce? The flower is perhaps one of the most complex and variable forms of plant expression in nature. The flower of the magnolia tree is a great example of a typical form (Figure 2.13). A flower uses folding geometry to unfurl itself as it opens, like a sail on a sailboat. The petals are usually a rounded curve, which radiate outward from a central disk in a circular pattern. These petals, when completely open, will form some kind of a cup shape with the plant's sexual organs extending from the central area, where the bright colors are hoping to attract insects in order to pollinate it with other plant's material (Figures 2.14 and 2.15).

Radial structures are a primary organic structure, and we can begin to see this in the flower of the plant. Although the petals themselves are a parabolic curve, they grow outward from the central node in a radial pattern. This is a recurring theme in organic structures, and along with the spiral it forms a key method of recreating them. Each branch, or petal,

FIGURE 2.13   A radial layout for floral structures.

FIGURE 2.14 (See color insert.)   Sunflower in the classic radial flower shape, although the seeds are grown in a spiral pattern. (Courtesy of Fir0002, GFDL 1.2, https://commons.wikimedia.org/w/index.php?curid=7613324)

FIGURE 2.15   A rose, which exhibits a perfect spiral in its petal arrangement. (Courtesy of M0tty, GFDL, https://commons.wikimedia.org/w/index.php? curid=36555673)

grows outward from the central core based on the vector of the curve, thus creating the circular pattern and appearance. Flowers come in multitudes of types, including spherical and spiral (a rose).

FRUITS

Fruits come in all shapes and sizes, but the primary shape of the fruit of the tree is very often a *bulbous* shape. A bulb, or bowl-like entity, has a narrow and a wide portion of the geometry, generally tapering at one end. The purpose of the fruit is to contain the seeds, and the fleshy part around the object is designed to be tasty, sweet, and colorful in order to attract animals to consume it, who will then spread the seeds through excrement or other means (like falling out of the fruit when being eaten by a bird or other animal). If you observe most common fruits of plants, they will almost universally have this bulbous, rounded, full shape, or an elongated version of it. It should be no surprise then that the human womb, the method for creating and nourishing new life, also conforms to this same shape (Figures 2.16 through 2.18).

The magnolia "fruit," which is somewhat pinecone-shaped, is a bolus that is the result of the flower closing (once pollinated), and then forming the outer sheath and internal seeds, which are bulbous shapes. You can see that the structure consists of multiple, smaller shell-like shapes which are made up of arc curves just like we learned in Chapter 1. The tiny hairs on the folded shells are once again tapered tubes, using that ubiquitous shape (Figure 2.19).

FIGURE 2.16 The bulbous apple shape, easily represented by an ellipse, lathed around a central axis. (Courtesy of Wikimedia Commons, CC BY-SA 3.0, https:// commons.wikimedia.org/w/index.php?curid=2094427)

FIGURE 2.17 Once again, we see our simple ellipse in action. (Courtesy of Wikimedia Commons, Arpingstone, https://commons.wikimedia.org/w/index.php?curid=13562039.)

FIGURE 2.18   The berry cluster is a bolus, but the berries are spherical! (Courtesy of Wikimedia Commons, GFDL 1.2, https://commons.wikimedia.org/w/index.php?curid=6215403)

FIGURE 2.19 (See color insert.)   The bolus, consisting of cupped shapes, around a central tubular core. (Courtesy of Wikimedia Commons, Hardyplants, https://commons.wikimedia.org/w/index.php?curid=21038136.)

VINES

A vine is basically a long, serpentine, branch that curls around other plants and objects that have a stable base. The vine doesn't have a stable trunk like a tree or a bush, so it uses other objects to provide that stability while seeking sunlight and nutrients. Kudzu is a common vine in the southern United States that was an import from Africa, yet became incredibly overpopulated to the extent of overwhelming entire regions. The vine grows very quickly and can bury entire areas if neglected. Figure 2.20 shows a kudzu vine with leaves. The structure of the vine is similar to all of the rest of the tubular-tapered structures, with the requisite random growth pattern.

FIGURE 2.20 A regular menace in the southern United States, kudzu is a creeping vine. (Courtesy of I, Gsmith, CC BY 2.5, https://commons.wikimedia.org/w/index. php?curid=2366652)

Creeping vines can easily be built with simple techniques like the extruded curve along a path with branching, as illustrated in Chapters 5 through 7. The cross section of the primary vine stem tapers from base to point, as do the outward branches, which often grow in a spiral pattern around tall objects such as poles, trees, and fences.

WATER PLANTS

Since underwater plants are a staple element of many scenes in games and animated features, they deserve some mention here as separate entities from ground-based plants. They have a very similar structure to ground plants, but the forms that the structure take are often specific or unique in some fashion. The morphology of the plant is usually based upon the purpose it must serve, which is derived from the fact that it has to contend with existence in a purely liquid medium.

Underwater Plants

Underwater plants live entirely underneath the surface of the water. For this reason, they are far more likely to be found in shallow waters, with very light fronds that collect sunlight. The milfoil has a whorled branch structure, in which the tiny fronds emerge from the main branch in a radial pattern (Figure 2.21).

Freshwater Plants

Freshwater plants have a distinct morphology from other plants, one that allows a top-leaf structure to settle on the top of the water surface, while the long stems reach the bottom of the pond or body of water, terminating in small, shallow roots that anchor it to the bottom.

Fanwort (Figure 2.22): Fanwort, common in Australia, is an excellent example of a spherical, radial pattern of growth. As you can see in Figure 1.26, the tapered tubes radiate outward from the center, but instead of a two-dimensional extrusion they occur in a three-dimensional pattern, forming a hemispherical structure. This spherical pattern is also indicative of regularity in organic form. Notice that the fronds that laterally branch from the main stem are dichotomous in nature! *So* you can see the varying structures we have been studying replicate themselves in multiple organic scenarios.

FIGURE 2.21   Common underwater plants, which have very specific and unique structures. (Courtesy of H. Zell, CC BY-SA 3.0, https://commons.wikimedia. org/w/index.php?curid=8907499)

FIGURE 2.22   Notice the radial branching patterns of perfect isotomous style.

Saltwater Plants

- *Kelp/seaweed* (Figure 2.23): This is a classically structured plant, with all the requisite features of organic growth.

  - *Tapered tubes*: The roots and stems are tapering tubular structures.

  - *Parabolic curves*: The fronds are flat, parabolic curved objects with a slight cup shape, similar to land-based plant leaves.

  - *Branching structures*: The roots and the branches follow the standard branching structure as seen multiple times before.

  - *Bulbous shapes*: The bladder is an air-containing structure that keeps the plant floating and upright.

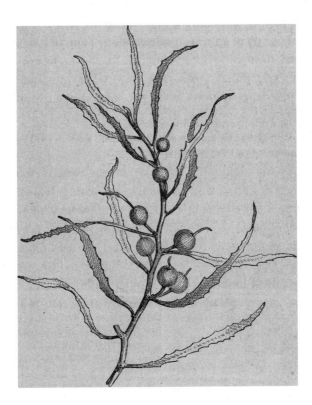

FIGURE 2.23 Kelp has large fronds and air pods which help it remain buoyant underwater. (Courtesy of Internet Archive Book Images, https://archive.org/stream/textbookofstruct00thom/textbookofstruct00thom#page/n276/mode/1up)

CONCLUSION

As you have seen in this chapter, there are a multitude of forms, patterns, and structures that are exhibited by plants, some unique and some common organic structures. One of the things about plants to keep in mind is that the majority of these structures have some mathematical basis and can be created in a procedural manner. Indeed, most games and films now "grow" environments more than individually model trees, shrubs, and roots. This is because the math behind branching, growth, and flowering can all be much more quickly and easily handled than individual models. The algorithms generating these structures can be based upon simple constructions as "descriptions" of a plant structure and then iterated and instantiated with deviations based on the environment and random elements in order to create a more realistic, lifelike world without resorting to making each individual plant. Indeed, with the amount of variation, growth factors, and multiple hierarchical branching in modeling plants, the ability of any one modeler or any team of modelers to create an organic environment would be nonfeasible at the worst, or extremely time-consuming at the very best. This is why software and plugins have been in progress since the very early days of computer graphics to solve the plant environment problem. They have gotten more and more sophisticated over time, and now it is all but unheard of to have to model an individual flower, plant, tree, or shrub.

So why have this chapter in the book? I believe that, as an organic modeler, the more you understand things like branching, leaves, hierarchies, and plant organic structures, the better your repertoire will be. Once again, the fantasy factor can be a huge unknown in your potential modeling career. The popular character Groot, from Marvel Comics' *Guardians of the Galaxy*, is part tree and part biped humanoid. In order to model him, the artist must have had some kind of understanding of tree structures and branching. Many other instances can occur when the plant physiology can be useful.

CHAPTER 3

Animal Physiology and Forms

INTRODUCTION

What is the difference between animal and plant life? Certainly, we can differentiate between them in various ways. One thing that seems to be a dividing factor is locomotion, or the ability to move of one's own volition. Plants, in the real world, can't get up and walk around. Not all members of the animal kingdom are possessed of the ability to move around (certainly a sea sponge can't), but it's a universal fact that none of the members of the plant world can. So we have many different methods outside of traditional biology to determine how we see plants and animals.

For our purposes, it's not so much in the DNA, but in the way the external aspect of the organism presents itself. Plants and animals, from a static perspective, have a lot of similarities. We should definitely go over these similarities before analyzing the differences! You wouldn't imagine you have much in common with a fern tree, but the truth is that organic shapes and structures are universal throughout the entire spectrum of life on Earth.

- *Tapered Tubes* Veins, arteries, and intestines are great examples of the internal plumbing that makes up our body. The tube and pump structures of the internal organs are prevalent among every form of life because it's how we transport liquids against the natural pull of gravity.

- *Segmentation* Nematodes and flatworms illustrate great examples of segmentation, but we can see it in complex animals like the armadillo. Segmentation is a result of growth patterns in which each new segment is layered on top of the previous. Some complex forms of animals, especially those with soft tissue externally like mammals, have very little evidence of growth patterns on the outside because we are basically born with all of our organs and our external structure. That is to say, we stretch, but we don't really build new structures as we grow like, say, a nautilus would do.

- *Branching* Hands and limbs are great examples of branching geometry in the animal kingdom. An interesting thing to note here is that on the external structure of complex animal life you rarely see nested branching past a single iteration. That is to say, you have five fingers and toes, *but* they don't branch off into more multiples of branches! That structure, however, is a part of your structure *internally*, in the arteries, neurons, and brachial forms of the lungs.

- *Radial Patterns* Radial patterns are evidenced in multiple forms through the animal kingdom, generally in the form of growth patterns that rotate outward from a central hub. The geometry of these patterns can often be attributed to a mathematical formula, and they are excellent candidates for procedural and mathematical modeling techniques.

- *Spherical Shapes* Spherical shapes are incredibly common in the animal kingdom, especially the most common structure of the eye and eyeball. The spherical shape lends itself to a visual distortion correct for the light that passes into the cornea and allows for a much larger range of view from the rotation in the socket.

- *Spirals* Spirals, as mentioned before, are mathematically shaped curves that change values exponentially over their length. You can see these in certain sea mollusks and crustaceans as well as the horns of animals like goats, buffalo, and narwhal.

- *Bulbous Geometry* The womb, the lungs, the heart, and the sockets of the mouth and ear canals are all great example of bulbous-shaped geometry. The head of an octopus can be used as another great example here, where it forms a roundish, but oval, socket.

- *Growth Patterns* All aspects of animals include the layering of growth. In some cases, as it does in humans, it ceases at a predetermined point of stasis. This means that once our full growth is complete, we do not continue to get taller or thicker (unless you're talking about fat, and certainly we all get more of *that* as we age etc.). Coral, however, continues to grow and grow indefinitely. Crustaceans don't live forever, but over the course of their life they continue to get larger, as do many fish species. As an organism grows, it often exhibits growth patterns that are like layers of sediment, slowly getting thicker and more complex with time.

- *Folds* Skin and membranes often form folding patterns in the animal kingdom.

- *Ridges* Hard-shelled animals often have sharp ridges, but these also can be found in the scales and fins of many fish.

- *Bolus* A rounded tube, generally found in single-cellular organisms and primitive life-forms such as a sea cucumber.

LEARNING THE STRUCTURE OF THE ANIMAL KINGDOM

Starting with the simplest forms of life, we can layer our understanding of common animal structures from the ground up. As we progress into more complex forms, such as reptiles, mammals, and other vertebrates, we will see the foundational structures repeat themselves and become more complex shapes. In this way we will begin to get a designer's grasp on these patterns and learn how to replicate them in a practical sense.

It becomes rapidly clear that the structures of all animals are made up of simpler, smaller structures that form a system, which in turn is a part of a bigger system. The curves, patterns, lines, and physical structures of such systems are always able to be broken down into smaller components. As we learn the variations on these structures, we can predictably model not only currently existing animals and organisms but also ones that never walked the earth at all! If you want to create fantastical beasts and alien life-forms, then understanding the fundamental structures of current life-forms is of vital importance. Fantasy creatures are almost always based in the realm of the physical properties possessed by modern or extinct animals.

SIMPLE SOFT STRUCTURES

We begin the animal world with microbiological life, which is coincidentally what we can consider "soft" life. Soft tissue is much different than the hard structures of the plant world that we covered in previous material on plants and plant-like structures, in that it is much more loose and pliable. Soft tissues are generally made of materials that can bend, stretch, and fold and have specific features of construction that make them difficult to create and construct in comparison to the much firmer, structured plant physiology.

Folds and Wrinkles

Folds are a vital component to any soft, pliable material. Folds and wrinkles are places where the skin or tissue is pressed against other tissue, causing it to fold into itself. You can see this in the fold of your elbow tissue, as it presses against itself. This is commonly known as *cleavage* in the 3D world. Cleavage is a particularly hard thing to create with 3D geometry because, unlike skin, polygons don't have any substance! So a polygon will interpenetrate itself instead of folding up like a piece of skin. Figure 3.1 shows some

FIGURE 3.1   Loose skin creates fleshy folds and cleavage between areas. (Courtesy of Bloodhound_Trials_Alton_2008.jpg: John Leslie ("Contadini"), CC BY 2.0, https://commons.wikimedia.org/w/index.php?curid=20124981)

animal examples of wrinkles and folds. Generally in 3D these techniques are done with various levels of physics calculation (such as for cloth) or careful manipulation of the structure to appear organic while still allowing for interpenetration. Penetration of one polygon into another is a very common occurrence when setting up organic models for animation, but one that is avoidable for the initial model in most places. We try to avoid modeling the wrinkles and folds in moving parts if possible, but for certain areas where there is no other option it becomes necessary, such as the jowls or folds in our hound dogs from Figure 3.1.

Folds and jowls are areas that gravity will have a major effect on, so when modeling them it's important to create a nice, rippling, curved downward flow. This will necessitate an oval shape.

Squishiness and Volume Retention

Figure 3.2 illustrates an amoeba, one of the simplest animal life-forms on the planet. As you can see, it has very few definable "hard" structures compared to our magnolia tree from Chapter 1. Instead, the amoeba is a tiny multicellular blob, with some organs to fuel the cells from the food that it ingests by absorbing it through permeable walls. Amoeba are great examples of the ability of something with a soft structure to shift its basic shape and

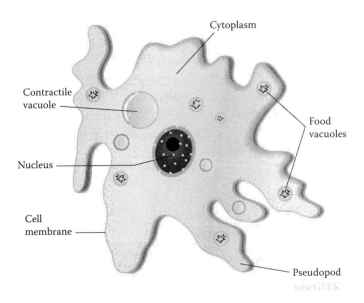

FIGURE 3.2 The amoeba, or "blob," has no defined structure but rather oozes inside a variable shape.

create limbs (in this case known as *pseudopods*) from its personal volume of material. This idea of volume retention is vital in modeling and animating soft objects! The very fundamental structure of early cartoon animation was (and still is in some regards) based on this principle of "squash and stretch," or the subtle bounciness of an object in relationship to its volume of material and physics. The squishiness of an amoeba, as it navigates through a droplet of water, can tell us a lot about basic animal life. Although the creature will create limbs to ambulate and to gather food, the basic volume of amoeba substance will not change. So if it extends a pseudopod to grab a bit of food, it will have to get thinner somewhere else. More complex animals can't really do this at all, because they have an internal skeletal and muscular structure that prevents them from changing shape at will. But in the microorganismal world it seems to be working out just fine.

Flagellum and Cilia

These are structures that resemble the vein of a leaf, or a tapered tube, but are constructed of a highly pliable material that can twist and turn in response to will contractions of tissue from the animal it belongs to. The main difference between cilia and flagella is the length and the shape of the motion. Flagella are longer and less numerous, but pump up and down in a wavelike pattern, either spinning like a spiral or creating a standing wave. These movements propel the animal through a liquid medium quite easily. Cilia are much more numerous and act in concert, swimming exactly the way you would with your arms, by pushing down against the body to propel itself forward. Figure 3.3 illustrates the construction and movement patterns of both cilia and flagellum, which are common to microorganisms. As you can see, the structure of a flagella or cilia is not much different than that of a leaf vein from the outside. A cross section clearly shows that the outward structure is a tapered tube! But this tapered tube can be willfully manipulated by

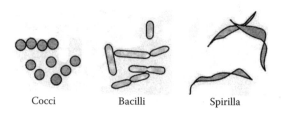

Cocci   Bacilli   Spirilla

FIGURE 3.3 Different microorganisms and the flagella. (Courtesy of C.K. Robinson, CC BY-SA 4.0, https://commons.wikimedia.org/w/index.php?curid=45678441)

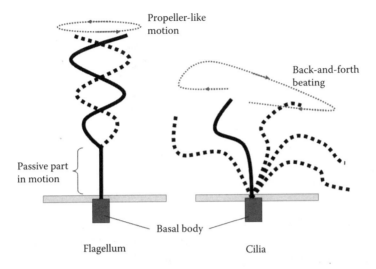

FIGURE 3.4 Movement types and patterns of flagella. Notice the sinoid wave and spiral. (Courtesy of L. Kohidai, CC BY 3.0, https://commons.wikimedia.org/w/index.php?curid=3874754)

the life-form to move it forward, backward, and in any direction it chooses at any speed it wants, provided it has enough energy (Figure 3.4).

Segments

Worms are a great way to explore segments and segmented creatures. A segmented organism consists of multiple and exact copies of an individual piece. The animal grows by adding segments on to the end of itself. The head segment is generally the primary unique segment, containing the eyes and sensory organs, including the "brain," while the other segments act in unison to propel the animal forward on land or swim through a liquid medium of some kind.

Segments are easily reproducible pieces that allow modeling by way of loops or procedural methods instead of organic workflows. Since each segment, like each branch of a tree, is a copy of the previous, segmented creatures can quickly be created using procedural, or mathematical, methods. This is far more efficient than using a "sculpty" method due to the expansive nature of the morphology. Segments appear again in the animal kingdom in the world of insects and arthropods, and indeed extend to all hard-shelled creatures from all levels of hierarchies in the steps of evolution. Outer shells and exoskeletons are generally segmented in some manner.

An insect has a segmented body, each segment neatly fitting onto the next, similar in many ways to a modern sports car, with the hard edges connecting at the seams. The soft tissues and vascular system are all inside the hard, external shell. This, of course, is a vastly different construction than our own body, which is soft and pliant on the outside but contains very hard structures underneath for structure and sup-

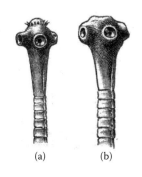

(a)　　　(b)

FIGURE 3.5 The segmented worm (a), with the head piece as a separate entity from the rest (b). (Courtesy of Wikimedia Commons https://commons.wikimedia.org/w/index.php?curid=34346)

port. If we want to model a segmented creature, we can certainly do it piece by piece. In fact, that is the preferred method for modeling a hard-bodied creature such as an insect or crustacean. Since there is no need of a seamless, skinned exterior, each segment can be created individually and fitted together as necessary (Figures 3.5 and 3.6).

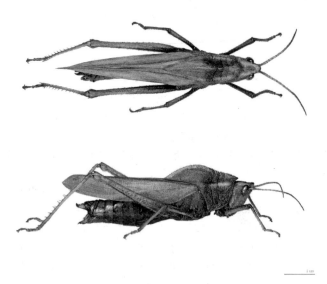

FIGURE 3.6 (See color insert.) A much more complex segmented animal, with multiple limbs and shapes. (Courtesy of Didier Descouens, CC BY-SA 3.0, https://commons.wikimedia.org/w/index.php?curid=18270423)

FIGURE 1.2 A French bulldog has a complex, folded, and adorable face that we cannot ever mistake for something made by a human. (Courtesy of Flickr, CC BY 2.0, https://commons.wikimedia.org/w/index.php?curid=1923093)

FIGURE 1.5 The VW beetle is a great example of something created by man in order to resemble something already present in nature. For that reason it has some organic features. (Courtesy of Spurzem—Lothar Spurzem, CC BY-SA 2.0 de, https://commons.wikimedia.org/w/index.php?curid=8360265)

FIGURE 1.10 A snail shell, an example of growth through a spiral. (Courtesy of H. Zell, CC BY-SA 3.0, https://commons.wikimedia.org/w/index. php?curid=24621809)

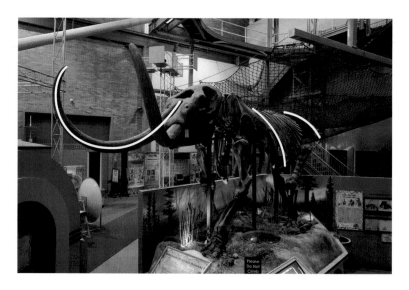

FIGURE 1.11 Multiple examples of our elliptical curve across a single skeleton. (Courtesy of Colts12871, CC BY-SA 3.0, https://commons.wikimedia.org/w/index. php?curid=33843793)

FIGURE 1.32   Radial floral structure of a magnolia flower. Note the petals with the cup (half-bulbous) shape surrounding the central bolus of the stamen. (Courtesy of Derek Ramsey (Ram-Man), CC BY-SA 3.0, https://commons.wikimedia.org/w/index.php?curid=11814157)

FIGURE 2.2   Growth causes random or seemingly random shapes to occur in the downward-growing roots of this tree. The shapes are developed over many years by multiple factors. (Courtesy of Wikimedia Commons, CC BY-SA 3.0, https://commons.wikimedia.org/w/index.php?curid=127103)

FIGURE 2.10 The magnolia leaf, which is basically two elliptical curves in a bilateral configuration.

FIGURE 2.12 A 3D modeled version of the magnolia leaf.

FIGURE 2.14 Sunflower in the classic radial flower shape, although the seeds are grown in a spiral pattern. (Courtesy of Fir0002, GFDL 1.2, https://commons. wikimedia.org/w/index.php?curid=7613324)

FIGURE 2.19 The bolus, consisting of cupped shapes, around a central tubular core. (Courtesy of Wikimedia Commons Hardyplants, https://commons.wikime-dia.org/w/index.php?curid=21038136.)

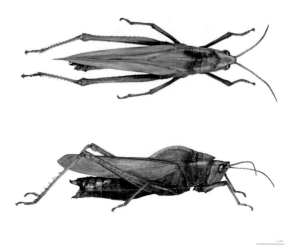

FIGURE 3.6   A much more complex segmented animal, with multiple limbs and shapes. (Courtesy of Didier Descouens, CC BY-SA 3.0, https://commons. wikimedia.org/w/index.php?curid=18270423)

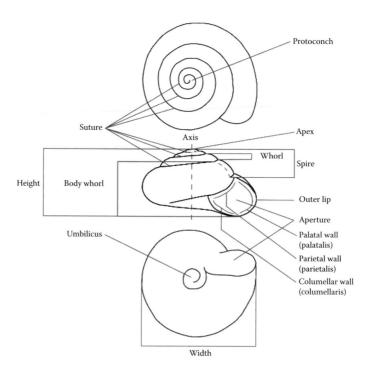

FIGURE 3.7   Spiral growth of a common snail. (Courtesy of Michal Maňas, CC BY 2.5, https://commons.wikimedia.org/w/index.php?curid=7545602)

FIGURE 3.17 An octopus, with wildly twisting tentacles. How different is this from our tree root structure? (Courtesy of Comingio Merculiano in Jatta Giuseppe—I Cefalopodi viventi nel Golfo di Napoli (sistematica): monografia, https://commons.wikimedia.org/w/index.php?curid=20146127)

FIGURE 3.36 Though a completely bipedal creature, the *T. rex* did not have a vertical spine. In this image you can see the swiveling of the hips that allowed it to walk on two limbs, balanced by the huge tail. (Courtesy of Wikimedia Commons, CC BY 2.0, https://commons.wikimedia.org/w/index.php?curid=39768754)

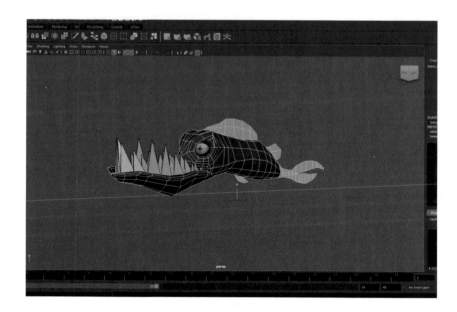

FIGURE 4.1   A fish model at very low resolution.

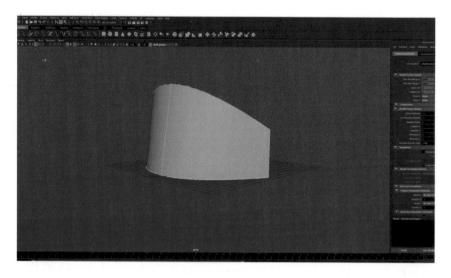

FIGURE 4.3   A simple NURBS-based loft between two curves.

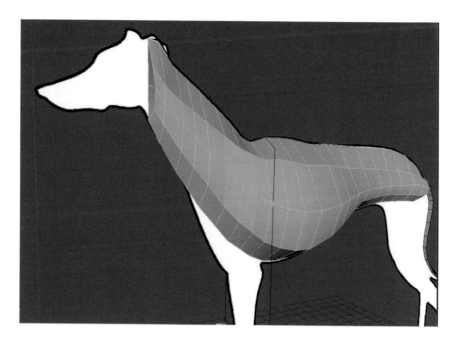

FIGURE 4.25 Adding the edge loops along the length of the spine allows us to create the nice curvature of the cross section.

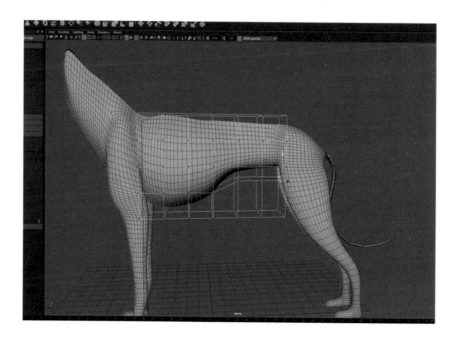

FIGURE 4.33 Using a Lattice to fine-tune an area.

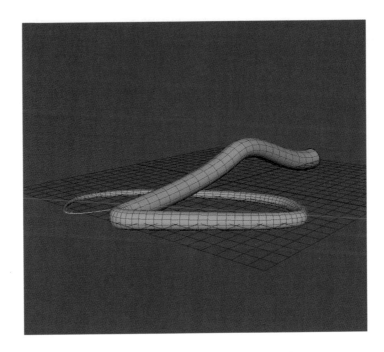

FIGURE 5.4   Some simple changes to the shape of the path curve create a much different piece of geometry.

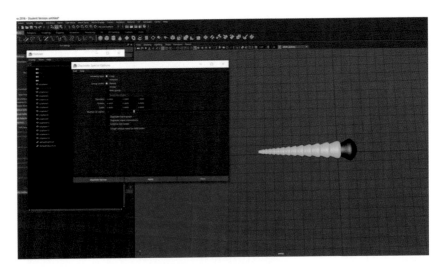

FIGURE 5.7   Result of modeling with duplication.

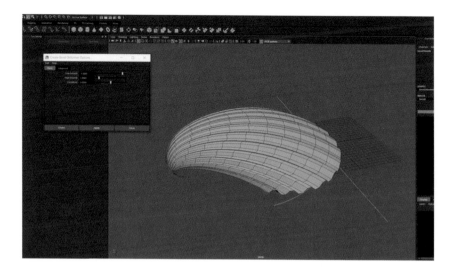

FIGURE 5.51   The second bend to the base curve rounds out the form.

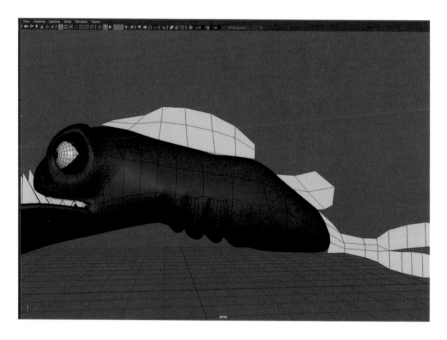

FIGURE 5.63   Making the same belly fat rolls as before, but only selected areas have increased detail.

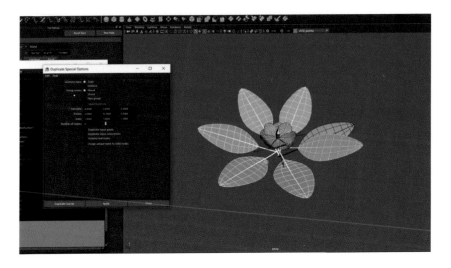

FIGURE 6.6 Modeling by duplication allows me to create a spiral growth around the central stem.

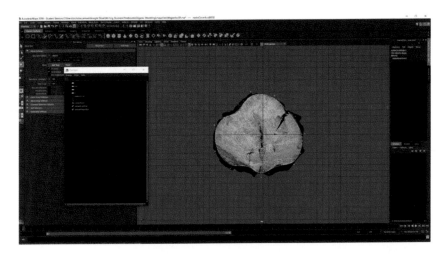

FIGURE 6.10 I match the vertices of our circle to the shape of the trunk.

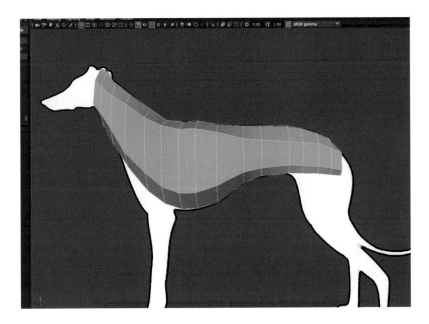

FIGURE 7.10   The middle edge loop will provide us one more point in the curve of the torso from top to bottom.

FIGURE 7.35   Pulling the legs down with another extrusion to the ground plane.

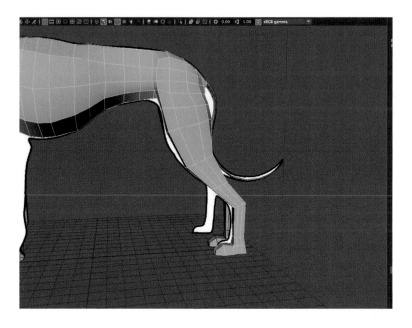

FIGURE 7.42 The resulting shape has the same contours with fewer vertices.

FIGURE 7.63 The ear from a perspective.

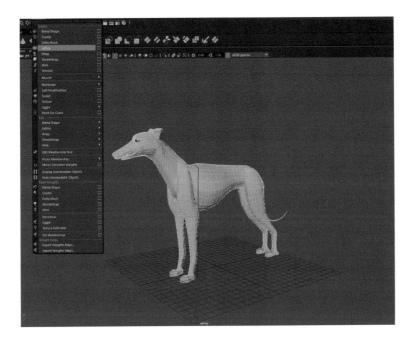

FIGURE 7.72   Creating a lattice to tweak the model.

FIGURE 8.3   A closeup of a bee's abdomen, which clearly illustrates the segmented construction. (Courtesy of USGS Native Bee Inventory and Monitoring Laboratory, Beltsville, USA,—Andrena-nuda,-female,-abdomen_2012-08-03-17.01.27-ZS-PMax, https://commons.wikimedia.org/w/index.php?curid=24746483)

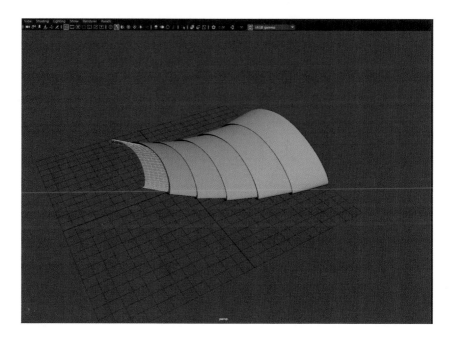

FIGURE 8.11   Each segment slightly fits into the previous.

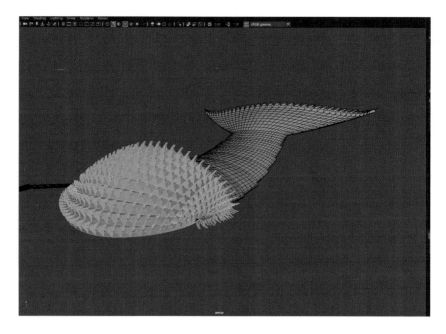

FIGURE 8.22   Some fancy spiking for our trilobite.

HARD-STRUCTURED ANIMALS

Hard structures are structural and protective elements that provide functional support for more complex movements and protection against elements. The hard structure is usually found in an endoskeleton (internally existing hard structure) or an exoskeleton (externally existing hard structure). These support systems provide the animal with an extremely functional advantage in many cases. The important thing here is not the evolutionary development of the bone material, but the structural shapes and forms we find it in. Hard-structured animals include things like (bony) fish, reptiles, and mammals! These all have some form of external or internal structure that is firm and rigid. Hard structures are important for providing structural support to animals that are above a certain weight and size. The pressures of gravity and water can place tremendous strain on organs, which increases with the mass of the animal. Cartilage, bone, and chitin are all hard materials that can offer protection and structure for locomotion to a complex and high-mass organism.

Arthropods (crustaceans, arachnids, and insects) form the second part of the equation, since they have their skeletons and protective layers on the outside of the organs, protecting the inner soft tissues. Insect geometry and structures are externally hard and structured with a definitive set of segments and hierarchical relationships, just like the internal skeleton of a mammal might be. The external structures of arthropods are quite varied in shape and structure; however, the characteristic is to have strong ridges and sharp angles, as opposed to internal skeletal structures, which are known for being far softer and more rounded in terms of the curve angles. This is most likely because if you had sharp angles *inside* your body, you'd constantly have your skeleton puncturing the skin from inside out every time you fell down!

Modeling a hard-bodied animal presents both a level of ease and complexity. On the one hand, the hard shapes are easier to manipulate and lay out for animation and movement, but on the other hand the multiple parts require an assembly structure much like the parts of IKEA furniture. Keeping track of all the little things and how they articulate can be quite a headache with hard-bodied animals, especially if they are extremely complex. The shapes and curves of the pieces themselves are often complex and time-consuming. This is also a very similar task to modeling an automobile or spaceship, in that there are many parts that fit together in specific ways. Many industrial styles of modeling can be adapted quite well to the modeling of hard-bodied creatures.

Shells

Crustaceans with a soft body and hard outer layer are prominent in the world's oceans. There are a few land-dwellers in this family as well. From the conch shell to the land crab, each one of these animals has a soft, inner body and a hard, outer layer. Shells are created by secreting the substance chitin, which rapidly hardens and takes form. The segments and shapes of shells vary widely, but they all have similar characteristics that follow mathematical rules in the same manner that plants do. If you look at Figure 3.7, you can see the outline and schematics of a snail shell, which follow a simple, flowing spiral pattern. Because of their mathematically congruent lines, shells are a great candidate for modeling procedurally

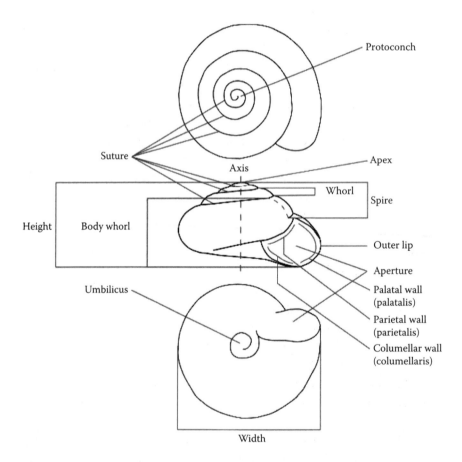

FIGURE 3.7 (See color insert.) Spiral growth of a common snail. (Courtesy of Michal Maňas, CC BY 2.5, https://commons.wikimedia.org/w/index.php?curid=7545602)

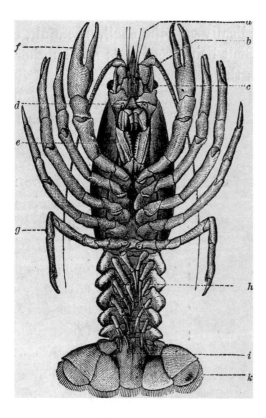

FIGURE 3.8 A complex crustacean, constructed of hundreds of segmented pieces. (Courtesy of Internet Archive Book Images, https://archive.org/stream/comparativezool00orto/#page/n290/mode/1up)

vs. organically. A hybrid of both can also be useful, where the initial form is procedurally generated with curves and the rest is tweaked afterward. Many of the forms you can see are examples of tapered tubes with hard ridges on the edges, both organic structures that we have seen in many other places previously (Figures 3.8 and 3.9).

Legs

Legs, of course, are the next stage in locomotion from fins. Developed from the lungfish-type of early land-walkers, the leg is all-important in moving the creature from one place to another. But legs evolved in varying ways across the animal kingdom, both from insects and from fish that were able to move out of water for brief periods of time, with vastly different structures designed for the same basic purpose; to move in a nonliquid environment.

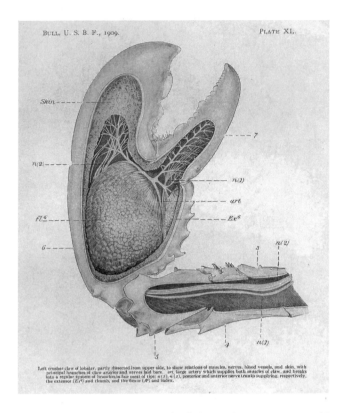

FIGURE 3.9 The lobster claw, with multiple hinged moving parts. (Courtesy of Francis Hobart Herrick, https://commons.wikimedia.org/w/index.php?curid= 42504734)

Crustaceans and insects developed multisegmented legs, which allowed them to move quickly across uneven and unstable terrain (whether submerged in water or on land). The structure of these legs are multijointed entities with a high level of complex curvature. As we begin to study hard structures such as exoskeletons made of chitin and endoskeletons, we will see that the structure of the curvature becomes more complex and complicated. Figure 3.10 shows the leg structure of a common spider. As you can see, there is a much more complex structure underlying the shape of the legs, with prominent ridges and arcing curves. Although the basic organic structures are present, they have been brought up one level of magnitude in complexity.

Insect, crustacean, and arachnid legs are all very similar to the spider leg design in Figure 3.10. In Figure 3.11, you can see a common insect leg diagram compared to a human. Although all the structures are from

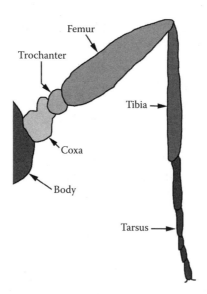

FIGURE 3.10 Wedged exoskeleton shapes, jointed together but separate pieces. (Courtesy of Nwbeeson, https://commons.wikimedia.org/w/index.php?curid=10789726)

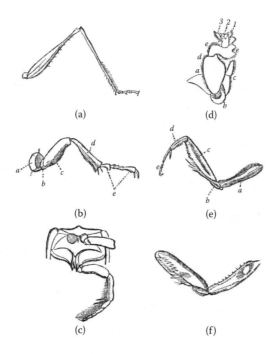

FIGURE 3.11 Various legs of insects. (Courtesy of Wikimedia Commons, https://commons.wikimedia.org/w/index.php?curid=12134252)

vastly distant relatives in the animal kingdom, the purpose of such is greatly similar: to propel us forward against the action of gravity on a ground surface of some kind (as opposed to swimming through a liquid or flying through the air). Each leg will have unique properties based upon its particular usage; however, the hierarchical layouts of the structures are all very similar. The joints are designed to hinge at certain points in certain ways, allowing for kinetic freedom with certain constraints, which in turn make it possible to locomote the entire weight of the body in a balanced fashion. This understanding of the underlying structure of the anatomy is crucial if you want to create organic models that will be animated! I can't stress enough how a solid understanding of kinetic movement will improve the usability of your models to the rigger and animator. It is very easy, as we will see in Chapter 6 ("Organic Modeling Methods"), to create a visually sound high-level "sculpture" of an organism without having a properly planned out structure for the underlying mechanics of movement and proper deformation. As we move into the higher level organisms, we must take careful note of the internal structures as much as the external.

MULTISTRUCTURED ANIMALS AND VERTEBRATES

As we move up to the higher vertebrate category of animals, we find a new structural form emerges. The increasing size and weight of the animal suddenly strains the limits of the hard shells and protective casings of the arthropods. A new level of complexity must occur; and a calcified skeleton is the answer to provision of structure that allows greater flexibility and strength to withstand the rigors of movement and gravity or water pressure.

The most important thing about the soft-bodied structure is that it's multilayered in construction. There is a hard skeleton at the center providing the scaffolding for a tremendously complex system of vascularity (blood, veins, intestines, internal organs), which feeds energy to muscles, tendons and ligaments, which are in turn covered by thick layers of skin. Modeling this is a tremendously difficult task because the artist must not only account for all of this internal structure, but provide for eventualities that it will deform based upon a complex internal structure that doesn't actually exist in the model itself. It is a very delicate balance, and because it is so difficult it's important to understand the internal mechanics of the animal type in order to prepare for it properly.

Organic modeling techniques, as described in Chapter 4, are a great way to go about modeling something as complex as a soft-bodied creature based on a vertebrate structure.

Fins

Fins are appendages for swimming in liquids, which of course are vital for sea creature locomotion (although not necessary for locomotion underwater). Vestiges of these near-universal ichthyic entities are observable in embryonic development of almost all mammal species, even if they never see a body of water.

Fins possess a fairly unique architecture, with different types from different animals. There are dorsal fins, pectoral fins, anal fins, and caudal (tail fins). Of course the fins of cartilaginous fish such as sharks will have different structures to the fish with bones, since they don't possess the spiny structure with the webbing in between the spines. Figure 3.12 clearly

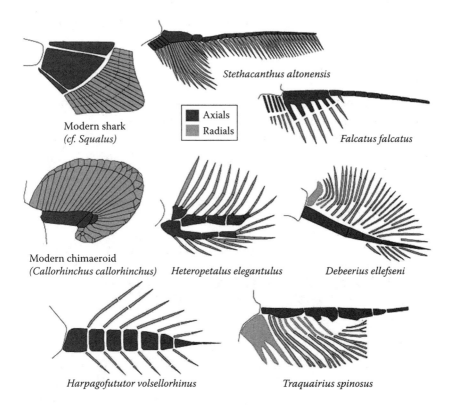

FIGURE 3.12   Despite the many forms of fish fins, they can all seem to be made from a common structure. Does the structure resemble a plant leaf at all?

illustrates the basic structures of the fins of fish that have definitive skeletons, including a shark fin (which technically doesn't have a skeleton, but heavy cartilage is pretty close in terms of modeling).

Constructing the fins of a bony fish should be a structural procedure. You can see in Figure 3.12 that the spiny structure of the bones is extremely similar to the structure of a leaf or even a segmented worm. Each segment of the bone is a similar, but slightly smaller, version of the previous one. As each bone line fans out away at an angle from the parent, it creates a wide, thin surface, perfectly suited for swimming since it can create the maximum drag with minimal effort. The angle of the structural support bones grow in a radial fashion, not so much unlike the spokes of a wheel or the petals of a flower!

Cartilaginous fish, such as sharks and rays, have no skeleton but still have a very similar fin substructure to bony fish. The main difference would appear in the rounded edges of the cross section, where the skin is heavy and thick compared to a bony fish. This results in the distinct triangular shape we are all familiar with from movies and television as it "breaks water" on the surface (Figure 3.13).

Arms

The difference between arms and legs in many types of animal is nominal. For the reptilian family, there really are no "arms" to speak of. Figure 3.14 shows a typical iguana, which represents a four-legged (tetrapod) creature, with an internal skeleton and organs to match. The front legs are not "arms" in the sense that they are used solely for locomotion on the ground,

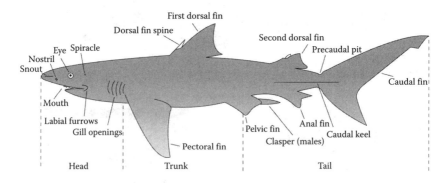

FIGURE 3.13 The nonbony fish. Note the sharp edges on the shapes of the fins. (Courtesy of Chris_huh, https://commons.wikimedia.org/w/index.php?curid=1754799)

FIGURE 3.14 A reptile has four limbs that extend outward from the trunk at the shoulder. (Courtesy of Crabx123, CC BY-SA 4.0, https://commons.wikimedia. org/w/index.php?curid=40866986)

but the front legs are anatomically very differently structured than the rear legs! This is because the method of locomotion requires a pushing from behind and a pulling from the front.

As we progress into more and more complex animals, the arms become more and more flexible, mobile, and used for nonlocomotion purposes. The crustacean families of organisms, as well as the insects, often have "claws," or appendages that are useful specifically for catching and manipulating food or their environment. These pincers, claws, and grabbing types of limbs can have very complex structures due to the mechanics necessary to use them (Figure 3.15).

Moving up the evolutionary scale in terms of complexity, we can find limbs that no longer serve the purpose of locomotion at all but allow the animal to perform complex mechanics and even use tools to some degree. These underlying structures of skeletal anatomy are vastly different than the ground-walkers because they are endowed with multiple uses and a high range of flexibility and mobility. Figure 3.16 shows the full anatomy of a lobster claw, which is used by the creature to manipulate and grasp food as well as defend itself from potential predators. Figure 3.15 shows the comparative anatomy of multiple mammalian armlike appendages, where the purposes of the structures are quite clearly more than just locomotion. Arms are so complex and pervasive in the animal kingdom that an

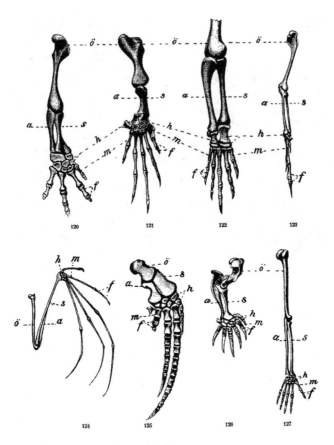

FIGURE 3.15 A pan of multiple arms and arm skeletal structures. (Courtesy of Wilhelm Leche, http://runeberg.org/lecheman/0102.html)

entire volume could be written about them and still not cover the subject comprehensively. The good news is that most armlike appendages have similar characteristics, which we can derive and condense into categorical anatomical structures.

- *Shoulder socket*: This is the ball-and-socket joint area where the level of flexibility really separates the structure from the legs. Legs meant for locomotion have a limited range of motion, in order to be tight and structured enough for constant movement. Even if you're a yoga master, your hips only have so much range of motion—anything else would prevent you from walking and running correctly! But the shoulder structure of a human is vastly different (as is that of primates) because of the need to lift the arms up above the head and climb, swing, or otherwise grab on to something. This flexibility is noticeably absent in most modern reptiles and amphibians, although we do see a good deal of it as we move up into the more complex mammalian species.

- *Elbow*: The flex of the elbow is not as important here as the *direction* in which the elbow can aim, which is derived from the high level of rotational range of motion in the humerus socket. This makes it possible to move, grasp, and manipulate objects and surfaces in multiple ways and directions.

- *Radius/ulna*: The rotational potential of the radius/ulna in the forearm of the arm is instrumental in creating even more of a flexible appendage for multipurpose use. This allows the entire grasping mechanism (the hand) to rotate completely around a 180-degree arc of motion. Most of this functionality is unique to bipedal humans and to some primates.

- *Wrist*: The wrist is another joint that has multiple uses, depending upon the use for which it is intended. On four-legged animals with little to no use of "arms," it exists as mostly an ambulatory entity; that is to say that its primary purpose is for locomotion, and its secondary purpose for grasping and manipulating things. Humans are the only *known* nonextinct species that use the arms and hands entirely outside of locomotion. This statement includes birds, even though of course an ostrich or penguin doesn't use the hands/wings/arms for locomotion much; but they don't serve other purposes. Many bipedal dinosaurs, such as the famous example of the *Tyrannosaurus rex*, had small non-locomotive arms with some level of wrist articulation extant, although the purposes and use are not entirely known at this time. Speculations are that they were used to tear and rip flesh for feeding on a dead carcass.

- *Hand and fingers*: Nearly every species of tetrapod has smaller, radiating appendages extruding from a flat, angled surface that we know as a "hand" or "foot." These jointed appendages have the ability to curl around objects and surfaces, which becomes incredibly useful in climbing, walking across slick surfaces, and, in the case of arms, grasping and manipulating objects. The morphology of all hands in the vertebrate kingdom is somewhat similar, although millions of unique forms exist for specific adaptions. The fingers and toes are the only existing multibranched structures in tetrapods, since the general outward structure of our bodies is bilateral (equal on both sides). Only in the fingers and toes do we see multiple branches from a single stalk, which otherwise are only binary (two arms, two legs, two eyes, etc.).

Tentacles

Tentacles are flexible appendages, used both for locomotion and grasping, generally used by underwater creatures in the octopus and squid family. These are animals that have little to no firm skeletal structure, such as vertebrates do, but still possess a wide range of movement and complexity of form that is somewhat unique in the animal kingdom. They present specific challenges for modelers because of their high level of flexibility and general "squishiness."

Tentacles are extremely uncommon in real-world Earth creatures outside of this phylum; *however,* they seem to be extremely common in alien and fantasy-based creatures from science fiction and otherwise! For this reason among many, it's extremely important to understand the nature and anatomy of this very unique appendage. Tentacles come in multiples, generally using an equal radial branching structure, but not necessarily by rule (especially when dealing with the fantasy kind). The real-world tentacles of octopii and squid are thick, rubbery, muscular structures with round, bulbous "suckers" on the bottom that aid in grasping and holding on to prey or anchor objects. In Figure 3.16, you will notice that the squid have an extra pair of tentacles (outside of the standard shorter, radial ones) that have a unique "diamond" shape, which assists the creature in grabbing prey. The most important thing to consider when modeling or preparing to model a tentacle-based creature is the incredible flexibility and shape-morphing capabilities that these appendages possess. Due to the distinct *lack* of skeletal structure underneath or surrounding the appendages, they can twist, squish, and elongate to a much greater degree than any other type of limb. In terms of the modeling structure, you must be prepared to design the basic geometry to allow for this flexibility!

Wings

There are many, many flying animals in the world of biology, but we can categorize them quite easily. True flight, as opposed to gliding, is evidenced by the animal being able to generate actual lift with wings, therefore being able to move from the ground to the air with some level of ease. There are

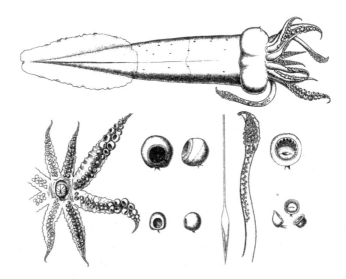

FIGURE 3.16 Squid have no spinal column, and although they have bilateral symmetry they also possess radial structures in the tentacles. (Courtesy of William Evans Hoyle, https://commons.wikimedia.org/w/index.php?curid=18703952)

FIGURE 3.17 (See color insert.) An octopus, with wildly twisting tentacles. How different is this from our tree root structure? (Courtesy of Comingio Merculiano in Jatta Giuseppe—I Cefalopodi viventi nel Golfo di Napoli (sistematica): monografia, https://commons.wikimedia.org/w/index.php?curid=20146127)

currently three existing animal types with the capability of flight, which does not include dinosaurs such as pteranodons and pterodactyls, but they should also be included when considering the means with which to model a flying creature. Wings are complex structures, but they all have the commonality of aerodynamic functionality, which includes a specific shape and contour that is unique in the animal world. Figure 3.18 illustrates a common bird wing, making note of the delicate curvature and structure of the arm.

The curves of the wing structures are unique to the flight mechanism, but also connected by utilitarian properties (Figure 3.19). When modeling these structures in Chapters 5 through 7, you will see how the commonalities guide the construction of proper shapes. Often in the realm of 3D fantasy games and production art, wings are extremely common and derive from vastly different morphologies. The dragon wings in Figure 3.20 are clearly derived from a reptilian concept, which can only come from dinosaur structures like the pteranodon in Figure 3.21! Of course, we must consider that the typical "dragon" of medieval mythology (and common in fantasy games) is a six-limbed animal, which is virtually unknown in the natural world. There are many examples of four-limbed dragon morphologies, how-ever, and these tend to have wing structures that are more "bat-like" than reptilian. Figure 3.22 illustrates a four-limbed dragon, which clearly has a more bat-like structure than the classic six-limbed dragon in Figure 3.20. Smaug, the classic Tolkien dragon from The *Hobbit*, was depicted in the films as having a bat-like structure, where the wings would

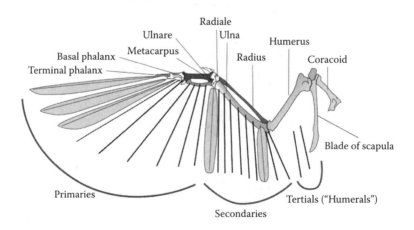

FIGURE 3.18 Typical bird wing, similar to our fish fins, but these are for swimming through the air! (Courtesy of L. Shyamal, CC BY-SA 2.5, https://commons.wikimedia.org/w/index.php?curid=21271855)

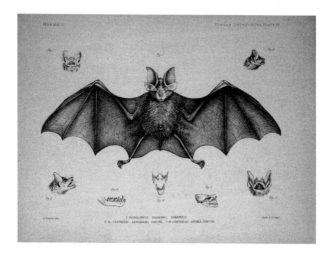

FIGURE 3.19   The bat achieves flight, but with a much different wing structure than a bird. (Courtesy of Flickr user Philbert Charles Berjeau, http://www.flickr.com/photos/biodivlibrary/sets/72157627799685671/)

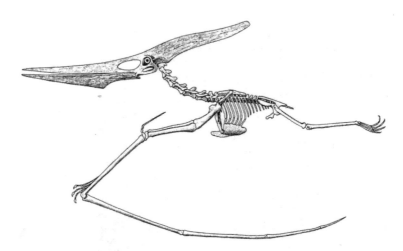

FIGURE 3.20   The pteranodon, with a radical wing structure based solely upon what was once a pinky finger! (Courtesy of George F. Eaton, https://commons.wikimedia.org/w/index.php?curid=7809433)

fold into the arms as flaps of skin. But the arms, unlike that of a bat, had wrists and fingers that could be articulated. This is technically not a form we see in true flying creatures, but it *is* prevalent in "gliders," or reptiles and mammals that have flaps of skin allowing them to glide from tree to ground, escaping predators. This is a great example of why modelers, riggers, and

FIGURE 3.21 A typical six-limbed fantasy dragon, where the wings are extra structures coming out of the back. (Courtesy of LadyofHats, CC0, https://commons.wikimedia.org/w/index.php?curid=53285235)

FIGURE 3.22 A more anatomically correct dragon, in which the wings are the arms, as in a bat or a pteranodon. (Courtesy of David Revoy/Blender Foundation, CC BY 3.0, https://commons.wikimedia.org/w/index.php?curid=22488156)

animators need to have a fine-tuned understanding of organic geometry and kinematics! How can you create a mythological beast that looks real if you can't deconstruct and reconstruct the piece in a convincing manner? The new level of realism in films has created a demand for creature-creators that have a very good understanding of organic forms and geometry.

Insect wings are varied and unique in and of themselves. They perform the same essential function as rodent, dinosaur, and bird wings, but the weight differential is exponentially smaller, so they are constructed in a much lighter and more ephemeral manner. Figure 3.24 illustrates common insect wing morphology. In keeping with our "fantasy" concepts, you can see the fairy in Figure 3.23 has insect-like wings (usually dragonfly, butterfly, or mothlike wings) protruding from its back. Likewise, the "angels" of modern mythology are usually depicted with birdlike wings including feathers (Figure 3.25).

FIGURE 3.23 Fairy wings are much like insect wings in this old woodcut. (Courtesy of Internet Archive Book Images, https://archive.org/stream/cu31924105428415/cu31924105428415#page/n537/mode/1up)

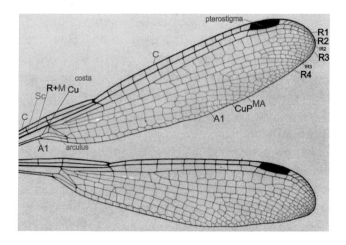

FIGURE 3.24 The dragonfly wing, with multiple cellular structure. (Courtesy of Bugboy52.40, CC BY-SA 3.0, https://commons.wikimedia.org/w/index.php?curid=14723570)

FIGURE 3.25 Wing of beetle Cetonia unfolded. You can clearly see the long, thin hard-shelled lines that create the structure of this insect wing, which has rippling curves at the edge, in a fan-like shape. (Courtesy of Siga, https://commons.wikimedia.org/w/index.php?curid=2002712)

The Spine

What is the spine? What good does it do us? What makes it so important to understand in modeling for vertebrates?

Other than the fact you would collapse into a human "skin puddle" without it, we can determine many things about the spine and vertebrates in general, as it pertains to modeling. The spine is structured in a very ordered and congruent manner, with multiple pieces that fit together and allow for an incredible range of flexibility while providing a thick sheath of bone for the protection of the massive and complex central nervous system, which connects the single most important part of our body (the brain) to all the rest of it. The spine is a complex structure that will define how to model and deform the main bulk of the creatures you will be creating. The geometry of the creature must flow with the spine, and indeed we can use the spinal physiology as a handy method of "wireframing" our models with an internal structure before creating a single polygon or curve.

The spine can be seen as manifesting in one of two directions, which will heavily influence your modeling techniques and layouts. There are "horizontal" designs, which incorporate most of the animal species (alive and extinct), and "vertical" designs, which will encompass solely human-like bipedal hominids. There is a tremendous difference between the two designs, so it's vital to determine just which you will use to design your own creature.

The horizontal design of vertebrates is a much older and highly functional setup. As you can see in Figure 3.26, the classic fish structure is a good beginning for understanding the function and purpose of the spine. The bass skeleton, a typical boned-fish typology, has a thick tail that sways back and forth in one plane of movement to propel the fish forward. The spinal structure of this animal is almost completely straight in the horizontal plane, making his back end directly behind his skull. This works perfectly for locomotion in a liquid medium, because he can see in the same direction he is moving, even if he angles upward or downward to change the depth level. So when modeling a fish, or similarly structured

FIGURE 3.26 A typical fish skeleton, with multiple spiny bones flanking the central spinal column. (Courtesy of Flickr user Francis Day, http://www.flickr.com/photos/biodivlibrary/8539693202)

organism, you will want to make the "flow" of the geometry move in this direction, which will not only enhance the appearance of the model, but also greatly ease the rigging and deformation later (Figure 3.27).

This fish has been modeled with the geometric flow of the horizontal spine kept in mind. Notice how the edge loops and contours are similarly spaced and laid out to the skeletal design.

Tetrapodian animals, from which we stem, are four-limbed creatures, who use the four limbs for locomotion. If we look at the anatomy of a simple amphibian, which are the oldest examples of the evolutionary scale, we can see the spinal system at its most primitive and essential architecture. The spine begins at the base of the neck and extends almost straight back from that segment, all the way to a tail (see below) at the end. The form has changed little from that of a fish, with the exception of added limbs (evolved from fins) that are now articulated enough to carry the creature across land, lifting the abdomen slightly off of the ground. When building a tetrapodian organism, the main difficulty is not in constructing the horizontal flow of geometry but in the limb extrusion from the body! Unlike arthropods and insects, the jointed parts of a soft-bodied animal like the newt in Figure 3.28 have complex folds of skin and surface texture, forming dimples where the hard skeleton extrudes out from the body. Luckily, in a creature as simple as this newt, we can see that the legs extend almost completely on a horizontal plane, allowing for some simple modeling tricks, which we will explore in Chapters 5 through 7.

Of course, not *all* amphibians have this typical four-legged structure! Figure 3.29 is a great example of a unique mobility adaptation in the

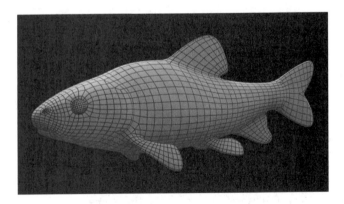

FIGURE 3.27 A 3D fish model, retaining the basic structure of the outside of the fish in Figure 3.26.

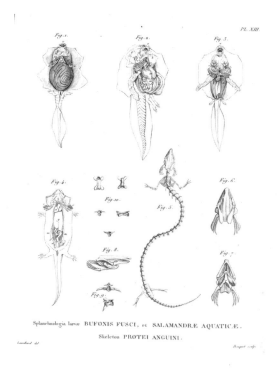

FIGURE 3.28   Newt skeleton, or the origin of limbs in vertebrates. Notice how they extrude nearly perpendicular to the spine. (Courtesy of A. Humboldt (1769–1859), https://commons.wikimedia.org/w/index.php?curid=8287891)

FIGURE 3.29   The frog has uniquely tailored back limbs for its unique form of locomotion. (Courtesy of Alejandro Linares Garcia, GFDL, https://commons. wikimedia.org/w/index.php?curid=8076221)

common frog and toad, where the architecture of the creature is designed for hopping. The skeleton and especially the hind legs are beautifully structured for just this kind of purpose! When designing and structuring hopping animals or even semihuman versions (like the Toad from The X-Men), you'll always want to reference the frog and toad anatomy to understand the dynamic mechanics of the movement. The spinal column of a toad or frog, despite the initial appearance, is absolutely horizontal! Like most nonhominids, the spine of the frog is distinctively parallel to the ground and extends directly behind the head.

Continuing our trip down the spinal path, we can see how mammals and more complex animal forms began to develop distinct features of the spine that aided in their survival. In Figure 3.30 you can clearly see the anatomy of the modern horse, which unlike the reptilian and amphibian models has a strongly curved spinal node leading into the neck! This allows the animal to have the neck high above the level of the legs and trunk, able to see from a higher vantage point and reach vegetation higher

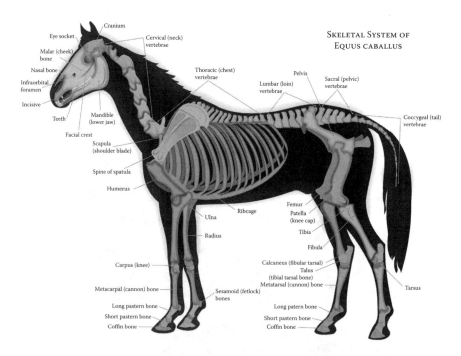

FIGURE 3.30 The horse, like a dog, has limbs that extrude slightly out of the spine and then straight down, making it very powerful and fast. (Courtesy of Wikipedian Prolific, vectorization process by The Photographer, CC BY-SA 3.0, https://commons.wikimedia.org/w/index.php?curid=44546089)

up in trees. These cervical vertebrae are very important in developing the structural anatomy of the powerful neck when modeling a four-legged mammal of any kind. You can notice that the angle of the *rest* of the spine, however, is completely horizontal and parallel to the ground.

Regardless of the species or level of evolutionary sophistication, the spine is a very important part of the general shape of the animal (Figure 3.31). A vertebrate gets a large part of the cross-section shape of the body from the shape of the vertebrae, which as you can see in Figure 3.32 has a distinct U-shape. The hole in the center protects the spinal nerve column and the wings give it needed support for the thick tendrils of ligament, cartilage, and other connective tissues that protect the vulnerable areas while providing for an incredible amount of mobility. One of the important things about recognizing the cross-section shape of the body is to mirror the spinal shape, which is almost always a U-shape along the length of the entire spine. A snake, as you can see in Figure 3.47, has this exact cross section throughout the entire length of the body, as does a fish. It is a tapering parabolic curve that meets in the center with varying levels of sharpness. The rounded, bulbous shape of the rib cage will determine how rounded this cross section is. For instance, in a frog and an elephant, the cross-section shape is very rounded because the rib cages are relatively wide. What the spine and skeletal structure can tell you about the animal is abundant—the size and extent of the rib cage can clue your modeling decisions in both the macroscopic and microscopic. It can help you rough out the contours of a simple shape as you strive to set up the rib cage and basic shaping, or it can tell you where the individual wrinkles of skin might go to define the spine in a high-resolution model for wrinkle mapping or normal maps.

The spine can be seen as your primary guideline for modeling your creature. The main length of the spine is the length axis you will model on, while the perpendicular axis to the spinal length axis will be your cross-section axis, which changes shape as you sculpt it along the length of the spine. The spinal top axis is the axis that we see looking down at a 90-degree angle to the spinal length axis. Modeling based up the spine allows us to slice the character up into pieces, like a ham, and adjust the changes in all three axes as we follow the spine from the skull to the tip of the tail.

So for a human, and some primates, the spinal length axis is equivalent to the y-axis in a Y-up world (Maya's default setting). This would mean that the spinal length axis is on the y-axis while the cross-section axis is the x-axis. The z-axis is our top view.

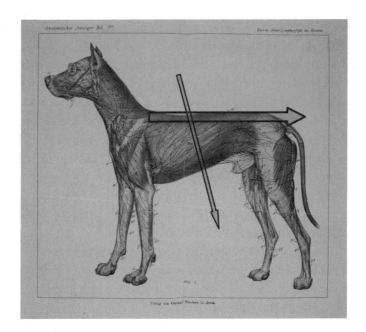

FIGURE 3.31   Vectors of the body as they pertain to the direction of the spine. (Courtesy of Hermann Baum, https://commons.wikimedia.org/w/index.php?curid= 6809940)

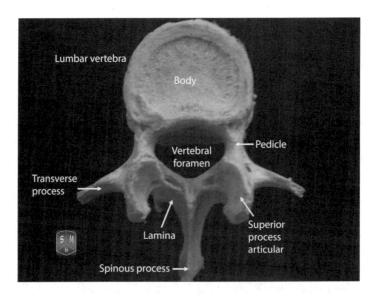

FIGURE 3.32   Layout of the vertebrae from a mammal. (Courtesy of Anatomist90, CC BY-SA 3.0, https://commons.wikimedia.org/w/index.php?curid=17155625)

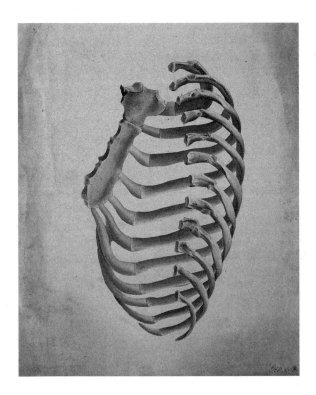

FIGURE 3.33   Notice how similar our rib cage shape is to that of a pear. (Courtesy of Wikimedia Commons, http://wellcomeimages.org/indexplus/obf_images/2e/38/ f380f5529b199b138b43671ec455.jpg)

For a quadruped, this schematic rotates 90 degrees around the x-axis. This means that the z-axis is the spinal length axis, the y-axis is the top axis, and the x-axis is the cross-section axis.

The human rib cage, depicted in Figure 3.33, and most animal rib cages, coincidentally replicate the bulbous shape as described in Chapter 1. Despite the multifaceted complex construction of the bones and structure of the rib cage of vertebrates, the essential form of the layout can easily be compared to other bulbous shapes, such as the female womb or a pear (Figure 3.34).

Bipeds

Bipedalism, as a form of locomotion, is not unique to humans! In fact, billions of years ago the dinosaurs, and subsequently the birds, got it pretty much covered. But the human mechanism and the aviary mechanism of bipedalism are vastly different. Dinosaurs, and some modern flightless

FIGURE 3.34 Once again, the pear shape is repeated across a wide spectrum of organic geometry. (Courtesy of Rhododendrites, CC BY-SA 4.0, https://commons.wikimedia.org/w/index.php?curid=54215885)

birds like the ostrich, employ bipedalism with a horizontal spine and a tail to balance it out. The advantages to bipedalism are many and varied. It can often speed up mobility (but not necessarily) and allow the free use of the forelimbs (arms) for grasping and manipulation of plants. It also provides a much higher vantage visual point to spot both prey and predators before they spot you.

As you can see in Figures 3.35 and 3.36, the bipedal dinosaur has a completely horizontal spine and rotates the main trunk of the body via the hip sockets, pivoting the balance between the bulk of the front mass and the length of the massive tail behind it like a seesaw! This makes a difference to the modeler in that he must imagine the neutral position of the creature in the original stance of the model, and not necessarily the staged position that it would be standing in when the skeletal reconstruction is assembled. So in order to build something like a *T. rex*, one would have to imagine it not standing upright with the spine at an angle to the ground, but horizontally, as in Figure 3.36. This is probably more of a natural locomotive state for the giant extinct creature than the more upright position (Figures 3.37 through 3.39).

FIGURE 3.35   Bipedal dinosaur drawing. The spine was still a horizontal structure, and the hips swiveled to bring the beast onto two legs. (Courtesy of Bugboy52.4, CC BY-SA 3.0, https://commons.wikimedia.org/w/index.php?curid=5731266)

FIGURE 3.36 (See color insert.)   Though a completely bipedal creature, the *T. rex* did not have a vertical spine. In this image you can see the swiveling of the hips that allowed it to walk on two limbs, balanced by the huge tail. (Courtesy of Wikimedia Commons, CC BY 2.0, https://commons.wikimedia.org/w/index.php?curid=39768754)

The Tail

Tails come in a myriad of shapes and forms, but there is a similarity that's vital in getting the geometry and structure correct! Once again, we have a tapering tube that commands the contouring, bringing us back to the original forms of organic life on Earth. But a vertebrate tail is a much

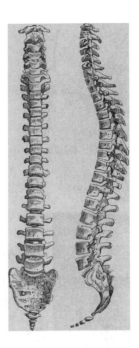

FIGURE 3.37   The human spine, and the only one in known existence to be vertical (perpendicular) to the ground! (Courtesy of Internet Archive Book Images, https://archive.org/stream/anatomyphysiolog00mayc/anatomyphysiolog00 mayc#page/n33/mode/1up)

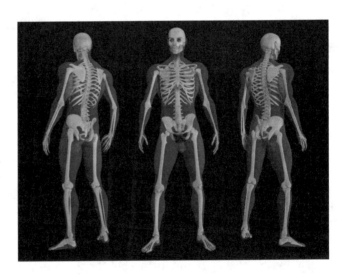

FIGURE 3.38   Humans are vastly different from all other species in their upright and perpendicular construction. (Courtesy of Bernhard Ungerer, CC BY 3.0, https://commons.wikimedia.org/w/index.php?curid=4256709)

FIGURE 3.39   Even an ape is not fully erect—they still walk on four limbs most of the time. (Courtesy of Vinnie Lauria, CC BY-SA 2.0, https://commons.wikimedia. org/w/index.php?curid=3792566)

more complex shape—cross sections will often have a distinctive triangular shape with slightly curved sides. The purpose of tails is multifaceted, and often the form will follow the function in this regard. Almost all vertebrates, with the exception of humans and hominids, have a tail of some sort that is used in locomotion, balance, sensory input, and defense from predators. The tail is a vital part of the spinal cord, but it's a unique part of the animal because it terminates the spine, and because different tails are structured around the intent and use. The tail evolved with the spine and still remains as vestigial in the embryonic development of *all* vertebrates, including us!

Fish Tails

Fish tails, as you can see in Figure 3.40, are the termination of the spine. The end point is usually a thick, muscular, rounded area surrounded by the actual fin structures, and the tines that make up the structure in between the webbing of the fin are also bones! It's important to note that any of these fin structures in bony fish are actually tiny, fingerlike bony extrusions. In fact, this is most likely where our fingers, and the fingers of all land-dwelling animals, are derived from (Figure 3.41).

Reptile Tails

Reptilian and dinosaur tails closely follow the form of the spinal column as it runs down the spinal length axis of the animal. This tends to give it a strong triangular profile shape, which tapers with a slight exponential curve down the length. You can see in Figure 3.42 the thick, meaty stock of the tail and the exponentially tapering profile. Figures 3.43 and

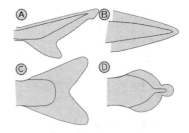

FIGURE 3.40   Various fishtail shapes. (Courtesy of Wikimedia Commons, https://commons.wikimedia.org/w/index.php?curid=975773)

3.44 illustrate a digitally generated shape using an extruded profile curve on a path to approximate this same exact shape in 3D geometry.

Mammalian Tails

The mammal and other vertebrates have a huge variety of tail shapes, many more than we could list! The forms of tail are generally dependent on the form of locomotion and environment of the natural habitat. The squirrel skeleton in Figure 3.45 shows a bushy tail high off the ground, with a curve that extends over the animal's head, but another member of the same classification, the common rat, who is mostly a ground-dweller, has a thick, ropelike tail with no fur at all. Yet they are both rodents. The morphology of a tail will always be first and foremost dependent on the termination of the bones that make up the spine, and

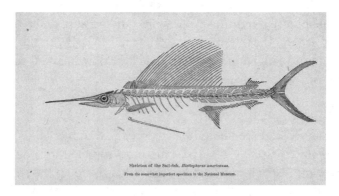

FIGURE 3.41   Another fish skeleton, showing the spiny bone nodes that make up the fins and tail. (Courtesy of George Brown Goode, https://commons.wikimedia.org/w/index.php?curid=42648690)

FIGURE 3.42 The iguana tail is a long, tapered shape that has a triangular cross section. (Courtesy of Rjcastillo, CC BY-SA 3.0, https://commons.wikimedia. org/w/index.php?curid=23122320)

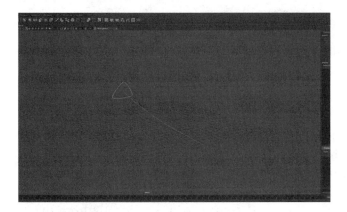

FIGURE 3.43 The lizard tail cross section in 3D.

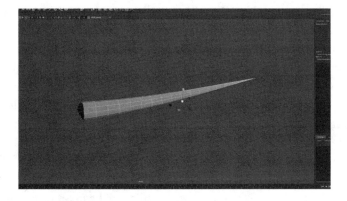

FIGURE 3.44 An extruded version of the iguana tail.

FIGURE 3.45   A tail with a strong upward curve. (Courtesy of Wikimedia Commons, https://commons.wikimedia.org/w/index.php?curid=24381924)

those bones will almost always have a strong taper from base to tip. This is why the tapered tube structure is almost always a perfect method of generating this structure in most animals. In a few specialized animals, such as the beaver, platypus, or mammalian aquatic creatures, the outer morphology of the tail element will vary greatly from the inner morphology (Figure 3.46).

Serpentine/Legless

Snakes, eels, and legless lizards are all great examples of slithering organisms that developed a unique and extremely complex method of movement. This morphology is also one of the most widely used in fantasy, science fiction, and other 3D/CG enterprises due to the highly emotional impact reptilian "slitherers" have on the human psyche. Hence, it would be very expedient for the 3D organic modeler to develop skills in this area. The snake, which is our prototypical slithering entity (eels live underwater, where the mechanics of movement are vastly different), moves across the ground by creating friction with a complex rib cage anatomy and a curling action.

The snake consists of two basic structures; the head and the tail (which is the entire length of the body). As you can see in Figure 3.47, the snake

FIGURE 3.46 The rodent tail, often a circular tubelike shape. (Courtesy of De Sève (dessin), C. Baquoy (gravure), http://gallica.bnf.fr/ark:/12148/btv1b2300254t/f38.item)

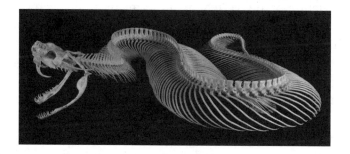

FIGURE 3.47 The snake has a head and one giant tail. (Courtesy of Stefan3345, CC BY-SA 4.0, https://commons.wikimedia.org/w/index.php?curid=46063244)

is a giant rib cage. Those ribs shape the snake, just like they do everything else; however, this reptile's unique form of locomotion has removed the vestigial appendages and left only a head and a tail (Figure 3.47)!

Muscles, Skin, Scales, Fur

I would be remiss here if I didn't mention the advent of skin. Having a skeleton on the inside doesn't do you much good if your organs are

falling out all over the place!
The muscles, ligaments, connective tissues, and skin covering
them provide the fleshy, squishy
part of the creature! Some creatures, as we can clearly see in the
arthropods, insects, and other
exoskeleton-type animals, have
all of their squishy parts on the
inside of their body (Figure 3.48).
Therefore, when modeling them

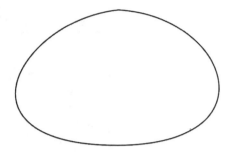

FIGURE 3.48   An ovoid shape, often the cross section of a mammalian tail.

we don't need to focus on the soft parts and in many ways can model them
in much the same way as we model a car: in segmented, jointed pieces.

Muscle and skin, however, have a much less rigid and defined system.
Since they are highly permeable and elastic they change shape and wrinkle with folds in multiple places in multiple ways, which have been giving
3D organic modelers headaches for decades. Modeling folds and wrinkles
is extremely difficult and notoriously tedious. There are many ways to get
around the difficulties, but solid shapes without these folds and wrinkles
are far easier to work with.

The structure of any vertebrate, in terms of its shape and topology,
can first be understood with the skeleton. As we have seen, the structures of the skeleton provide the framework upon which the rest is built;
we can derive the basic shapes in 3D from simply matching the rough
areas of the bones. But the outer layers of the skin and organs provide
just as much information about how to shape and model the creature.
There is where we really focus on secondary and tertiary elements of
the geometry.

Muscle shaping is very rounded. It consists of the fibers and the fas-
cia, which are all essentially tubelike structures of stretchy, flexible tissue,
stretched between two ends. Because the tissue is pliable, we can see and
feel them flex, at which point the shape can drastically change. The volume
is retained, however, in the total shape. In 3D modeling, we must pay careful attention to the muscular structure of the animal in order to create a
realistic appearance. Muscles are layered tissues, sometimes with multiple
muscle groups lying on top of one another. Figure 3.49 shows a human leg,
with the muscular structure revealed. This layering reveals that certain
muscles are long and lean, while others are thick and bulbous (like the
gastrocnemius, bicep, or glutes) and taper out as they reach toward the

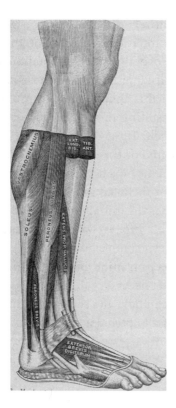

FIGURE 3.49   In this anatomical cutout of the human lower leg, you can see how the bulbous shapes of the muscles deform the skin that stretches over them, all supported by the hard, solid bones beneath. (Courtesy of Wikimedia, https://archive.org/stream/appliedanatomyk00bowe/appliedanatomyk00bowe#page/n196/mode/1up)

point of insertion. The important thing about the muscle structure to keep in mind when modeling is that they often define the details of a particular body part as well as the overall shape of an area. Major muscle groups, like the glutes, the pectorals, the gastrocnemius, the biceps/triceps, and quadriceps, can clearly define the overall shape, while the smaller muscle groups such as the abdominals will define the detailed areas by use of indentation.

When modeling an organic creature, you will let the major muscle groups guide the overall shape of the torso and limbs. This is always done first, as the primary pass on the creature in low resolution is occurring. That is where the shapes of the legs and arms are created, paying close attention to the silhouette and front view.

Indentation is an entirely different surface feature than that of the major shaping. Indentation is the variations on the surface from the normal vector, and not the overall shape. Indentation occurs when you have overlapping muscle and bone areas, and those changes in shape cause a "divot" to occur, which is simply offset from the height of the previous muscle or bone, resulting in a variation between the height of the surface compared to itself. These divots and ripples are the result of the difference between them. For this reason, musculature and the shaping of these areas must be done on a higher resolution polygonal mesh. This can be hand-sculpted or included in a high-resolution version as a tool for normal mapping after the initial model is complete. When modeling the organic method, this process would not take place until the low-resolution model has been completed.

Another thing to keep in mind is that the indentations in the surface of the muscles aren't necessary to have a good, solid organic model. The outer appearance can have the shape that the skeleton and muscles give it without sporting sculpted deformations!

CHAPTER 4

Organic Modeling Techniques

INTRODUCTION

What is an organic modeling technique? There could easily be an argument made to the effect that 3D modeling, in its current form, is entirely *nonorganic* in the sense that the nature of the medium requires a strictly technical approach. And that is not entirely untrue, in the sense that you won't achieve professional results as a modeler for animatable content (as opposed to just a sculpture) if you don't have technical expertise, ability, and understanding of the best way to approach the task.

What this section will do is explain to you the choices a modeler has when tackling a complex organic structure, the reasons that certain methodologies are used for certain cases, and how to make that decision tree on your own with scalable, high-level results! There's a lot that goes into the art of 3D modeling, and one of the most important aspects of this discipline is to fully comprehend the task at hand and how to determine the best path to the completion of that task. There are very organic, "sculpting" methods of generating curves and detail that work great for sculptures, but most 3D organic models are intended for rigging and animation, and it's imperative that they be modeled for that purpose. This means that the final rendered product is *not* the objective goal you should be considering as a modeler. In fact, the layout and structure of the geometry as well as the final appearance of the rendered model are both equally important when making modeling decisions.

What are some of the tools at our disposal? What are the decision trees that we will be looking at in order to better guide our modeling decisions? Luckily, the structure of the organism we are modeling, as outlined in previous sections and chapters, can help guide us along our path. The type of organism and the structure of that organism will give you clues as to the best method of construction. So all of those "biology lessons" in previous content will definitely count for something when learning how to determine the best course of action.

Detail versus Complexity

Some of the important concepts to understand in this segment are the combating needs for the end result model. Level of detail and adaptive complexity are two things that often become mutually exclusive, or at least fight with each other on a sliding scale. A high level of detail will necessarily make the need for complexity high, as it is very difficult to model something with a lot of detail without adding a lot of geometry. Adaptive technologies such as Non-Uniform Ration B-Splines (NURBS), Bezier surfaces, and subdivision surfaces offer some ability to increase or decrease the local level of complexity adaptively; however, there is always an increase in difficulty or several caveats that one faces with each of these higher-level forms of modeling (described in more detail below). The basic polygonal quad mesh offer customized detail at the expense of global adaptivity, but great strides have been made in the ability to localize and globalize increased detail in the polygonal model! Also, for reasons of increased computing power and real-time rendering ability, simple polygonal modeling has become more prevalent in recent years than it was a decade ago. Note here that polygons are *always* the end result of the rendering pipeline, even if you don't immediately see the conversion process, which for some 3D content creation packages is always under the hood.

The model in Figure 4.1 has a huge amount of fine detail, but the polygon level is incredibly high, making it sluggish to display and difficult to rig for animation. The model in Figure 4.2 has a much lighter level of detail, but as you can clearly see the edges are not smooth, and the deformations will be clunky and difficult to create smooth areas from. This conundrum has been very difficult for modelers and 3D artists to hurdle; if we increase the level of complexity we can achieve superior results in rendering and smoothness, *but* we exponentially increase the complexity and necessary computing power to properly set up, rig, and animate. The search for balancing these two elements of 3D modeling has been a long-standing

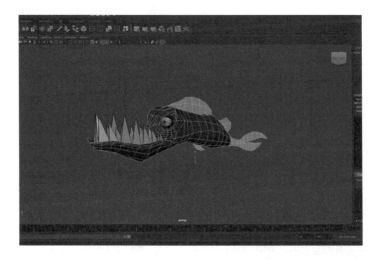

FIGURE 4.1 (See color insert.)   A fish model at very low resolution.

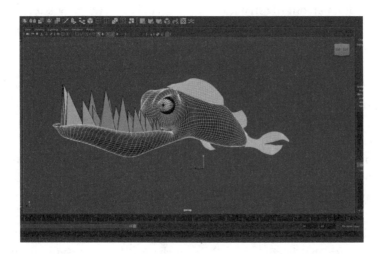

FIGURE 4.2   Our fish character with several iterations of smoothing.

balancing act and remains a problem even with the higher processing and graphics power of the modern computers. Even *if* the computer could process billions of polygons a second, our brain couldn't catch up with it, which means that some form of superadaptive geometrical layout must be created to bridge the gap between what we as humans can process, and what the computer can process. This is especially true in games and interactive entertainment, since the real-time processing speeds necessitate a much lower level of polygons drawn. A rendered frame for a film can take as long as 1–2 hours to render at full resolution and even have things rendered in layer passes for later composition with the background or other elements. A game needs to process 60 frames per second with *every* visible polygon and texture map in the rendering pipeline! For this reason, creating scalable structures with reasonable amounts of polygons is the function of every organic modeler in the real-time arena. But how can we achieve this?

There are several answers, and combinations of various techniques to increase perceived or potential detail without changing the *actual* amount of polygons in the modeled mesh. In this section, you will learn some of these adaptive polygonal techniques and how they are used to model organic shapes with a natural workflow. When you're dealing with computer technology and limited resources, there will never be a 100 percent effective method of modeling something like you would sculpt a piece of clay (at least not with existing technology), because there is a sincere need to plan and map out the structure of the model to match the use of it inside an interactive environment. The model itself is only the beginning; you need to also consider the eventual use as a rig and animated character.

Adaptive Geometry

Adaptive geometry in 3D uses the exact same principles as vector graphics do in 2D. The geometry is high level, which in less fancy terms is just a description of a space inside of which geometry is rendered, converted to as many triangles as necessary for the intended level of resolution. This is also the way text is rendered in your web browser or word processing document; the vectors that make up the font will appear just as smooth at any zoom level. This is because instead of looking at pure pixels (like in a typical JPG image) you are looking at pixels rendered inside the description of space that is contained inside a shape. The shape can be filled in with as much detail as possible when it is necessary to do so. So the number of pixels can increase or decrease as needed to fill in the space of the shape that the text consists of. This is simple vector graphics at work and is at the heart of computer graphics technology. The vector describes the shape, and the shape is filled in with a number of pixels determined by the size and resolution of the display.

In 3D graphics this same concept is achieved through a similar manner but calculated in three dimensions using curves and calculating the area contained by them (or through some other curve-based operation). There are many different terms for this in different modeling programs, but *skin* and *surface* are common terms that describe the contained area stretched out between two or more curves and then rendered to polygonal geometry in an adaptive manner. Any two or more curves can be turned into a surface by lofting them, which generates geometry between them through describing the space that they contain. This is done with either NURBS or Bezier curves, and the resulting surface will then be tessellated, or converted dynamically into triangles for actual rendering display on a screen. The triangles then act in a similar manner to the 2D vector font shapes, where they are filled in with the appropriate amount of pixels based on multiple factors such as lighting, texture, materials, and so forth.

Although this is an incredibly succinct description of a computer graphics rendering pipeline, it's only partially consequential to our focus on the modeling aspect of the process! Lighting, rendering, and compositing are far outside the scope of this book. The important thing to understand in this section is the concept of adaptive resolution through modeling with curves and surfaces.

Figure 4.3 illustrates a simple loft between two curves, forming a NURBS surface. Figure 4.3 shows that same surface as it is seen by the rendering engine, converted into triangles (a process called *tessellation*). The important thing about NURBS and surface-based modeling is the ability to adaptively increase or decrease resolution fairly easily. As long as you don't need to branch anything off of a NURBS surface, the modeling technique can work quite well. A great feature of the surface is the ability to increase detail along one axis quite easily by inserting another isoparm anywhere along the surface. A disadvantage, however, is that we have to

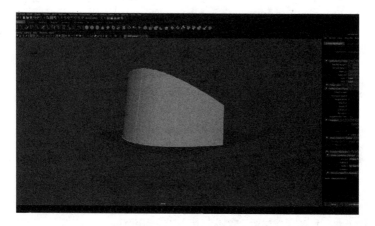

FIGURE 4.3 (See color insert.)   A simple NURBS-based loft between two curves.

insert the detail across an entire axis of the surface at once! This is actually really difficult to work with when the detail increases to a point where it becomes unmanageable (Figure 4.4).

One thing that NURBS is terrible at, however, is branching or extruding one surface from another. Unlike pure polygons, surfaces are entirely unable to be extruded in a branching fashion. The reason this is impossible is that the area that you are seeing isn't really a surface at all, but rather a description of an area in which the triangles are rendered by the software. It *is* possible to convert the surface to polygons and extrude from that, but as you can see in Figure 4.5 that ends up with a very awkward extrusion,

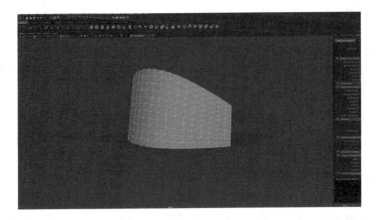

FIGURE 4.4   The tessellated version of the loft from Figure 4.3, in which we see the polygon triangles directly in the viewport.

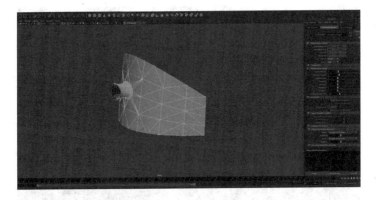

FIGURE 4.5   A branching form of NURBS, shown in triangles. Notice how uneven and unruly the geometry is around the protrusion?

due to the fact that the area that would be extruded as a rounded shape would have an impossibly complex and uneven layout of polygons.

Knowing what we do about the need for many of our organic models to have smooth and rounded branching features, we can clearly see that there must be a better way to construct our creatures than using surfaces. There most definitely is, and we will come to that in a short bit below.

So where are these surfaces useful in terms of organic modeling? They are, actually, quite useful in a number of places where we do not require seamless branching to occur. Any geometric shape that has multiple complex hard pieces without the need for a seamless skin is an excellent candidate for surface-based modeling! The great thing about arthropods, arachnids, and any other hard-shelled creatures is that the outside of the body is made up of individual pieces that fit together as segments and hence can be modeled with surfaces.

In fact, any hard-shelled structure without a soft skin covering is an excellent place to use the techniques of surface-based modeling. Simple bivalve seashells like clams, oysters, and mussels are great places to employ such modeling techniques. The interesting thing here is that both polygonal primitive and surface-based modeling can be used to model the same objects, with varying results.

Adaptive Modeling with Primitives and Edge Loops

The most common technique for organic flow modeling is to use simple primitives, mostly cubes, and edge looping. Edge looping is a particular form of polygonal modeling that mimics the surface geometric flow where there are U and V loops of polygonal edges, able to be inserted, edited, or removed as an entire line across the geometry. Polygons can then be modeled and edited in a similar manner to surfaces, *but* include the advantages of polygons such as divisible faces, easy branching solutions, and individual triangulation.

An *edge loop* is contiguous lines of polygonal edges. As long as we confine it to this definition, we can understand how they operate in layman's terms. These loops can be connective, in that they form actual circles (hence the term "loop"), or they can be nonconnective, flowing flat until they terminate at both ends. Edge loops can be selected and manipulated as a whole quite easily; however, in order to use these selection tools the loop in question must be situated in between two other edge loops. This means that somewhere along the line there will be an edge loop "termination," or point where the contiguous loops are completed. Likewise, there can be "half loops," or contiguous lines of edges that do not come back together as a circle. Using the half loops can be an excellent way to insert detail in a semiradial manner into a certain area without disturbing the rest of the topography, for instance in the area of an ear or a shoulder, to help round it out without adding detail across the rest of the model (Figure 4.6).

UV edge loops are edge loops that flow in the U and V of a surface, or the up and down vectors of what would be a flat surface if placed upon a plane. You can see in Figure 4.7 the flow of the edge loops as they are highlighted, illustrating what an edge loop actually consists of and how it fits into the entire piece of geometry. It is very similar in workflow to NURBS surface isoparms, with the added flexibility of polygon quads.

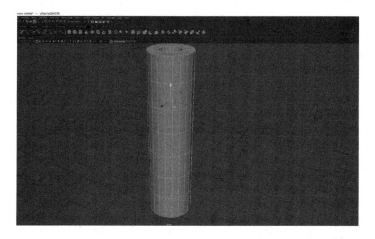

FIGURE 4.6   Illustration of an edge loop in the cross section.

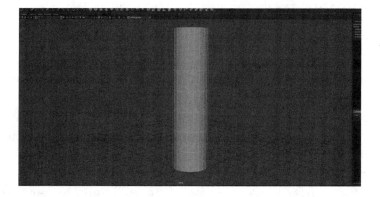

FIGURE 4.7   A vertical edge loop, along the length of the object.

The resolution is not adaptive, as would be a NURBS surface; however, it is possible to increase it by using a polygon smooth (see Figure 4.8) or manually inserting more edge loops wherever necessary.

In order to create proper UV edge loops, the geometry must be prepared and approached in a very specific manner. Individual polygons can't just be placed here or there; rather the entire surface must be laid out as if it were a continuous tube, as you can see in Figures 4.9 and 4.10. The rows and lines of edge loops are contiguous polygonal edges, all contained between two other sets of polygonal edges. The nice thing about this layout is the ability of the modeler to put extra levels of detail into certain

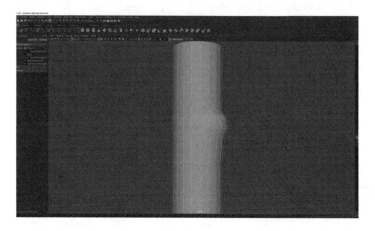

FIGURE 4.8   Inserted detail in a looping manner.

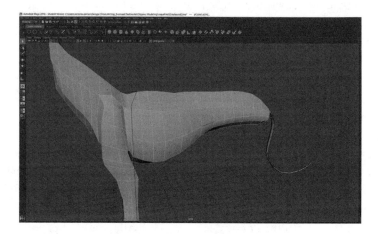

FIGURE 4.9   The U and V of edge looping.

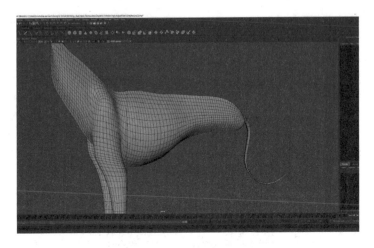

FIGURE 4.10 The smoothed version of the edge looping created a nice, even flow to the surface. Without proper edge looping the smoothed version could be very chaotic.

areas of the model that require it, while leaving the rest in a more primitive state! The disadvantage here is that in order to keep the integrity of the edge-loop formatting, you absolutely must add detail across the entire surface that you are working with, or at the very least the contiguous edge loops available. It *is* possible, and indeed highly likely, that you will work with the edge loops eventually constricted to certain areas that require extra detail in local places, as opposed to across the entire mesh. This will happen as you narrow down the areas that require extra detail. In order to properly connect the areas, the polygons can be triangulated in certain areas to patch them together without losing the single, continuous surface layout. In Chapters 5 through 7, we will explore the exact process of this locally edited resolution in far greater detail (Figure 4.11).

Edge looping has multiple distinct advantages, both in workflow and in rigging/deformation/animation. Edge loops can be globally added, removed, and edited as units, which speeds up the workflow and ability to rough out polygon models quickly and efficiently. Inserting the detail where needed and making a change to the entire edge loop at once increases the speed and the proper parameterization of the geometric flow of the resulting polygonal mesh, something that is very important for texturing, rigging, and rendering. Having evenly spread-out polygonal faces increases the ease of use of any model, especially one that is going to be rigged and animated.

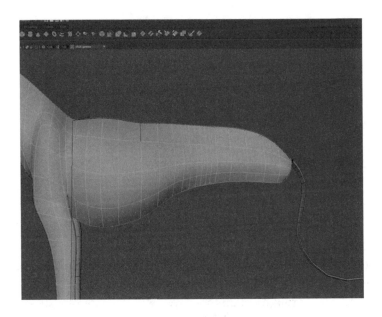

FIGURE 4.11   Inserting cross-section edge loops.

Radial edge looping is the real gem of polygonal edge looping, in that it allows us to create radially adaptive areas inside of cross-section polygons for the purposes of creating vital organic shapes such as eyes, antennae, shoulders, limbs, and almost anything else that is structured in a radial or circular manner! Organic geometry contains a myriad of radial shapes, which exist inside of cross-section shapes, and for that reason it's an almost universally recognized and utilized technique for proper polygonal organic modelers. Figure 4.12 shows a very simple, yet deceptively deep radial edge-looped structure, resembling an eye socket. The speed and simplicity with which this structure can be modeled and detail increased (or decreased) makes it a very powerful tool for organic modeling. In order to do the same with NURBS surfaces, one must go through a series of hoops with projected curves on surfaces, trim surfaces, and fillet surfaces, which in the end produce little useable polygonal geometry for organic deformation and animation. Radial edge looping presents one of the simplest scalable and powerful modeling techniques for organic structures! It's also worthy of note here that the radial structure was created inside of a UV edge-loop structure, which means that anywhere you want in an edge-looped model you can create a radial shape and add detail to just this area, making it incredibly efficient for things like mouths and eye sockets, where you want more detail surrounded by less detail, especially if they

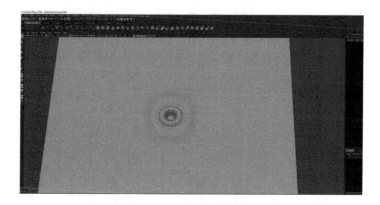

FIGURE 4.12   Radial edge loops inside of cross-section edge loops.

are intended to be animated in some way. Edge-looping techniques give you the best of both worlds in this regard.

In Chapters 5 through 7 of this book, you will learn step-by-step instructions on how to create radial edge loops inside of cross-section edge loops for the ultimate in selectively adaptive organic modeling.

Adaptive Modeling with Polygon Smoothing

Polygon smoothing is the process of taking a rough, or low-detail, modeled polygon and "smoothing" it by increasing the geometry and rounding the hard corners as the geometry is globally smoothed. Figures 4.13 and 4.14 illustrate the various elements of polygon smoothing as basic concepts and what can be accomplished with this operation. Smoothing is a powerful detail enhancement utility because it allows the user to model in a low-resolution "rough" manner, while producing a much higher resolution version after the low-resolution model has been roughed out. It can be used in adaptive rigging as well, in the sense that a low-resolution version of the model can be modeled and rigged and a smooth operator applied to the low-resolution model with the deformation still in the active history or "downstream" of the object. This allows the low-resolution object to be controlled by the skeletal rig while the smoothed result is what you see when you render the animation. This is a simplistic way of increasing the resolution of the resulting rendered animation but a good example of this technique of starting with a low-resolution model and using that to drive the progressive resolution of the end result. This process, however, is only useful if you are working with prerendered output such as film and video, and not at all useful for real-time games and interactive

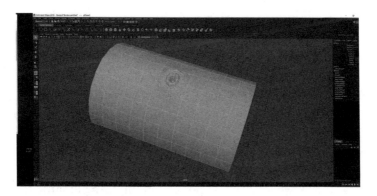

FIGURE 4.13   Radial area inside of a curved cross-section area.

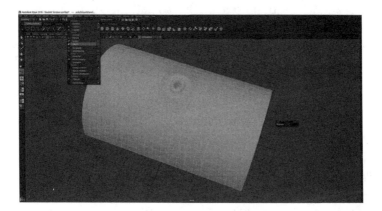

FIGURE 4.14   One iteration of smoothing.

entertainment, simply because these operators are fairly costly in CPU time and could rarely be processed at 60 frames per second! Outside the exponential increase in processing power with quantum computing, the interactive smooth and low-res object driving the high-res output is less likely to occur. There are people working on the compression of such techniques, however, and it's possible that sophisticated algorithms that compress the information could be worked out, which could allow us to use this technique in real-time applications.

In the process of modeling, however, the polygon smooth operator is a great way to up the resolution of the original rough model on a global scale! Figures 4.13 and 4.14 show a model in rough original and with a polygonal smooth operator applied (respectively). You can see how the number of polygons has doubled, but the resulting model is much smoother and rounded, which is perfect for organic structures. High-quality modelers, however, generally accomplish this increase in detail with the resulting rounding on their own and only in the areas that need it. This is a much more efficient way of modeling, because it allows you to only place the higher levels of detail in the areas that need it and leave the rougher areas with less detail. This is not possible when globally applying the polygonal smooth to a polygonal model, because it operates on all the faces at once (Figure 4.15).

Polygonal smoothing is all about creating a rounded curve from a hard angle, and this is why it's such a powerful tool in the organic modeler's arsenal. It allows us to create rough-hewn shapes that are easier to work with and complete our model as a smoothed, rounded result. Because Poly Smooth works best *globally*, it's something that happens toward the end of the modeling process and not too early. One must prepare for the end smoothing operation to create the rounded areas without too much loss of volume and detail. Often modelers completely eschew the Poly Smooth for anything but a general guideline to what the completed model will look like, and instead of using the polygon operation they will create the smoothness interactively and efficiently only in the needed areas of detail.

So what is the best use of the polygon smooth tool for organic modeling? Polygonal smoothing can quickly show you what the object will look like with the resulting increase in detail and rounded areas, which are ostensibly flat or angular. There are many 3D packages (including Maya) that will give you a quick preview of the geometry as it is smoothed, giving you an idea of where you might need alterations in the current geometry.

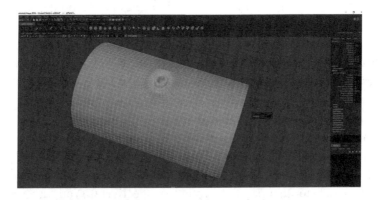

FIGURE 4.15 Two iterations of smoothing.

Another common technique is to run a polygonal smooth on the object as a whole and then remove certain edge loops from areas that do not require them. This way the mesh becomes more evenly spread out and easier to work with larger-scale deformation or rigging but is still adaptive in the areas that need the extra detail. It's a similar workflow to putting the loops in the areas you need them, but in reverse.

Adaptive Skinning with Wrappers

Adaptive rigging and skinning can also be accomplished with wrappers and geometry-based deformation. A low-resolution object is modeled, rigged, and animated, while a much higher level model is created from the original low-resolution version. Also a high-resolution character can be created, with the resulting low-resolution geometry generated from a polygon reduction tool automatically (which is often not the best way of generating geometry because of the low-resolution and poor resulting geometry). Wrappers for deformation were once a long-standing technique of very high-end "film-based" rigging and animation; however, newer and more realistic techniques have been pioneered and installed over the past decade, such as virtual muscles and muscular-based deformation systems. I am most mentioning it here as a methodology for using low-resolution models but receiving a high-resolution result.

Adaptive Detail with Normal Mapping and Ambient Occlusion

At some point in the previous two decades of computer graphics, somebody had the brilliant idea to substitute higher geometrical detail in polygonal models with the *illusion* of higher geometrical detail. In order to simulate higher detail without the detail, they used the rendering engine to apply a texture map that contained information about a polygonal object's normal values, or the tangential angle to the vertex, which determines by a large part how smoothly the light flows across the geometry. If this sounds complex, that's because it most definitely *is* complex, and you actually don't need to know all the details. The important thing to understand, however, is that if you can map the way light diffuses across a surface through a texture, you can create the illusion of detail in places where there isn't actually any detail! The surface can appear to have variations of height and levels of smoothness that you couldn't otherwise get without the addition of extra geometry. This "normal map" is based upon a higher level piece of geometry being compared to a piece of a lower level geometry with a similar topology. The mapping of the normal from the higher resolution geometry makes the lower resolution geometry appear to have a much higher level of detail. This trick is often used in organic models, especially with characters because the wrinkles and folds in skin or clothing can be created with good results on an otherwise low-resolution polygonal model! There are caveats, of course. The normal maps only work in static lighting and the normals will not change with the deformation of the character, which means that the wrinkle in skin and normal-mapped detail will not adjust with the radical changing of the positioning due to animation and skeletal movement. So it's limited in some manner of speaking, but still a powerful and useful tool in creating more detail with less geometry.

Normal mapping is now considered an essential element of high-quality content for real-time character models, and hence you should understand the basic mechanics. Creating normal maps is usually an automated process undertaken by the modeler after creating an extremely high-resolution version of the model that will actually be shown in the game. Once the sculpting of the high-resolution model has been completed, the normal maps will be generated based on the offset between the lower res model and the higher res model, then mapped to the UV mapping already in place (which is another process entirely).

Ambient occlusion is essentially a texture-based operation, but it should be included in this section because it provides some similarity of the illusion of detail as a normal map, and hence is very useful for the modeler to understand. Ambient occlusion is the process by which light is indirectly blocked by the folding or rounding of the skin. Areas of the body like eye sockets, wrinkles, and the inside of the knuckles are places where light generally and intermittently (when the wrinkles are deeper) cannot penetrate, and they are thus darker than other areas. Real-time 3D lighting is very expensive, and since these areas are constantly changing (indeed they are usually, but not always, in places of folding skin), they aren't great places to use normal mapping since the normal would have to update with the animation and deformation of the geometry. In these cases ambient occlusion maps can do a lot of work for less processing power, where the darker wrinkle areas are filled in with a shifting map, which adjusts to the depth of the wrinkles or simply to the movement of the joints in the rig. Ambient occlusion can add significant depth to an otherwise low-resolution model by faking the occlusion of light that occurs on the skin. Textures and advanced techniques using them can often give us far more leverage in the detail of a model than adding a bunch of geometry to achieve a similar result. For this reason our models can be as only as dense as we need them to be for deformation, and not so dense that they become unmanageable! Thanks to the advent of these new texture-based geometrical detail, the trend of organic modeling has gone toward minimalism and away from complexity. We can now focus solely on the deformation needs of the model over the rendering needs.

ORGANIC MODELING WORKFLOW AND METHODOLOGY: VERTEBRATES

So how do we put all this seemingly disjointed information together to form a cohesive method of action? After learning everything we can in general terms about the structure, shaping, design, and curvature of the organic world, how do we then go about determining how to succeed in creating them?

Organic modeling workflow, like anything else in the technical industry, requires a solid strategical approach to be successful. "Organic" in terms of modeling workflow is somewhat of a misnomer; it's organic because it involves an organic object (even if it is a car shaped like an insect), *but* the workflow is "organic" because it resembles the act of sculpting more than engineering. There are definitely sculpting-based modeling software packages, most notably Z-Brush and Autodesk's Mudbox. These are tools for a sculpt-like modeling workflow, where the artist uses virtual 3D brushes to pull and push high-resolution geometry as if manipulating clay. The advantage of these organic modeling workflows is the ability to create high levels of detail and a very smoothed, rounded result that can include difficult modeling techniques like wrinkles and folds quickly and with good parameterization. The downside of these modeling packages is that they can often produce unusable geometry for rigging and skinning, especially for use in real-time development characters for games. That being said, they often have polygonal reduction tools for re-parameterizing the high-density meshes generated, which can then be adjusted for output to a game engine. Organic sculpting software packages such as Mudbox and Z-brush also have a very steep learning curve and are often used more by sculpture-driven artists or high-level modelers with years of experience in varying venues. They are also often used in conjunction with another 3D content package (like Maya, 3D Studio, or Blender) to adjust, tweak, and re-parameterize the sculpted model. Indeed, most basic modeling is started with the more standard workflow and then "enhanced" with the sculpt programs (and perhaps 3D painted with textures), then parameterized and sent back to the original content software for cleanup and rigging.

So it's far better to have a total command of the initial organic modeling skills using the standard content-creation software rather than specialize in the sculpted versions. This book is dedicated to teaching and understanding the basic and foundational skills in organic modeling and not how to use sculpt software.

The organic modeling workflow presented in this book is intended to get the beginner to intermediate modeler off the ground with a staple of knowledge and techniques that can be used to rapidly produce quality organic creatures of all kinds. The workflow is designed to set up the modeler with everything they need to start producing solid work, using a system that also makes it the most efficient and structurally sound for use in a rigged, animated environment. I can't state enough here the importance of strategy and proper planning when modeling! If you start with a cube and kind of just mess around with it until it look similar to what you're trying to model, it will end up looking like a rounded cube vaguely resembling your original goal. If, on the other hand, you take pictures of what you want to model, lay them out proportionately as reference images, set up your modeling workflow to be efficient, and follow proper guidelines in terms of structure and modeling technique, you can start to create good work quickly with less effort.

The "organic" part of organic modeling will be the result of proper planning and setup, when you are freed from technical constraints or an array of decisions needing to be made about how to proceed. When you have set up the modeling environment properly, the process will cease to be onerous and tedious and instead feel more like you're "breathing" life into a lump of clay. Unfortunately, that lump of clay has to be prepared a certain way in order to make the modeling experience more fun and organic! Once you set yourself up properly, the act of modeling will be a lot more fun and creative.

The step-by-step process I am outlining below is fairly specific to vertebrates, but many of the techniques here can certainly be adapted for other types of animals. Since the vertebrates like fish, reptiles, dinosaurs, birds, mammals, and humanoids are the *most* difficult to model and have identical structural considerations, I have chosen that for my series of steps and examples, which move in a very particular order for this purpose. In Chapters 5 through 7 of this book, there are multiple examples of invertebrates and plants that can be modeled in various other ways. Chapter 8 of this book deals with nonorganic modeling techniques for organic creatures or pseudo-organic structures. This series of instructions should go hand in hand with Chapters 5 through 7, where I go into detail about the specific steps as I model a vertebrate animal using the methodology outlined in this section. The steps below should be adhered to in the order that I have outlined them, for the sake of the fastest and most efficient final result.

Reference Images

Reference images, properly laid out in your modeling package, are essential for proper and easy organic modeling! I can't recall how many times I have started working with a polygon primitive in order to just "sculpt" something without any planning or reference images inside of my modeling software. It rarely resulted in anything worth using in a professional manner. Even if you have reference images *outside* your modeling software, you absolutely must edit and import them to your software as image planes on the 3D grid. This is so you can quickly and easily edit the edge loops and geometry rough shape to match the proportions preset by your reference images.

Importing and choosing your reference images will depend on the type of animal or creature you are modeling. This will depend on the structure of the spine or the alignment of the creature in two dimensions. Figure 3.26, for instance, is the side profile of a fish. This fish would be set up to be modeled from the side, which would be facing the x-axis (either Y-up or Z-up here; the x-axis is always the long axis of the ground plane). Why is this important? We want to model the creature in its most natural state as well as use our Symmetrical Modeling to cut the amount of work in half and speed up the process, assuming that this model is intended to be perfectly symmetrical.

Most complex animals, from insects to dogs, can be split in half along the z-axis (in a Y-up world). This is because their spine extends from their neck backwards, and even with the long necks of giraffes, camels, and horses, there is a strong horizontal spine along the x-axis. This is because the spine supports the legs, which extend along the y-axis in some form until they reach the ground. This is the *primary spinal axis*, and it is the most important view of the reference images because it will give you the absolute best shape to work with when using a simple primitive object, such as a cube. The flow and shape of the horizontal geometry will be heavily determined by this reference image.

There are exceptions to this side-view layout, most notably the human or bipedal model! Since the spine of the human is almost completely straight, the axis that you begin the human shape with is the z-axis, and not the x-axis. It is important to note here, however, that the humanoid biped is still bilaterally symmetrical along the z-axis, which means we want to slice him right down the middle of the z-axis, looking forward. The modeling phase where we "rough out" the basic shapes would occur in this z-axis for the bipedal humanoid, as opposed to the x-axis for the quadruped, insect, fish, or any other horizontally aligned spine. Dinosaurs are always laid out on the x-axis, as you can see in Figure 3.35 because although they are bipedal, they have spines that terminate in long tails and hence the length of the body is the most prominent in terms of shape.

There are also several animals, such as a starfish or jellyfish, that have radial symmetry, a trait more common in the plant kingdom than anywhere else (think of flowers or fruit), are generally most exemplary being modeled from the top-down, or the y-axis in a Y-up world, because they exist and navigate along this plane; therefore, we generally place the reference images along the y-axis and work from there.

The secondary view is the second-most important view for modeling the rough shapes, and it generally follows the length of the spine as well. This means that the "long-spine" axis other than the primary axis is the second axis you will work with. The third axis is usually the one that gives you the least information, because of foreshortening and the fact that essential parts of the anatomy of a creature are obscured along the length of the spine. Any top and side view would illustrate this through the images of a fish; the primary axis (side) gives us vital information about its shape, and the secondary axis (top-down) fills in the gaps of the model that we need to get the entire shape looking roughly like the reference images we have laid out. The cross-section axis is that third axis, where it would be like making a fish steak (if you've ever seen those horseshoe-shaped salmon steaks at the supermarket, then you know what I'm referring to). This can give us some clues to the contouring of the body of the animal, but in circumstances like a humanoid biped there is only so much information we can glean from this image; the ribcage and the hips obscure way too much about the nature of the shape. In partially bipedal animals, like a chicken or a raptor, these are almost useless because the animal is partially on two planes at once. We don't ever want to forget that we're working with a three-dimensional, complex shape, even in the simplest of creatures, and the roughing out of shapes based upon flattened images only gets us so far!

Figures 4.16 and 4.17 shows some simple image planes being used to set up the proportions of the animal we want to model. I have shown it

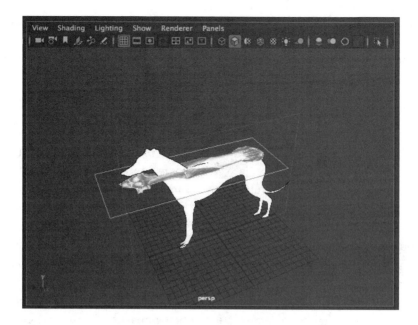

FIGURE 4.16   Proper setup for reference image planes.

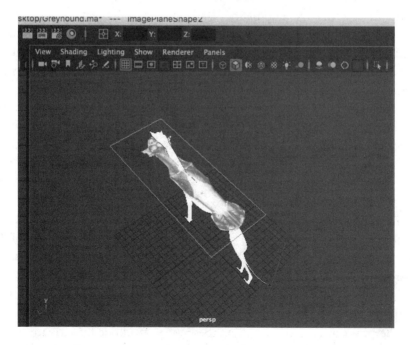

FIGURE 4.17   The image planes are there for you to match the proportions of your intended outcome.

in perspective to illustrate how both top-down and side views were set up to create proper proportions, which we will use to begin our modeling process. These should be excellent guidelines to aid us in the start of our organic model.

Polygon Primitives

So what do we use to begin the process? This could depend heavily on the intended model structure; however, there are really only two to three options for most animals. Radially symmetrical models could start with a sphere or hemisphere, and tubular structures of course would begin with something like a cylinder. But the most common and flexible polygonal primitive we can use is the simple polygon cube! You can't get simpler and easier to manage. Six sides, six quads, twelve triangles. With edge-loop modeling techniques, we can turn this into anything we want. Some amazingly detailed models have started life out as a simple cube.

The polygon cube has several excellent properties that we can exploit immediately. It has scalable resolution (albeit globally). It has the potential to be symmetrical (more on this later). It can be used to simply and quickly create a rough shape based on a few modeling actions in a short space of time. Also, with edge looping, has the ability to adaptively increase resolution in certain areas while leaving others rougher with fewer polygons, and this is what the organic workflow is all about. We also have the ability to quickly and easily pull out and extrude specific shapes as blocks of space, which can be quickly manipulated into higher resolution contours.

The biggest con of the cube-based organic model is the fact that novice modelers will often miss the process of rounding out the curvature of the model to make it shaped properly, which can leave the end result looking "cube-like." If this happens too far down the road, it's very hard to return to a rounded shape. This is why the process must be approached in certain steps to properly set up the iterative resolution and correct curvature.

Basically anything can be modeled using a cube to start with, and indeed the cube has become my staple organic modeling departure point. We can really think of the cube as our lump of clay, provided we use it properly.

Symmetrical Modeling Setup

In the physical organic world, as previously mentioned, there are three types of symmetry: asymmetrical, radial, and bilateral. When recreating something as a 3D model, we really want to use similar dynamics to do the least work possible for the most result. Indeed most creatures, including humans, aren't truly bilaterally symmetrical! Your heart and internal organs are all over the place inside of your body and even your facial features are slightly crooked or offset from one another. If you took a straightedge and measured from the tip of one ear to another, chances are you would find that the line was slanted.

But in 3D modeling, in order to get the maximum amount of efficiency and reusability, we want to create our models with total symmetry. Most of our organic structure will be totally symmetrical across the x-axis, in that if you flip the model from the positive X to the negative X (considering a few simple rules about vertices on the mirror axis), it would form a perfect mirror. This is a great deal for you, since you'll only have to model one side at a time. Keeping track of two sides at once while modeling quickly becomes a tribulation, especially when selecting vertices or edge loops. Often times you will eventually completely forget a step on one side, and then be several steps behind on the other. Symmetrical modeling is absolutely an essential tool in a fast and easy organic workflow.

The cardinal rule of symmetrical modeling is that the model *must* be symmetrical along one axis! This may seem like a simple thing to achieve, but the center vertices can *never* stray across the symmetry axis or the model won't mirror properly. You would be surprised at how many people have created agonizingly mangled geometry because they did not adhere to this incredibly important rule. If the vertices in the centerline stray across the X-Zero Axis, they will definitely cause problems. So no matter what setup you are using to accomplish your symmetrical modeling, you definitely want to keep this in mind.

There are several ways to set up for proper symmetrical modeling. Each has its strengths and advantages.

In-Software Symmetrical Selection Tools

This is when the software package you are using includes tools that will automatically select the opposite subobjects (like vertices, faces, and edges) for you when the mode is turned on. This is a great tool to have if you don't mind double-checking the software's work on occasion, and at times needing to manually fix the selection. Also, the problem with this symmetrical modeling setup is the constant accidental selection of subobjects on the opposite side; keeping track of and adding to selections is one of the most challenging aspects of 3D to even advanced users. I often refer to this as "selection kung fu" in my college classes, and not for lack of a good reason! There are so many tricks and subtle ways to get the right selection of vertices that when the amount exceeds what you can reasonably keep track of you begin to make mistakes. The software-based symmetry tools are very useful for many purposes, and they have been developed long enough to be fairly reliable; that is to say, they will work for you most of the time as expected, provided everything is 100 percent kosher from the beginning of the process. Things that can really screw up the symmetry tools of an object are:

- Offset or incorrect object pivot placement of parent polygonal object

- Imported geometry from non-Maya geometry format (DXF, OBJ, 3DS, IGES, FBX)

- Poorly designed geometry

- Nonsymmetrical geometry

The Mirrored Instance

Mirroring the instance of an object is a great way to *see* the mirrored result but only work on one side at a time. This involves slicing your original primitive (let's assume it's a cube) in half and then deleting one side. You must absolutely make sure that the half left conforms to our symmetrical modeling rules; hence, we will always make sure that there is a defined centerline of your object, and that centerline vertices are lined up on the X-Zero Axis! Otherwise you will have crisscrossing when you mirror the object. The next step is to create an *instance* of the half-object you are currently working with. An instance is a node that shares the same geometry input but can be placed anywhere else in the scene. You can move it, rotate it, or scale it, but the geometry will always be exactly the same as the original object. It is not so much a copy of an object as it is a *hologram* of the object, being placed somewhere else in the scene but only getting its geometrical subobject placement from the original object! Now we want to make sure that the object's pivot point is somewhere along the X-Zero line and scale the instanced version −1 in the *x*-axis. It should flip to the other side of the *x*-axis, making it a perfect mirror image of the original object.

This is perfect for symmetrical modeling because you can work with only one side at a time, but seeing the object as it will appear once it is mirrored. Every change you make to the original object, including edge-loop additions and extrusions, will be perfectly mirrored on the opposite side, which gives you the freedom to work with only one side at a time, but the preview of the finished product! This works well because you can see the depth of the construction and the thickness of the object, which may be obscured or difficult to determine without the opposite side previewing. Being able to see the full version of the model, without the burden of being responsible for all those extra polygons, is a fast a flexible way to model organically. It prevents mistakes with the symmetrical modeling process (like moving center vertices across the *x*-axis) or having to reevaluate the thickness of your model. When you have completed making changes to the original model, you can delete the instanced version and do a polygonal mirror to get the full model.

The Half Model

This is where you begin the basic structure of the model, and then lop off half of the rest along whichever axis is the symmetry axis. It basically follows the same procedure as the instanced half methodology with the exception that the instance is never created and mirrored. This is significantly different because while it reduces visual clutter, it also reduces clarity in terms of the visualization of the final product! From my personal observation, the more advanced experienced modelers are best suited to this type of setup because they have been doing these types of models for a very long time and have the benefit of repetition and a strong visual model in their mind. They are not in need of the other half of the model to show them what the final result is going to look like in the end.

I would highly suggest that beginning to intermediate modelers *not* use this approach, because the full 3D visualization will be better suited to giving you a strong sense of the widths and thicknesses of things not immediately obvious, such as the waist, ribcage, and hips of an animal. As an aside here, I believe it is important and worthy of note that any model with proper edge-looping can be resymmetrized quite easily at most points during the modeling phase, and without major loss of work. *If* you find yourself at a point where you have screwed up the symmetry or middle line to some fantastic degree, simply delete half of the model and make sure all the pertinent points are centered along the proper axis! This is actually a pretty useful solution to fix models that get out of hand or topology that has somehow lost its even parameterization and natural flow (Figures 4.18 through 4.20).

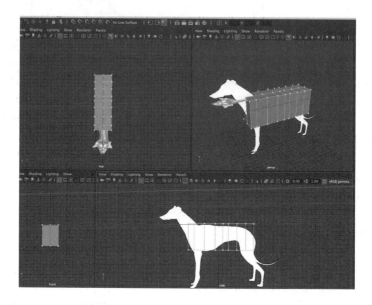

FIGURE 4.18 Setting up for symmetry means that you only work the model on one side, mirroring the actions on the opposite.

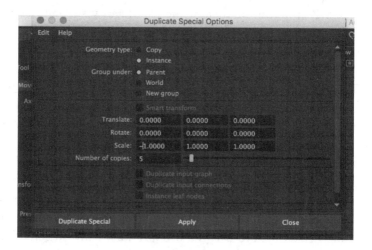

FIGURE 4.19 Mirroring with an instance.

Rough Sculpting with Cross-Section Edge Loops

Once the reference images are set up and the symmetrical modeling has been initiated, the next step is to rough sculpt. Far from what the name would imply, the modeler does less sculpting than positioning of edge loops and vertices, as well as inserting edge loops into the areas that need

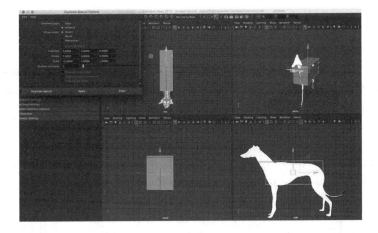

FIGURE 4.20   Anything you do to one side will automatically occur on the other side, inversely.

more detail or a more pronounced curve. The key in this stage is to insert the *least* amount of detail possible while adhering closely to the rough shape and curvature of the animal. Figure 4.21 will show you the simple half cube (with symmetry down the *z*-axis) shaping our reference images of a greyhound. There is a minimal amount of edge loops flowing down the *y*-axis, in which we will manipulate in that axis to give us a good profile shaping of the animal along the spine. For both humanoids and tetrapods, we will leave a box at the end to represent the head, which of course will be filled in later with the requisite detail. For now, representing the head with a plain box gives you proportionate clues without fussing over areas that require heavier detail (which you will fill in later).

Phase 1: Shaping along the Spinal Length

For vertebrates, which will usually be the bulk of your organic models requested, the shaping goes along the *length* of the spine. Don't try to do limbs at this early point; those can be extruded much later. Our real goal in this rough, cross-section edge-looping face is to set the areas with the most needed definition and parameterize the model with a nice, even, but efficient topology. As you can see from the figures below, the basic shaping at this stage is done with simple, elegant transforms of the vertices. In this stage, the cross-section edge loops are kept nicely aligned with the two-dimensional plane that we are working in (in this case it is the *x*-plane). One thing to keep in mind is that we want these edge loops to be almost completely straight up and down! Don't offset the top from the bottom or create any zigzag shapes. This will vastly improve the future of the topology and result in a nice, clean, contoured mesh.

Inserting edge loops can be done easily in areas with needed detail. Here we want to work *only* in the vertical y-axis, or whichever axis is perpendicular to the spine. For the tetrapodal (four-limbed) animals it's usually the y-axis, and for bipedal humanoids it's usually the x-axis. You can see that the inserted edge loops are necessary to better define the shape of the model along the length of the spine. We insert these edge loops first and foremost, because they are vital in laying out the foundation of the animal. Once you begin to throw in more and more edge loops along the perpendicular length of the spine, the model begins to get extremely complex, and you lose the ability to work rapidly and cleanly. So putting detail in the foundation level of sculpting can be done with some discrimination, hopefully resulting in evenly spaced edge loops with heavier division where the curves need more attention. Don't try to overmodel the curvature too much, because this is what the polygonal smoothing operation or the normal maps can provide at the end of the process. We want to use the minimum amount of polygons necessary for the most organically appearing shape in 3D, and often this can be done without adding a ton of extra geometry. The shaping and contouring is far more important than the amount of triangles in giving the model correct proportion and appearance. An overrounded model loses some of the important elements of good shaping (Figure 4.21).

FIGURE 4.21   Creating the basic profile shape.

Phase 2: Shaping on the Cross-Section Perpendicular Axis

Here is where we look at the animal torso/spinal length from the perpendicular angle of the spine as it flows down the length (top-down or *y*-axis for nonbipedal humanoids and side view or *x*-axis for humanoids) and adjust the edge loops and geometry accordingly. The geometry can be tweaked to move the points and tapered to match the reference images as much as possible. This second step should be nice and simple, especially using what we know about organic structures so far! The rib cage is the bulbous part of the torso, and hence it should be wider than the neck or the stomach areas, which are generally (but not always) tapered from the rib cage area. Some notable places where this taper doesn't always happen are in reptiles and amphibians, where the taper occurs much further down the torso, where the rib cage tapers off into the hips and tail. Generally speaking, the further up we go on the evolutionary scale away from fish, the more we find the scoop of the belly, as in Figure 4.22, which is relatively narrow in this perpendicular view to the spinal length. Of course, fat deposits can have a huge effect here as we can see in very obese humans,

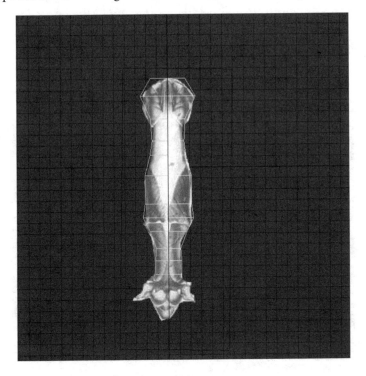

FIGURE 4.22 Editing our model from the top-down, which is the perpendicular axis to the spinal length.

where the stomach actually bows outward and creates a "Grimace" effect). Elephants and mammoths had a flaring from top to bottom, for instance, instead of the taper we see with a more svelte creature meant for speedy movement. This is the reason that we use the reference images! The reference images allow us to tell exactly where the model should taper or expand in the perpendicular axis.

The tapering tube of the torso, complete with the tail in the case of most animals, eventually results in a "lumpy snake" or limbless, bulbous tube. This is perfectly fine, since it follows along with the topology and structure of the vertebrate animal, which is evidenced in the skeletal image matching what you will expect to see as the underlying structure of the animal.

In Phase 2, you may find it necessary to insert edge loops perpendicular to the long-spine axis to increase the level of detail. It's important to note, however, that we are still only slicing the model along the perpendicular axis to increase the level of detail. The cross section, seen in Figure 4.23, is still a single, solid polygon. The reason for this will become abundantly clear in the next phases, where we truly start to round and shape our model. For now, we only want to add detail and shaping in the one, edge-looped axis. You will see that this can get us very far in our basic shaping of a complex animal with the most efficient amount of polygons possible. This low-polygon approach can be used to create level-of-detail models quickly and intuitively, or just make the process more streamlined and efficient.

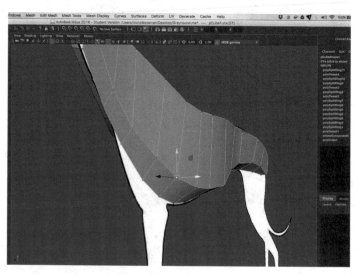

FIGURE 4.23 Beginning to taper the torso in the front view, as the shape flows down the length of the spine.

Phase 3: Shaping the Cross Section

"Bodyworlds" is an art and medical exhibit by Polish anatomist and artist Gunther von Hagen, in which the human body is exhibited in various forms of dissection, frozen in action or sliced into pieces and preserved with a plasticization technique that he created. One of the amazing things about this taxidermist-like exhibit is the ability to see animals and humans "sliced" like pieces of ham and stacked to see how the shape occurs and changes over the length of the spine. As gruesome as it might sound, the exhibit allows the shape of the cross section to be revealed, which is something that can't be accomplished in the natural world unless you want to get a hacksaw and a dead animal, which is pretty messy (not to mention gross).

The cross section of an animal is the shape that you would get if you sliced it paper-thin and traced that piece of paper. It's elusive because it changes as it flows, moving along the solid line of the spine just like the Extruded Curve along a Path, which we used to create the tapered tube as a major organic structure in Chapter 1. What is the definitive cross-section shape? In Figure 4.24, we can see that the shape drastically changes over the length of the spine! It's very hard to pin down. It's not going to be the same in one area as it is in another; however, we can definitely expect that it will follow some rules in the case of a vertebrate. There will almost

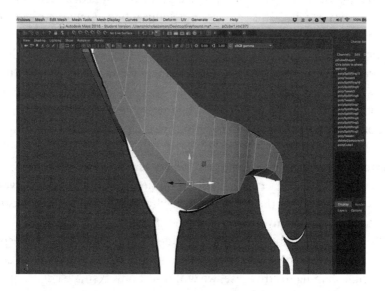

FIGURE 4.24 Depending on the animal, there will be an inward slant to the belly or an outward angle.

always be some version of the parabolic curve. This curve, as laid out with two to three Bezier points, can provide us with a huge amount of flexibility in the cross-section shape along the length of the spine. An older form of organic modeling with NURBS, which closely mirrors the "slice of ham" concept, in which multiple curves are lofted together over the length of another curve in order to form a flowing change in the shape of the cross section. The bulge in this curve can change shape as it flows down the path of the spine, and indeed almost every single animal or human is unique in the particular flow of this cross-section shape! This cross section, however, is vital to creating the accurate three-dimensional shape.

Before we add any extra edge loops running down the length of the spine, we should first create the shape of the cross section by adjusting the positions of the pertinent vertices into the rough-hewn shape of the curve in Figure 4.23. You can see in the cross section in Figure 4.24 that we have four vertices making up the shape of the half cross section. I have ordered them from the center-top to the center-bottom, from 1 to 4. Because of our Symmetrical Modeling setup, Vertices 1 and 4 *must* stay where they are in the perpendicular (here it is the x-axis), but they can move up and down in the cross-section axis (here the y). In order to turn our square into a curve, we must first squeeze or pinch Vertices 2 and 3 closer together in the cross-section axis to create a rounding effect. This simple action will generate an approximation to the parabola and give us the contours of a vertebrate that we need to start with! This can occur globally at first, applying to the entire model, and then be tweaked on a per-edge loop basis afterward. Adjusting Vertices 2 and 3 on the x-axis (or y on a bipedal humanoid) now will allow us to create a unique cross-section rough shaping for each edge loop individually, which is how we begin to fully realize the object as a three-dimensional sculpture and not just a cube that kind of resembles the creature. Each cross section will be shaped individually, but we are still in the rough stages of modeling. We still have a slightly rounded cube! The most important thing to remember in this stage is that the spine is usually raised up at the apex of the parabola. This apex can be easily contoured based upon the curvature (or lack thereof) along the spine, which is why it's so important to look at the skeletal structure of any model we are building.

Now the edge-loop detail must be added along the length of the spine. Once again, we want to add the least amount of detail necessary to create the rough shaping. In this case, we will insert only a single edge loop that runs along the length of the spine. As you can see in Figure 4.25 all of our previous work in a smart and structured order has paid off, and by simply

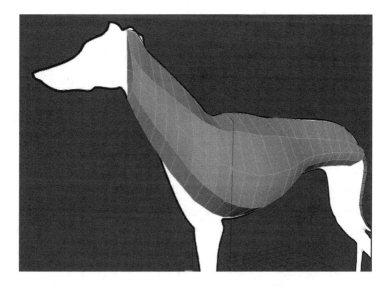

FIGURE 4.25 (See color insert.) Adding the edge loops along the length of the spine allows us to create the nice curvature of the cross section.

pulling the vertices out individually from the new edge loop outward on the x-axis we have a reasonably shaped model!

Phase 4: Contouring the Creature

Now that we have the basic spinal length modeled and roughly shaped with the mid-rib edge loop added, we must individually edit the geometry vertices to create a unique shape for all the varying parts of the model as they exist along the spinal length. Contouring the vertices means that for every edge loop along the spine, we must individually tweak the vertices of the loop to better fit into the three-dimensional shape of the cross section. *So* once again, referring to our slice-of-ham visual model, each slice must have a slightly different shape, which we individually edit. There are rules, however, to this editing. We want the parameterization of the model to flow nice and evenly, and along the major contours of the structure. Therefore we want to keep the continuity of the edge loops nice and straight along the normals, or perpendicular axis to the subobjects. Without getting into the math of it, we simply need to make sure that if the spinal length flows along the x-axis (quadrupeds and serpentine structures) then the vertices we are individually editing would move very little along that axis, unless we are editing the entire edge loop. This way there is no "wavy" geometry. There is absolutely no gain from offsetting these edge loop vertices along the length of the spine! It just creates a UV and deformation nightmare later for texture artists and character riggers. Having nice, clean, even edge loops is the key to having a top-notch model.

The contouring is usually the most painstaking and tedious part of the modeling process. While every modeler has their preferred method of tweaking the vertices, it's important to mention here the direction, or component space, options we have to edit the positions of the vertices relative to one another.

- *World space*: This moves the components relative to the world, which is advisable only in certain cases. While it highly depends on the model and the layout of the spinal length, I tend to use this transform space very sparingly with individual vertices, because there is a tendency to lose the natural flow of the parameterization. There is, however, an occasional use for world space in the movement of the entire edge loop as a unit, but larger offsets will still have a tendency to lose the flow of the model.

- *Object space*: This transform space is usually only different from the world space if there is some special consideration for the model, and it's not laid out on the standard *xyz* axes. The proper setup and layout for organic modeling method is to use the world space layout to create your geometry, but in the rare case that you need to model something in an offset space this will be the corresponding space to the world when you are modeling.

- *Component space*: This uses the component selected or averaged components' normal space for the components selected (if more than one is selected). This space is *excellent* for pulling vertices out and generating a thickness in the model based upon the flow of the model, as opposed to the world. Component space uses the normal of the component, which is the perpendicular angle from the triangular face. So pulling a vertex using component space along the normal never upsets the general flow of the geometry. That being said, using the UV or two-dimensional space relative to the face the vertex is attached to utterly ruin the flow of the model. The general rule of thumb here is to only move vertices in component space when you want to create dimples (negative normal space) or lumps (positive normal space) on a model. This can be great for brush-based modeling on high-detail meshes, because you can create nice surface aberrations that more closely resemble an organic creature.

The contouring process can last a while, as the modeler examines and reexamines his or her work, tweaking and iterating small changes that can have a very big effect on the final product. One thing that we will need to ensure here in this phase is that the flow, or the normal average, of the cross-section edge loops, goes along with the shape of the spine. This means that the cervical and sacral vertebrae, which tend to be offset in curvature from the rest of the spine, should have the edge loops following their flow, and not straight up and down on an axis, as they originally were! You can see the example in Figure 4.25.

Selective Detail Inclusion

Inserting detail into the model during the contouring stage is always a quandary. The more edge loops you create with the Insert Edge Loop tool, the more detail you can work with, but the more vertices you must contend with. The trick is to insert just enough edge loops to get the shapes perfectly modeled without adding so much that you aren't able to globally edit it later. If there is too much detail in an area *before* it has been properly shaped, it will take forever to sculpt. The good news is that edge loops can be deleted all at once if you need to remove detail areas and go back to a rougher shape, without any loss of geometrical constancy. This is why keeping your edge-loop modeling completely clean at first allows you to iterate up or down in detail quite easily, somewhat mimicking the NURBS modeling process. One thing to ask yourself when you begin to insert detail into certain areas is if it's really necessary. Every time you add in an edge loop, take a minute to assess whether that edge loop is going to make your life easier or more difficult down the road. As a general rule of thumb, we can see that adding an edge loop perpendicular to the length of the spine (the y-axis in a quadruped or the x-axis in a bipedal humanoid) only adds detail to a localized cross section and will be far more manageable than adding an edge loop along the entire length of the spine, which adds more detail across multiple edge loops! This means that we need to add the fewest edge loops along the length of the spine and only towards the end of the contouring process. This will ensure that we don't create more work than we need to and that the model has nice, evenly spread parameterization and no unnecessary geometry.

Transitioning Detail Areas

Inevitably, you will come an area that requires much more detail than another. This can happen in transition areas, such as the head and neck. The head of many animals will require many more polygons than the neck, which is a variation on the circular, tube shape and thus requires far less edge loops along the length of the spine than the head, which will require many more of these long edge loops to shape areas for the eyes, mouth, and ears. How do we transition between a high-detail area and a low-detail area in a single model? There are several ways to do this, but the most geometrically sound way of transitioning between one and another is what modelers refer to as a "T-edge," or an area where one edge loop terminates into the center of an edge, as in Figure 4.26. Technically, you can leave it just like this. The 3D software (Maya in this case) will triangulate the resulting five-vertex face automatically. This can present a problem, however, as evidenced in Figure 4.27, where I illustrate the auto-triangulation of Maya vs the manual triangulation by using the multicut tool to ensure the quads are cut properly and evenly into the triangles. While Maya will auto-triangulate the quads, it doesn't always do so in an even manner (being up to an algorithm instead of human judgment), which can have adverse effects on the deformation later. It's always best in these cases to manually triangulate the T-edges and ensure an even parameterization for the transition between a heavily

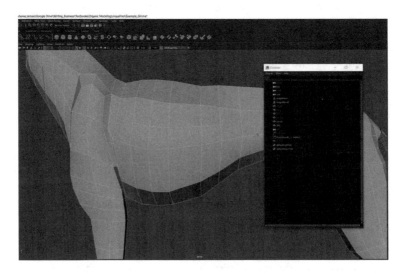

FIGURE 4.26 Adding in a partial edge loop, but the T-edge presents problems.

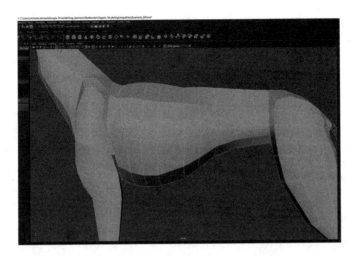

FIGURE 4.27   Properly triangulating the ends of a T-edge.

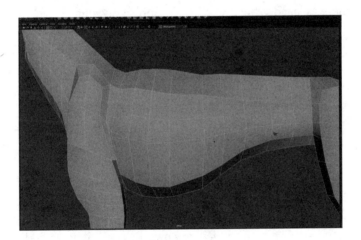

FIGURE 4.28   The improper triangulation of a T-edge, caused by letting the software choose for you instead of manually editing the termination.

detailed area to a lighter-detail area. You can see in Figure 4.28 how this technique can give us many more vertices to shape our model in one certain area while leaving adjacent areas lightly detailed.

Limb Extrusions

Quadrupeds

Since tetrapodal animals have vastly different limb mechanics than our own bipedal bodies, let's focus on these for a moment in terms of limb extrusion! Limb extrusion is a very important part of the organic design methodology because this is where the real power of polygonal modeling shows its true color. A curve-based modeling method, such as NURBS, must be based upon a single surface, with infinite complexity, length, and width, but no depth. This means that you absolutely cannot "branch" a surface as a single skin. You can create fillets and contiguous branching surfaces only with multiple surfaces, and they retain their attachment through painstaking setup and later skinning with joints for the rig. If everything is not done perfectly correctly, the surface will not be able to deform or be modeled as a single surface. If and when you try to convert these surfaces to contiguous polygons, the nature of the trim surfaces and the projected curves (which serve to generate the fillet or branching areas) will make it extraordinarily difficult to match the resulting polygonal output, making it nearly useless for real-time game engines.

What we really want is a single, flowing surface with adaptive geometry detail where we need it, but not where we don't. Polygonal modeling is excellent for branching these limbs off of the main spinal length. The branches can begin as a single quad and quickly be edited and modeled into a complex limb structure. The important thing is to get a good idea of how the limbs come off of the body in any model that you are working with.

You can see in Figure 4.29 that the front legs of the greyhound emerge and branch almost straight down in the y-axis, while the rear legs have a much wider, horseshoe-like shape due to the protrusion of the hip. That being said, both sets of limbs tend to flow downward more than outward, but we must choose the proper area to begin the extrusion from along the spine. This is the area I have selected in the model for this operation, based upon my photo reference. The quads defining the shoulder blades are extruded outwards first, and *then* downwards until they reach the ground plane. This allows for the slim area of "cleavage," where we would know it as an armpit. This area is important because it separates the humerus and shoulder mechanism from the ribcage. The humerus is the point from which the geometry will be extruded downwards, and in this case it is narrow and barely extrudes from the ribs.

The rear of the animal extrudes outwards much further and wider that the humerus, due to the fact that the hip-bone structure is defining it. If you could look at a dog head-on you would see that the rear legs are much wider and more powerful, which makes the dog an excellent runner. Select the proper faces to extrude into the hips, creating the area if need be by inserting edge loops to form a solidly formed area where the hips extrude from the body. Once that hip-bone area has been extruded at the proper width, we can extrude the legs downward by selecting the bottom faces of the hip extrusion and extruding them to the ground.

The limbs will be edited after the initial extrusion as was the extruded torso along the spine; the shaping will occur by creating more edge loops that follow the direction of the path of the bones that create the legs. Here, these lines do not follow along the world axes; therefore, it will absolutely be necessary to adjust the orientation of the edge loops to follow the flow of geometry. This is necessary because the animation and subsequent proper deformation of the creature will depend on this flow. When inserting edge loops, you can see that the inserted loop will average its orientation between the outer edge loops. This means that the main orientations should be set first, and the subsequent shaping loops inserted afterwards. If you look at Figure 4.29, you will see that the shaping of the leg begins at the top, and as each subsequent edge loop is created and edited it follows the path of the leg. In the ankle/foot area, where there is a radical shift in the orientation of the angle, we also shift the orientation of the edge loops. This ensures a smooth movement of the edge loops along the leg and far easier ability to tweak the shaping later.

Once we have laid out the edge looping on the limb extrusions, the shaping of the areas where they extend from the body should occur.

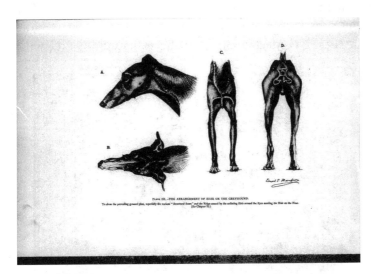

FIGURE 4.29 Detailed perspective drawings of the greyhound front head and front/ back view. (Courtesy of Wikimedia, https://archive.org/stream/cihm_35627/#page/ n112/mode/1up)

This will vary greatly from model to model, and once again it's a longer, slower process to slightly tweak the vertices that make up the rougher shape into the structurally sound wireframe for the parts of your creature that are defined by the bone structure. My suggestion is to really pay attention to these areas and get the best contours you can with the fewest vertices. You don't want to add the vertical edge loops in here just yet, at least not until you can get the general shaping correct! The vertical edge loops (or perpendicular to the spine in this area) will add much more detail than you need right now in the limbs, since we have these branches and the edge loops that are perpendicular to the main spinal length are now parallel to the flow of the limbs and will add a lot of extra vertices to edit.

Once we are done really shaping the hips and the shoulders, we can then insert the edge loop running perpendicular to the spinal length but parallel to the limbs. Only one edge loop here will suffice to begin pulling out the vertices on this edge loop along the normal, which will create the rounding of the limb cross section and make it start to look less like a cube. Proper contouring here is the key to having your end result look as non–cube-like as possible! It's a very rookie mistake to have the final result of your organic model looking like a dog-shaped cube. You want this to be representative of an actual creature, with a real organic flow to it.

As you can see in Figure 4.30, I have set up the basic shaping of the legs. The toes of the feet can be branched off, and this area will take as

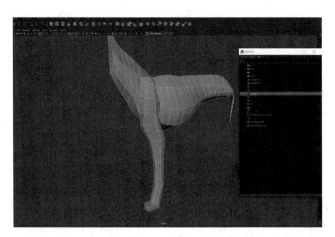

FIGURE 4.30   This is the simplest and most low-resolution shaping of the forelegs of the greyhound model.

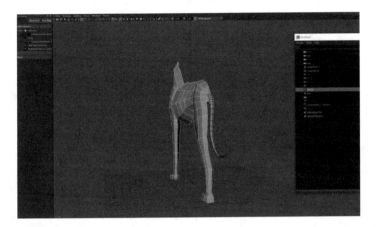

FIGURE 4.31   This is the rounded termination of the torso with the limbs, from the rear angle.

much time and effort to properly sculpt as the entire leg, which is also true of the human hand. The more branches from a single source, the more work you will have to do to properly model it. Indeed, human hands are some of the problem areas for modelers because not only are there five entities to work with, but none of them are on a plane that aligns with the world xyz axes! At least the dog has toes that are relatively short and align with the world z-axis almost perfectly, as Figure 4.31 clearly illustrates.

Shaping the Head

In the case of our current model, we have a diamond-shaped head with a long, extended snout. Figure 4.29 illustrates both the top and the side of the head, which is excellent for reference imaging. The two most important things about the head in vertebrates are the jaw/mouth mechanism, and the eyes! Both require some finesse and mechanics to operate properly for animation. Something to be aware of in this case is that the character might not require articulated jaw/mouth movement. If this is the case, then you won't have to mess with the proper radial edge looping or extension of this area. But most of the creatures we model should at least have the jaw open and shut properly at the very least. Long snouts, like the one in the creature we are modeling, are actually a lot easier than a human mouth, which requires very precise radial edge looping to create the proper structure. A short-faced dog, however, like our Frenchie in Figure 1.2, requires just as much work as a human, due to the deep folds in the skin. Luckily, the French bulldog doesn't have to convincingly talk like a human (unless this is the intention, but that's a whole different book).

In order to create the snout shape, we can extrude the jaw from the center face of the head and split it along the jaw line, shaping the rest from there and inserting edge loops to add detail.

Radial Edge Looping

For step-by-step instructions on how to properly radial edge loops specific areas of geometry, please reference that material in Chapters 5 through 7. It will guide you in the proper setup and tools to generate the edge loops and edit the result. But the question to ask here in this section is, "Why use radial edge looping? Where does it benefit us?" Radial edge looping is the practice of creating circular, or radial contiguous, faces inside of a polygonal cross section. This is something that is inherently unique to polygonal modeling and indeed was somewhat revolutionary in practice at the time of in conception (probably 2001 or so). It was a way of getting the best features of NURBS with the best features of polygons, especially as it pertained to organic modeling. The premise is fairly simple: we want to create an area of radial symmetry or continuity inside of a cross-section-style model. In order to add some type of circular form inside of a cross-section geometry, many more divisions would have to be made and a lot of sculpting be done in order to make the shape circular. Even high-density meshes with thousands to millions of polygons required sophisticated sculpting tools to generate spherical indentations (like the eyes), folding orbital muscles (the face and eyes), or any other tubularlike extrusion or branch from a main stem. With radial edge loops, a circular form can quickly and easily be built into a cross-section model with very little difficulty, and the level of detail can be completely different than the surrounding geometry, which allows for high-detail areas inside of low-detail areas with no compromise in geometrical flow. So places like the eyes and mouth will have many radial edge loops, while the surrounding quads will remain fairly low-resolution.

Many organic structures use the radial structure in form and function. The human mouth and eye areas are two such places, and both are extremely important in character modeling for film and games. Geometry that is built around a radial hub will easily be deformable in a radial manner, which is how we form the expressions of the eyes and make the mouth talk! Any orifice or circular protrusion on an animal should be considered for radial edge-looping techniques because of the powerful and efficient methodology. Eyes, ears, nose, and mouth are some very good places to explore the radial edge-looping methodology, since all are radial in structure (Figure 4.32).

The key to successful radial edge looping is to set up a *pole*, which is a crossing of vertices at a juncture. There are several ways to accomplish this; one of the simplest is to extrude all four faces adjacent to the pole (keeping them linked together) and to relatively scale them down to a tiny size. This will provide the basis for the subsequent radial edge loops, of which you can insert as many as you want. Although this is the simplest way of creating the radial structure inside the cross-section structure, it presents a challenge to actually use in practice, because most of the places you will be creating the radial edge loops will not be aligned to the world and will not have congruent normals. In the case that there is not a solid world alignment, you must take the longer route by using the multicut tool to triangulate the quads and cut your own inner radial edge to begin the setup. The reason that this works much better for nonaligned polygons is because we can then edit the structure of the inner edge loop congruent to

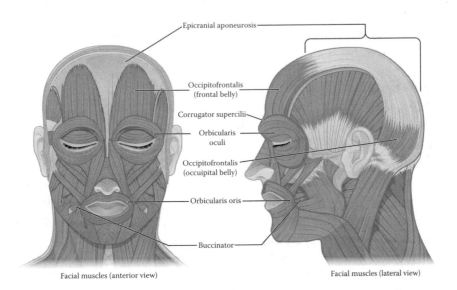

Epicranial aponeurosis

Occipitofrontalis
(frontal belly)

Corrugator supercilii

Orbicularis
oculi

Occipitofrontalis
(occuipital belly)

Orbicularis oris

Buccinator

Facial muscles (anterior view)

Facial muscles (lateral view)

FIGURE 4.32 The orbital muscles of the human face. (Courtesy of OpenStax, CC BY 4.0, https://cnx.org/contents/FPtK1zmh@8.25:fEI3C8Ot@10/Preface)

the normal of the surrounding faces and get a nice flow for the subsequent loops created. The flow of the surface is dependent on nicely parameterized normal and triangle placement. Once it gets messed up, it's really hard to fix.

Once the radial edge loop structure has been initialized, the modeler can then shape the structure by inserting edge loops and tweaking the shape of those loops. It is important to note here that the outer edge loops will take on the positions of the next nearest loop, so the ones closest to the outer edge will most likely be more "square" than the ones nearest the inner edge loop, which we will round out to keep things from being to linear.

Most modeling software will have convenient ways to select and edit entire edge loops, which can quickly form folds and indentations like wrinkles in the eyelid. Radial edge loops are an essential for any talking creature, because the mouth and lips are based upon the extremely radial muscles of the orbicularis ori (as are the orbicularis oculi, or eye muscles), which operate much differently than the main skeletal muscles. These muscles expand and contract in a circular manner, which creates the multitude of facial expressions that we are capable of. These shapes are so familiar to us and hardwired into our brain as recognizable pat-terns that we immediately notice anything odd or unnatural about them. Therefore, modeling the area as it is structured to move is vastly important in getting the deformation and resulting animation to occur correctly.

Global Polygon Smoothing

This is something I personally tend to avoid if possible, because it often creates more detail than you really need. Once the previous steps have been accomplished correctly there should really be no need for this; the "smoothed" model and the presmoothed model should have almost no differentiation in shape with the exception of two to four times as many edge loops! There is essentially no difference in the con-tour and 3D shape of the model exhibited, but the model will have twice the polygon count. Is this necessary? It might, for instance, aid in properly deforming the creature once it is rigged, but there are many places where we could manually add those edge loops in as needed without adding them globally, which is what happens in the Poly Smooth operation. The polygon edges that run down the long length of the bones are always the most troublesome to control the flow, so the cross-section edge loops pose far greater importance in deformation of most types of characters. The cross sections are usually responsible for the joint hinges and "bendy" part of the character.

A substitute for a global polygon smooth operation would be to create a normal map for the model by duplicating the object, running a Poly Smooth with several iterations, and then sculpting it in greater detail, either inside the primary content tool (like Maya) or exporting it to Mudbox or Z-Brush, in order to further iterate the detail. This results in a smoothed-looking model without the need for the extra geometry generated.

In Autodesk's Maya, and other polygonal-based modeling systems, the smoothed preview can be seen with a hotkey (usually "3") that shows you a smoothed version of the model without the extra geometry. If you can go back and forth between the smoothed version and the unsmoothed version without seeing much difference, then you know you've done your job properly!

Mirroring Geometry

When should you mirror the geometry of your model and merge the two sides? This is a hard question to answer, but definitely not until you feel like the model is as detailed as you want it, with all aspects of the seamless areas complete. This is not an action completely set in stone, since you can always select all of the faces on one side of the mirror axis (provided they are all still symmetrical) and delete them, returning to the Symmetrical Layout as discussed earlier in order to make more changes.

In Autodesk's Maya, as well as many other packages, there are automated tools for mirroring the geometry and merging the centerline vertices together. You can also do this manually, but it is better to let the software package handle the process unless there is some special circumstance that requires manually duplicating, flipping, and merging the objects. Once again, as long as your model is symmetrical there's a simple way to get back to the last step. Of course, if you intend to make nonsymmetrical changes in terms of topology, you won't be able to reset your symmetrical setup easily, so you might want to keep this in mind.

Fine-Tuning with Deformers

Once the essentials of modeling a seamless polygon organic creature are complete, there are multiple methods of making global tweaks and detail insertion to really fine-tune your model. There are times when you will want to sculpt little bits here or there, or globally widen an area or pinch an area. Deformation tools are tools that can proportionately adjust the entire model or selected areas while keeping the flow of the edge loops intact. While there are far too many of these to mention, a few of the modeling with deformer tools are worth mentioning here.

One other important thing to mention about the use of these deformation-based techniques for modeling is that they should *always* be either done after the model has been mirrored, or the mid-axis vertices omitted entirely. The nature of proportional modeling is that the vertices move in proportional relationship to the deformed point, which means that there is a high chance of offsetting the midline if those vertices are included in your lattice, cluster, or proportional modeling selection.

Lattices

The best use of the lattice in the organic modeling methodology is as a post-model, global tweaking device. Even if you did a perfect job of sculpting the low-resolution version of your model, you might need to globally tweak some areas that now have a lot more detail than the original ones. A lattice can scale down the detail needed and only require you to transform a few points in a localized area in order to get the adjustments you need. One good example of this is the distal taper along the tail of a creature; perhaps you find you need a little extra taper or shaping along the length of it but the length-edge loops are too dense to tweak the individual vertices. A lattice would be the best way to go about tweaking an entire area by simply transforming a few vertices.

A lattice works by creating a low-resolution, nonrendering "cage" in the shape of a rectangular solid with the ability to control the amount of subdivisions at the time of creation. It is notable here that unlike standard polygons, the cage of the lattice structure must be set in stone at the point of creation. If you try to increase the subdivisions after the lattice points have been moved, you will get wildly unpredictable results. In many ways, a lattice can take you back to a point where you had much less detail and were able to make global tweaks to the shape without individually moving vertices. If the offsets are done in a proportional manner, the topology will stay solid (Figure 4.33).

Nonlinear

Nonlinear deformers use 3D-wire nodes to create a single offset along some kind of curve. A bend is the most commonly used, and indeed is absolutely excellent for something as simple as a tubular structure that you

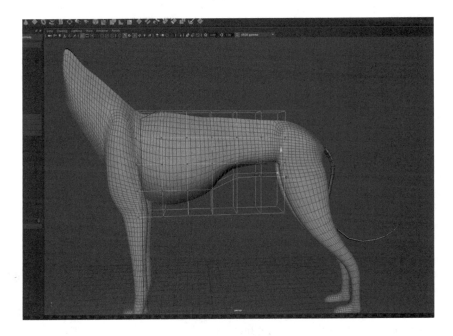

FIGURE 4.33 (See color insert.)   Using a Lattice to fine-tune an area.

want to adjust the curvature of. Flare/tapers are the second-most common, and they can be used for the same purpose, especially with the length of a fairly straight object, like a fish or a squid's head.

Proportional Modeling/Soft Select

Proportional modeling allows us to tweak a single vertex and have the influence of that transform spread out to others based on distance. In Maya this is called a "Soft Select." Maya has a toolbox control set of the falloff radius and calculation based on one or another algorithm. This is nicely convenient because it allows the modeler to edit swaths of an area with claylike properties, where the surrounding areas will deform in the same direction but perhaps with less percentage of movement, which falls off in intensity over time. These soft modeling techniques work much better with more vertices and are not nearly as effective with an extremely efficiently modeled, base-resolution mesh (Figure 4.34).

Clusters

Clusters are the deformation-based equivalent of Soft Selection, in which a selection of vertices is given a transform with weighted values, allowing

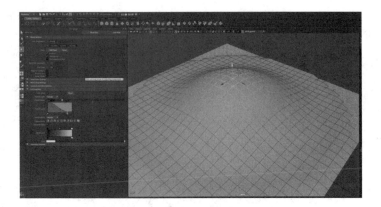

FIGURE 4.34 Using the Soft Select to move vertices proportionately.

you to edit, animate, and tweak the values after the deformation has been made, unlike Soft Select, which makes the action a permanent offset. Clusters can be useful when you want to animate the values later or need to retweak your model after the fact.

Sculpt Polygon Tool

Sculpting polygons uses the Artisan Toolbox in Maya and allows the brush tools to be intuitively used to tweak the surface. As with the Soft Selection, this works best in a higher resolution polygonal mesh and is not extremely effective with low-resolution models! The sculpting toolset in Maya 2016 is fairly comprehensive, but the most important tool is the sculpt tool, which allows you to push and pull the vertices of a model based on the normal

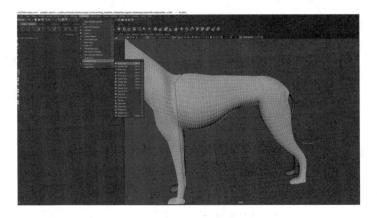

FIGURE 4.35 Added geometry make sculpting feasible.

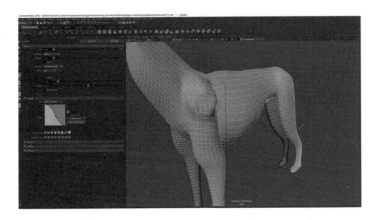

FIGURE 4.36   Using the sculpt tool.

of the surface, which is like pushing or pulling a piece of clay. The ability to pull and push vertices based on the surface normal (or perpendicular angle) is a great tool for creating indentations and ripples on the model to simulate the musculature underneath the skin (Figures 4.35 and 4.36).

CONCLUSION

The workflow in this section has been outlined in great detail to give you a very clear picture of the proper process with which to build a complete, seamless, well-formed polygonal model of any organic creature with a spine! If you follow the basic rules of the procedure and each step in the correct order, the hierarchical layering of complexity should make the modeling process easy, relatively rapid, and accessible to anyone with basic 3D modeling skills.

The real challenges in the final, high-resolution model hinge upon the crucial final sculpting and tweaking of detail, which often involve a greater need for high-level artistic skills and experience. But the foundational shaping of the creature you are working on should be 75% complete by the time you get to the last shaping steps outlined in this section. You will see in Chapters 5 through 7 exact, step-by-step detailed instructions for the same process discussed here in theory. Using these two sections you should be able to confidently model any vertebrate out there. Happy modeling!

CHAPTER 5

Modeling Essential Organic Structures

The essential organic structures listed in previous chapters can easily be created with the multiple component approach. That is to say, each of these component structures can be modeled in certain ways that will facilitate larger, more complex organisms. In this way we can begin to develop the skills and abilities to model anything organic in nature. The instructions in this section are written using Maya 2016 as a base modeling package; however, they can be extrapolated to any current modeling software today (Blender is a perfectly apt free open-source software package that can be used in lieu of Maya). All of the techniques illustrated are condensed to the simplest and most universally available modeling tools, and although the parameters and the interfaces may appear slightly differently between modeling packages, these tools and options are generally held as universal and absolutely essential in any 3D modeling software suite.

Modeling in these practical chapters is done entirely with polygonal outcomes in mind and not with NURBS, B-splines, Bezier surfaces, or subdivision surfaces. This is for both simplicity's sake and the desire for a universality of technique and toolsets. That being said, I often use Bezier splines as modeling tools in Maya, in which implementation is somewhat lacking but far simpler (and less accurate) than NURBS curves. Bezier curves and B-splines are easier to use and lay out, but the implementation of 3D Bezier curves is very different in varying modeling software packages. They are, for instance, far more flexible and easy to use in 3D Studio than Maya and have been an inherent aspect of the software, while Maya incorporated NURBS initially and only added the Beziers as an afterthought. This is one of the areas where there is no perfect answer to the quandary, and one must use the toolset that is easiest in the package that is best suited for the task. If you are not using Maya it shouldn't matter all that much, however, and the basic information and techniques presented here will work with everything provided some minor tweaks are provided.

Some of the major types of structures will be covered in step-by-step tutorials in this section:

- Tapered tubes
- Tapered segments
- Radial edge looping
- Branching
- Ridges
- Folds/ripples

TAPERED TUBING: EXTRUSION ALONG A CURVE WITH TAPERING SCALE

From the pine needle, to the human heart, to the roots of a tree, the tapered tube is one of the most recurring and common forms that you will encounter when modeling any type of organic creature. The process is a simple one, and should be in the arsenal of every organic modeler.

Step 1: Laying out the Tubing

Building the tube requires two curves: the profile curve and the path curve. The profile curve provides the shape of the curve and the path curve provides the shape of the 3D geometry as the profile curve "flows" down the path curve, creating the end result. You can see this as a very similar process as a pasta maker! The pasta is made by squeezing a dough substance through a circular opening, which determines the 3D shape based on a 2D profile. If we add in a scaling value we can quickly and easily create a tapered tube in any shape we desire, with adaptive geometry tessellation controls (which can increase or decrease the level of detail with relative ease). Figure 5.1 illustrates the Pasta Principle of the Extrude Along Path concept.

First, create the path curve with a simple Bezier three-point curve. This will create the length-shape of the curve in 3D. I am going to leave it

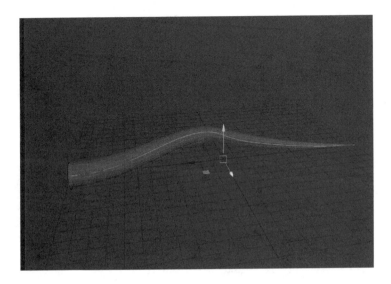

FIGURE 5.1 A simple tapered tube, with a profile curve and a path curve.

completely flat, however, and we can see how the edits to the shape of the path curve will trickle down to the resulting geometry.

Next we will create the profile curve. The profile curve provides the tubing shape. It is possible to have an "open" curve for the profile curve in this operation; however, in the world of organic creation we don't see a lot of open-shaped extrusions such as this (one notable exception would be mollusks and gastropod seashells), and in this case we are intending to create a "tube" that is totally closed. In this instance I will create a simple primitive circle and use it for the base profile curve. The shape can be edited after the extrusion, which gives us a surprising amount of control over the end result (Figure 5.2).

While it isn't necessary in the case of an Extrusion Along a Curve for the profile and path curves to be spatially aligned, it's generally a really good idea to set them up visually in order to see the results trickle down in a meaningful manner. For this reason, I have used the Curve-Snapping tool to line up the Profile Curve to the First Vertex of the Path Curve (which we can see in Maya indicated with a square selection box).

The next step is to select first the profile curve and second the path curve and open the Surfaces > Extrude Action box. The action is a curve-based modeling technique, although we are going to be generating polygons for the sake of this tutorial. We will be choosing the path as the creation position, although the way we have it set up it won't matter whether the path

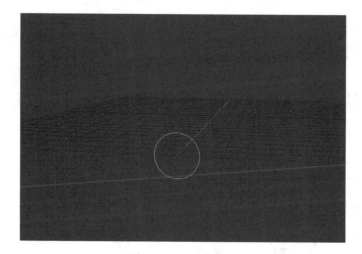

FIGURE 5.2   The profile curve and the path curve.

or profile is the point of creation (since they should be physically situated exactly the way we want). Once we have the parameters dialed in (in this case I'm creating a polygonal output from the resulting surface with specified detail levels in quads) we can click on Create and the tube will be generated, as you can see in Figure 5.3. Not very exciting, right? Let's add the Tapering aspect of the geometry by changing the Scale value in the Attribute Editor to a value of 0. What this will do is create a uniform taper between the original profile curve and the end of the Extrude, resulting in

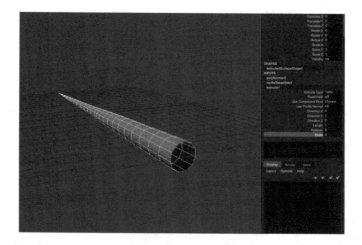

FIGURE 5.3   A 3D tube, which has been created but not tapered. The geometry looks very even and symmetrical, which does not have an organic appearance.

a tapered tube! Although this doesn't seem very exciting, it's an incredibly powerful organic modeling tools for anything that has this type of geometry. A starfish, an octopus, a creeping vine, and the horn of a goat or devil character can all use this simple technique for creation! In Figure 5.4 you can see some slight alterations to the path curve and the resulting change in the tapered tube, which now resembles the twisting form of a tree root. Figure 5.5 shows the exact same technique used for a creeping, winding

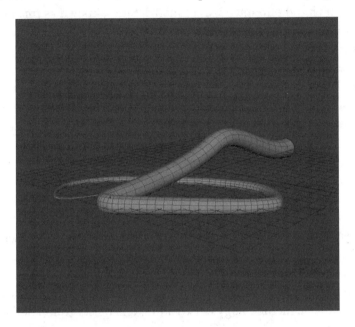

FIGURE 5.4 (See color insert.) Some simple changes to the shape of the path curve create a much different piece of geometry.

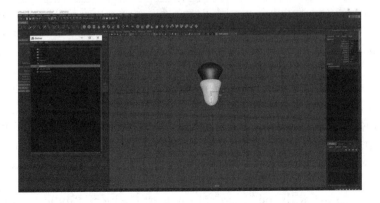

FIGURE 5.5 A simple segmented offset to make a wormlike structure.

vine for a plant. The tapered tube shape is incredibly versatile and will serve the organic modeler well in the creation of a multitude of species and life-forms, both fantastical and real.

BRANCHING GEOMETRY: FROM ONE COME MANY

Branching geometry is an incredibly complex subject. So complex, in fact, that books could be written about it, and indeed they have! In fact, an entire branch (no pun intended) of mathematics, known as *fractals*, have been built upon it. What should we know about branching geometry as it pertains to organic modeling?

There are several different types of branching geometry, but there's only one really good way to model them, and this should really be good news to the organic modeler. This means that there is always a go-to modeling technique for modeling branching structures for plants or animals. There are two important things to discuss when we look at the practical aspects of branching: the structure (mathematically) and the morphology, or how that structure manifests itself in the geometry. Mathematical modeling of something like a tree model will be much more procedurally based, and indeed it is the basis for all of those landscape and tree-generators that are so easy and open for our use. In fact, modeling an environment for a real-time game is often now a matter of "growing" it in the virtual sense with previously created growth algorithms and not individually modeling each component. But the heart of these tree-growing technologies is the basic geometric methodology of extruding one object from another with proper geometry.

TAPERED SEGMENTS

If you've ever wanted to model a tapeworm (and who hasn't), then this is the section for you! It's a simple operation to model tapered segments, which is based upon modeling with duplication and procedural trans-forms. Since the bodies of many segmented creatures come in the form of self-replication on a per-segment basis, this is the perfect technique for this kind of organic structure.

Since the segment model of an organic structure is quite common, especially in simpler animals such as worms and types of insects (or at least parts of insects), it's going to be something a modeler comes across more than once! It's also incredibly easy to implement.

First, I start with the "head" of my worm, which is indicated by the darker and slightly larger polygonal primitive (generated from a sphere with some mild scaling). Right behind this head is the template segment, which we will use as a "mold" or repeatable object.

The next step is to open the Duplicate Special Option box in Maya, where we have an array of options to make multiple copies with offsets to the transforms of the copies. These options allow us to offset each subsequent copy by the relative amount illustrated in the dialog box, giving us a range of duplicate modeling results possible. In this case, I will offset each copy (of which I have chosen 12 copies to make) by one unit in the z-axis. This will make it still partially reside in the space of the previous copy, and due to the tapered shape of the segment the copy will fit over it, obscuring the lower half. This is called *interpenetration* and is perfectly acceptable in the instance of a segmented type of model. Usually the top piece is shaped in such a way that you don't see the interpenetration break the illusion of solid matter. I also scale each copy .9 in the *xyz*, which will ensure the model will taper in all axes uniformly as it duplicates. The taper is not necessary; in fact some worms and nematodes don't have any taper at all as they segment. In this case, however, it's nice to see the range of options we have when modeling with duplication (Figure 5.6).

Figure 5.7 shows the result of the operation. Each segment fits perfectly on top of the other and slightly decreases in size! Even some insect limbs are constructed in this manner, with each subsequent segment fitting inside the previous.

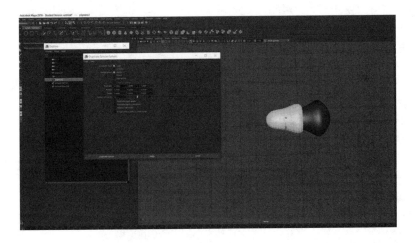

FIGURE 5.6   Duplication with transforms allows you to create multiple versions of the same object in different places and scales.

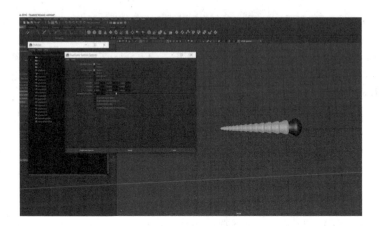

FIGURE 5.7 (See color insert.)   Result of modeling with duplication.

RADIAL EDGE LOOPING

The concept of radial edge looping is a complex one, but it is very simple to implement once you understand it. It is also one of the foundational skills in building scalable organic structures with variable resolution. There are several methods of generating these structures, and I will show you three methods here, each one with its own set of difficulties and advantages.

Concepts

Radial edge looping is the methodology with which we create radial structures on organic creatures. These structures are everywhere in the natural world, generally depicting an orifice, ocular structure, sphincter, or diaphragm-like muscular structure that moves or changes shape in a circular manner. Radial edge looping allows you to easily and quickly build these types of geometric structures inside UV edge-looping structures, which means that you can add large amounts of detail inside an area of lesser detail without altering the flow of the geometry.

Take a look at Figure 5.8. In the lower left corner you will see a structure that looks like a spider's web. This is a perfect rendition of the radial edge looping inside of UV edge looping. The radial part of the geometry is shaped in circular loops, while the rest of the geometry is shaped going across the surface. This means that we can add as many edge loops into the radial section (increasing our detail) without changing the amount of edge loops across the rest of the surface. So if we need to increase the detail in the radial area, not only does the rest of the model stay as it is, it does

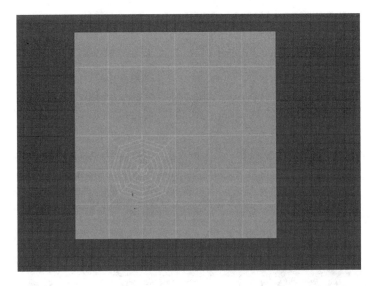

FIGURE 5.8　A radial structure inside a cross-section structure.

not interfere with the other edge loops at all. Compare this to Figure 5.9, in which I have subdivided the same basic area of space (four quads) uniformly. In Figure 5.9 the uniform divisions of the polygons have created a similar amount of polygons, but there is no circular structure *and* it completely destroys the continuity of the edge loops, due to the T-faces where the new divisions terminate. I can no longer model this globally.

Creating with Extrusions

The first step in creating a radial edge looping of any kind is to locate a pole. A *pole* is a vertex where four or more quads intersect one another. This vertex will be the center hub of your radial setup (Figure 5.10).

Once you have identified your pole, you can now select the quads that are adjacent to it; as you can see in Figure 5.11.

In order to begin the Radial setup, you will simply run an Extrude operation on those four quads, but instead of extruding the shell away from the original polygons, you will scale them (using the global scale option of the extrusion operation). This will create the box-inside-the-box structure, as you can see in Figure 5.12. Scale this as small as possible, as this will serve you as the innermost radial edge loop.

Next we will create a circular shape by scaling the outer four vertices inward, toward one another. This will create a natural circular shape for the inner edge loop (Figure 5.13).

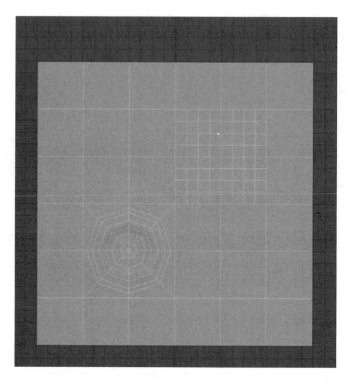

FIGURE 5.9 Trying to make a rounded shape from the increased detail in the right-hand corner would be nearly impossible, but it's easy in the radial section.

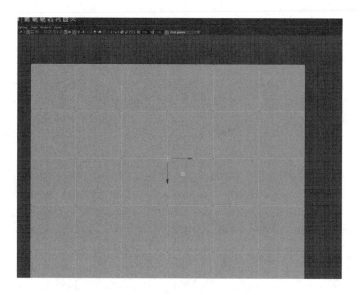

FIGURE 5.10 The pole of the radial areas, selected.

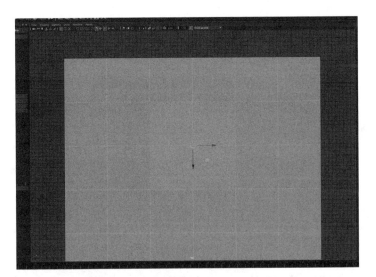

FIGURE 5.11 Preparing for the extrusion.

FIGURE 5.12 Extruded faces, scaled inward as far as they can go.

Now we will use the Insert Edge Loop tools, clicking inside of the radial area (but outside the inner radial edge loop that we just edited) and dragging it until we are almost to the outer radial edge loop, which will be the outer edge of the original quad faces that we began with. The edge loop will take on the shape of the closest adjacent edge loop, so you will see it change shape from circular (inner loop) to square (outer loop). Once you

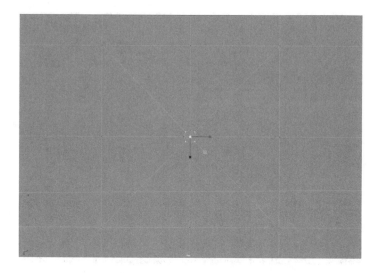

FIGURE 5.13   Adjusting the vertices of the inner loop to have a circular shape.

have inserted this loop, you can repeat the process of making it more circular by scaling in the outer corners inward, as you can see in Figures 5.14 and 5.15.

Now, in between the outer and inner edge loop, you can input as many edge loops as you like, each one of them being circular because both inner and outer edge loops have been edited to be circular in shape (Figure 5.16).

FIGURE 5.14   The outer edge loop of our structure.

FIGURE 5.15   Rounding out the outer shape.

FIGURE 5.16   Inserted edge loops will have a rounded shape as well.

The extrusion method of radial edge looping works perfectly well on a flat surface like this, where you have a definitive pole to extrude around. It does not work well at all in places where the surface is completely flat or at least planar in one world axis, which would allow the faces to be perfectly aligned when the extrusion is made. However, such is not always (an usually is *never*) the case in organic creatures.

Poke Face

Often you will come across a face or an area that does not have a pole to create edge loops around. Figure 5.17 shows such a polygon, with more than four sides and no central hub. In this case, we will use the Poke tool, which will create a vertex in the center of the face selected, triangulating the rest of the connected face (Figure 5.18).

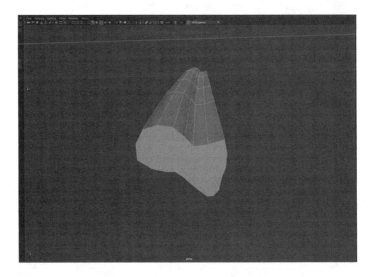

FIGURE 5.17   The flat polygon at the end of a complex extrusion.

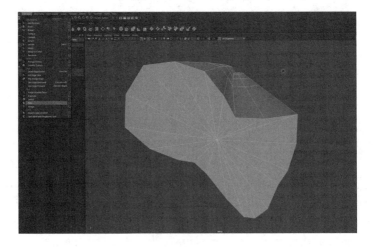

FIGURE 5.18   Using the Poke face to center a vertex and triangulate around it.

We can then select all faces created and use the Extrude method (as above) on this particular area, resulting in a radial edge loop structure where there was once just a single face. The final result, as seen in Figure 5.20, can be edited to create a nice, contoured, sloped surface where once there was single, flat plane (Figures 5.19 through 5.21).

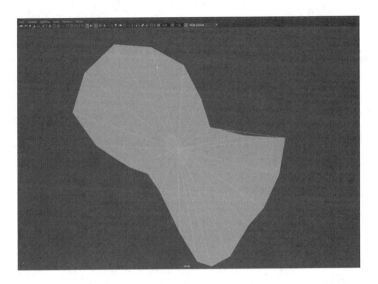

FIGURE 5.19   Making the inner edge loop.

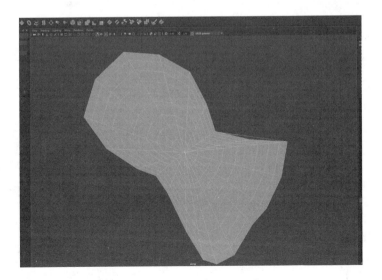

FIGURE 5.20   Inserting multiple edge loops.

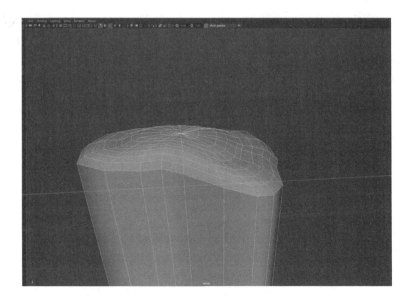

FIGURE 5.21   Pulling out the edge loops to round off the cap shape.

The Manual Method

Manually creating a radial edge-loop area inside of a UV edge-loop structure is the most likely scenario in organic modeling, since most of the
time it will involve inserting an eye socket, a mouth, an ear, or other
important feature on a model. Many of the areas in which you will find
this task will not be flat or aligned with the world, which will make our
extrusion method very difficult to manage properly. In this case, everything that we have done previously can be done manually, individually
cutting into the pole section the inner radial edge loop. The reason that
we do this is so we can have the subsequent radial edge loops totally congruent with the flow of the surface.

Figure 5.22 illustrates a curved surface that I wish to place a radial
edge loop inside of. The area I want to create is highlighted, with the pole
in the center. If I try to use the previously mentioned extrusion method,
the subsequent geometry will completely lose the rounded curvature of
the surface, which in turn makes the normal almost unusable in any
functional way. Figure 5.23 illustrates this result.

So how do we get the result we want? It's very simple. We simply use
the multicut tool, which operates like a scalpel, to cut in the structure that
will give us the radial edge looping we need but maintain the continuity

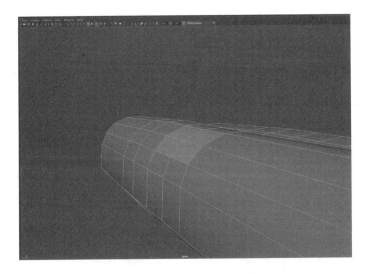

FIGURE 5.22   Selecting the faces for radial insertion.

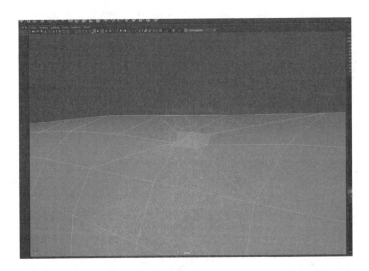

FIGURE 5.23   The result of trying to use the extrusion method: the continuity of the surface is destroyed.

of the surface. I first cut the triangles across the quads; as you can see in Figure 5.24, this sets up the quads and the pole for generating the inner edge loop ring.

The next step is to carefully make the inner circle using the multicut tool. You will want to make this circle as tight as possible to the pole,

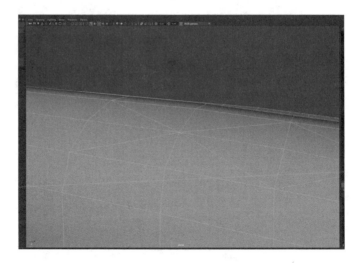

FIGURE 5.24   Triangulate the quads evenly.

so that you have the option to place as many edge loops in between the inner circle and the outer circle as you can (Figure 5.25).

Now simply insert the radial edge loops as needed and each one of them will maintain the flow of the surface contours. The reason this is so important is that when cutting an eye or a mouth or a tentacle sucker, any of these structures will keep the surface continuity and allow you to work across a complex, curved surface (Figure 5.26).

FIGURE 5.25   The multicut tool cuts the inner loop into the faces, preserving the continuity.

FIGURE 5.26   Inserting multiple edge loops.

BRANCHING

For the sake of organic modeling terms, we can organize branching structures into two main categories: self-replicating (plant-based) and bilateral
(animal-based). If you can place the typology into one of these two categories, you can easily begin to prep and create your geometry.

Self-replicating branching is what we typically see in a plant or even
bacteria, where there are multiple similar shapes that continuously branch
into identical (but smaller) shapes. Figure 5.27 illustrates the recurring
branching of a simple treelike shape, where every branch divides itself into
two branches recursively. This, of course, could happen to infinity, and the
structure would increment itself into a level of complexity so deep it would
crash any modern computer in seconds. There are many different forms of
self-replicating branching, some uniform, some nonuniform, but the main
concept here is that each branch is an almost-identical version of the parent
branch with the exception of scale (Figure 5.28).

Compare this to a common tetrapodal animal, and you will see an
entirely different method of branching, where the branches do not form
replicas of themselves but rather complex and segmented extensions for
particular purposes (generally locomotion). In a bilaterally symmetrical
branching model, each branch is replicated inversely on the opposite side
of the centerline, usually indicated by the length of the spine (if there is
indeed a spine). Bilateral and nonreplicating branches are the hallmark of

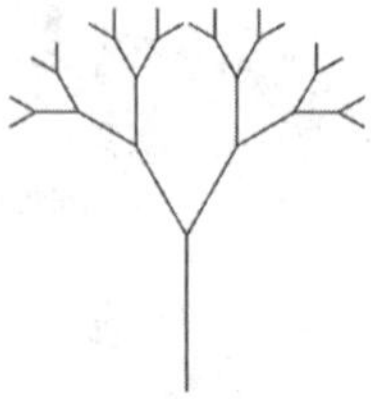

FIGURE 5.27 Self-replicating branching. This is a form often seen in bacteria and water plants.

FIGURE 5.28 Several iterations of self-replicating branching, often seen in yeast cultures.

FIGURE 5.29 Four-limbed vertebrate creature, typical mammalian and reptilian branching structure.

pretty much any ambulatory animal in the vertebrates, and of course we are a member of this phylum. Self-replication is not evident in this type of branching, as we can see clearly in the example of our own hand, which has five branches from the central hub of the wrist, whereas each joint of our arm only has a single branch (Figure 5.29).

The most important thing about these branching typologies and why we are having this slightly "biological" discussion is to understand the best methods of modeling different types of geometry. Self-replicating branching structures are much easier and more efficient to create with procedural mathematics like fractal equations, which allow for very high levels of fine-tuning in regards to the layout and design of curves and structural designs. Things like a nautilus shell or a willow tree could easily be constructed with procedural modeling methods, whereas something like an iguana would be much less successful. *So* when tackling a modeling job, it's always a good idea to begin with categorizing the necessary model into a biological structure, as opposed to just beginning the model and trying to get there in an organic method like sculpting clay. Most of your typical plant-based modeling, unless there's a need for extremely high detail, will be procedurally generated, or "grown" by algorithms that simulate the typical plantlike growth patterns. Any branching will be done in an automated way (often with the ability to randomly seed the equations) and would not really require individual attention.

Branching with Extrusions

In order to branch any kind of geometry into any kind of branching structure, the important tool to use is extrusion, much as we used it to create the tapered tube earlier in this chapter. The branched extrusion is created in a similar fashion to the tapered tube, only this time we will be using polygon edge loops as our profile curve, and a Bezier curve as our profile curve. The principle is extremely similar, however, and we can easily use it in multiple circumstances. Please read and go over the exercises in the previous section, "Radial Edge Looping," in order to perform these branching exercises using the same concepts.

We will begin with the simplest branching structure possible, as evidenced in Figure 5.27, which is a set of branches from a single stem into two divisions, which become tapering tubes that terminate in another two branches. First, we will begin with the concept of *symmetrical modeling*, as outlined in the previous Practicals section and Chapter 3. We have a simple cube, split down the middle. We will use the polygonal extrude tool on the cap node, splitting the end into two equal pieces and editing the resulting shell that was created to separate it from its base by an angle of ~45 degrees. This is so we can begin to build out our branches from the main stem and provide some room. Figure 5.30 illustrates this step.

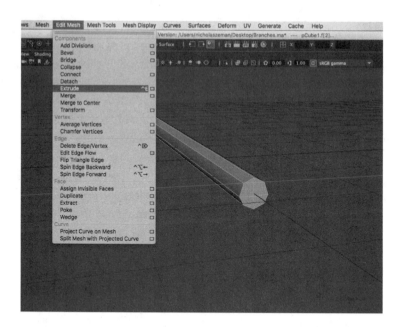

FIGURE 5.30 Dividing the cap.

Now we can repeat the process on each of the end caps that resulted from the original extrusion! It's the exact same process, repeated on the smaller caps. Now imagine that you were an organic "factory" employee, whose job it was to continue this process, each time selecting another face at the cap and scaling down the resulting extrusions by the same percentage value. After 40 iterations of this same action, there would be an incredibly high number of branches but an incredibly simple blueprint. This self-replicating branching structure is nearly identical to multiple microorganisms such as yeast and some fungi. The multiple extrusions can be done simultaneously, so that the extrude operation can continue, unabated, into infinity (or at least until your computer crashes). So what, other than budding yeast, would this even be useful for? For one thing, growth patterns and time-lapse concepts could easily be visualized with some simple scripting and automated branching functions, which are often at the heart of fractal imaging systems, which are a staple of shader noise filters and other procedural effects. All of those incredibly dense environment world creation software programs and tree builders also use variations of these functions in order to dynamically grow environments with multiple types of plants, bushes, vines, and trees. There are all kinds of minor tweaks that can go into the building of procedural plant types based on functions and input values. Sometimes, as in the fingers of the hand, there are terminations of more branches than began (more on this later).

Square versus Radial Branching Geometry

If we look at Figure 5.31, we can see that the basic branching structure will appear to be kind of cube-like and "blocky." Even in the smoothed view the basic structure of the branching is not very rounded or smooth, compared to Figure 5.32, which shows the bronchial branches of the human lung. Since we are essentially dealing with a tapered tube, branching into another set of tapered tubes, it's less than ideal to extrude multiple branches from a single, squared polygon as in Figure 5.31. Instead, we want the shape of the extruded structure to create a smoothly tapering form as it branches off of the parent. This is true for both bilateral geometrical shapes such as an arm or leg as well as plantlike forms like the branches of a tree. How do we achieve a smooth transition for our branches?

Radial Edge-Loop Branching

Radial edge looping is a perfect candidate to create a more viable, flexible, and detailed extrusion from any parent object. In this lesson we will learn

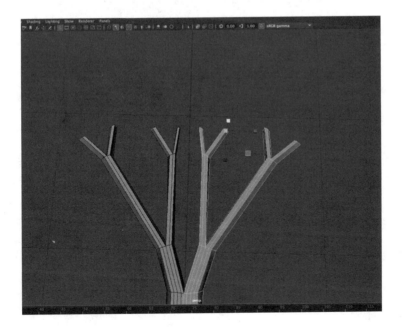

FIGURE 5.31 Each branch in turn branches again.

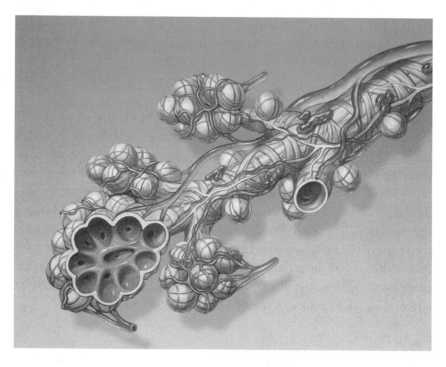

FIGURE 5.32   Bronchial branching in the lung. (Courtesy of Patrick J. Lynch, CC BY 2.5, https://commons.wikimedia.org/w/index.php?curid=1493050)

how to use radial edge looping for this purpose and set up a simple tree branch with smooth geometry extending from the parent.

First we will begin by creating a definitive point around which to generate our radial edge. This is referred to as our *pole*. Figure 5.33 illustrates the insertion of edge loops into the model to define the proper pole for our radial geometry (Figures 5.34 through 5.36).

Once the pole has been defined, we can now build the radial area by triangulating the quads around the pole and using the multicut tool to build the initial radial edge loop around the pole, as in Figures 5.37 and 5.38.

Now that the initial radial edge loop has been created, we can then use the Insert Edge Loop tool to insert a radial edge loop, which will define the base of the extruded branch (Figure 5.39).

The inner faces should be deleted and the radial edge loop edited to make it more rounded. Next we will do a simple edge extrude on the

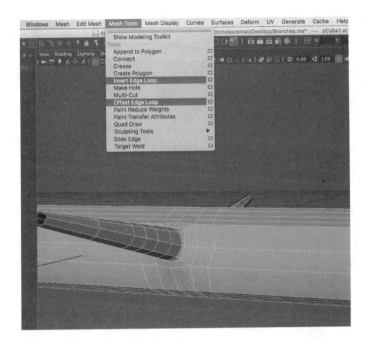

FIGURE 5.33   A radial branch.

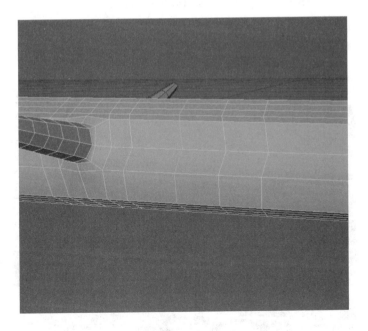

FIGURE 5.34   Choosing the cross section for the branch.

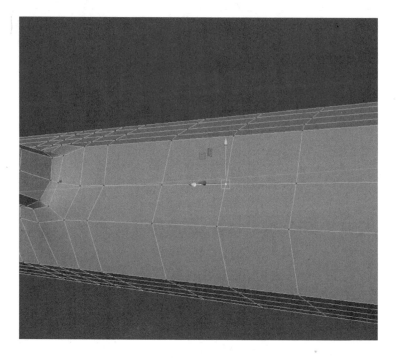

FIGURE 5.35   Determining the pole of the branch.

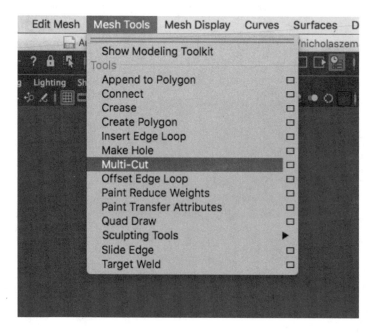

FIGURE 5.36   The multicut tool in Maya.

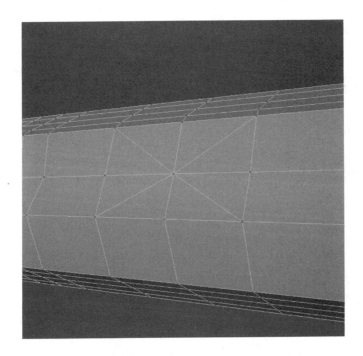

FIGURE 5.37 Beginning the radial structure.

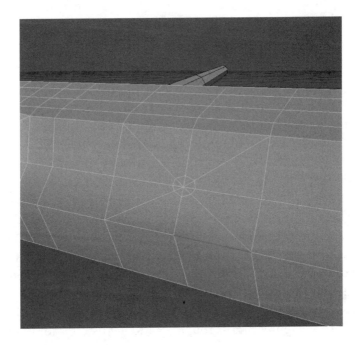

FIGURE 5.38 Building the inner loop.

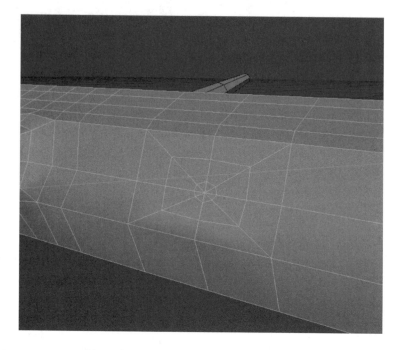

FIGURE 5.39   Building the outer loop.

innermost radial edge loop, as you can see in Figure 5.40. This is the simplest method of extrusion we can use. I created several divisions on the extrude, as well as a taper, which gives us the nice filleted curve.

It is also possible to extrude the edge loop along a path curve for more detailed branching, just as we extruded the curve along a path earlier in this section. In Maya, you will need to be in object selection mode, right-click on the edge loop you want to extrude, and *then* select the curve you wish to use as the path. I always align them exactly as I would want the end result to appear in the Perspective view. You can see in Figure 5.41 that I have set up a curve to use as a path and put the beginning of the curve exactly in the middle of the edge loop. Select first the edge loop you intend to extrude and then the path curve, selecting Extrude from the Edit Mesh pull-down menu. Maya will understand that you intend to use the curve as an extrusion path automatically. You must insert extra divisions into the extrude and put a value in Taper in order to see the extrusion take on the shapes of the curve! See Figures 5.41 through 5.44 to get a better idea of how to execute this.

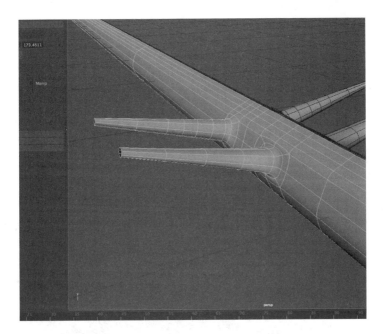

FIGURE 5.40   The radial extrusion, with a more rounded appearance than the straight extrusion.

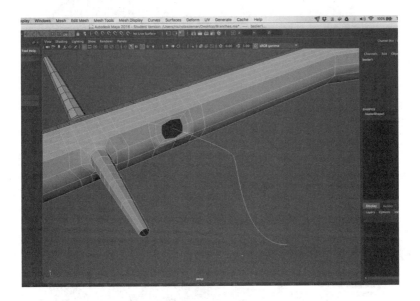

FIGURE 5.41   The path curve and the profile curve, which is the edge loop on the branch.

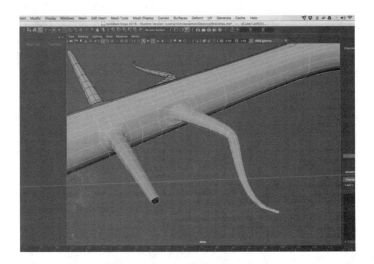

FIGURE 5.42   The resulting extrusion from Figure 5.43.

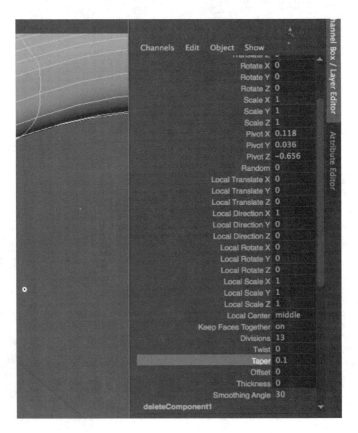

FIGURE 5.43   Using the taper to taper the extrusion.

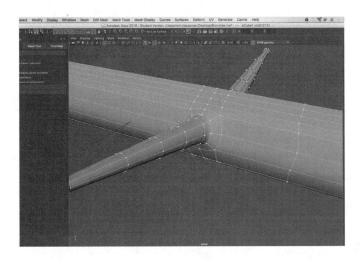

FIGURE 5.44   The proper shape of the branching area.

BUILDING RIDGES

There are several ways to build ridges into objects, but we begin with the analysis of exactly what a ridge is and how the morphology is represented in the organic universe. A *ridge* is defined as a raised up area, running the length of the object, branch, or limb of any creature. Ridges have a sharp profile, in which the raised area can be an acute angle (such as in a tooth) or a rounded edge (like in a clamshell). The ridges in our typical seashell in Figure 5.45 have a distinctive rounded appearance, which uniformly follow the length of the shell.

FIGURE 5.45   Classic ridges.

Curve-Based Ridges

How do we make ridges? There are multiple ridge-generation methods. When constructing a seashell, the ridges can be an integral part of the curve that is used to generate the model. Figure 5.46 illustrates the base curve for modeling, with the ridges built into it. The ridges for this profile curve have been created as one-degree, or angular curves, for the sake of better visualization.

Next, I will give the curve a bend using the Nonlinear Bend deformer from the Deform menu and position it with a bend in the curve, creating an arc in 3D for my ridge curve. This can be edited later if kept in the History! So the parameters are not set in stone (Figure 5.47).

In order to create the geometry as a surface, I then create a simple arc, using a Bezier curve with two handles to edit the sweep until it vaguely resembles the shell from Figure 5.45. Afterward I will convert it to NURBS to give me enough subdivisions of the curve for a nice sweep of the surface. Bezier curves in Maya are of great use in shaping the curve but less useful for creating geometry because they are only sparsely subdivided (Figure 5.48).

The next action is to create an extrude surface with the two curves, being careful to use the path curve as the normal, so that our ridge curve will sweep along the path and take on the orientation of the sweep, instead of remaining flat like the profile. I will also tweak the Scale factor to narrow the width of the extrude surface along the path curve, which will

FIGURE 5.46   Rippled curve that will provide ridges for our geometry.

FIGURE 5.47 I bend the curve with a Bend deformer to give it an elliptical shape.

FIGURE 5.48 The extrusion curve, based on the shape from a seashell.

create a similar shape to the shell in Figure 5.49. As you can see, the shape of the initial ridged curve has propagated itself into the surface geometry! This is a rather neat trick of curve-based modeling, in which you can rapidly generate the complexity of repetitive shapes like a ridge by making profile and path curves.

Finally, I add a second Bend Deformer to the profile curve, which will add another dimension to the resulting shape and give it the circular

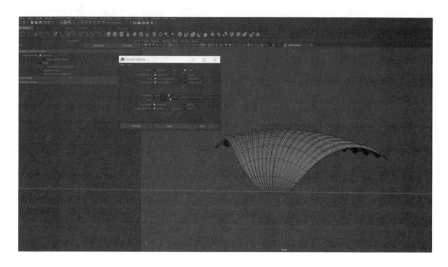

FIGURE 5.49 The extrusion of the wavy curve to the path curve produces a familiar shape.

appearance from the top view. This is not a perfect rendition of the shell shape, for the reason that work needs to be done to completely clamp the bivalve creature at the center, but it is a reasonably rapid prototype of the finished product, replete with the major ridge feature that we see in the geometry (Figures 5.50 through 5.52).

FIGURE 5.50 The Bend deformer.

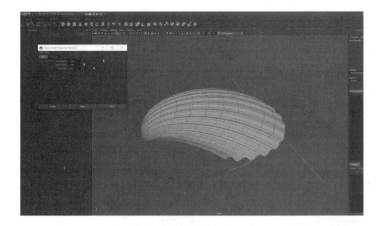

FIGURE 5.51 (See color insert.) The second bend to the base curve rounds out the form.

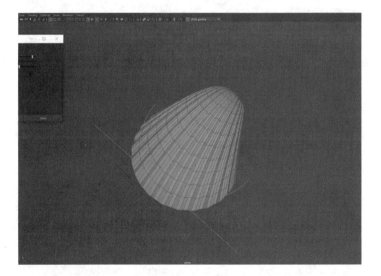

FIGURE 5.52 Upper perspective of the shell.

Extrusion Ridges

Another way of inserting ridges into geometry deals with existing shapes that you need to put ridges onto. This occurs when the basic shaping of an area has been completed, but the model in question requires ridged geometry. Generally this is a shape that has been rough-modeled with the organic methodology but after the basic modeling needs to have the detail of the ridge shapes inserted.

Here, in Figure 5.53, I have created a simple helix primitive with polygons, to simulate an already-modeled object in need of ridges. I have added several subdivisions running along the length of the path used to create it, as you can see in the edge loops spiraling up and around the object.

The next step is to select every other edge loop in the object running along the length of the polygon and then convert those edges to vertices. You can see in Figure 5.54 I do exactly this.

I then transform all of the selected vertices using the normal, or the perpendicular angle to the adjacent faces. Using the normal ensures that each vertex move inward based on the surface contour, which will uniformly indent them from the original flow, causing the ridges or rippling to take effect (Figure 5.55). Using a smooth afterward will smooth out the result, as you can see in Figure 5.56.

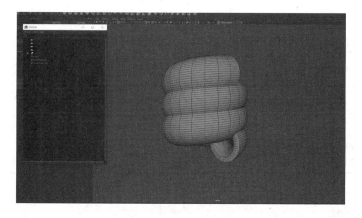

FIGURE 5.53   A spiral shape, created by an extrusion along a helix curve.

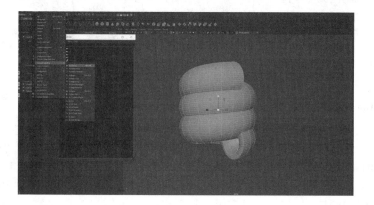

FIGURE 5.54   Editing edge loops.

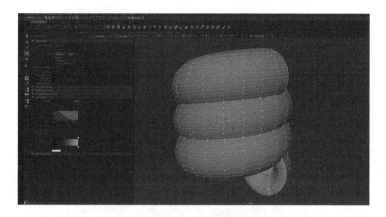

FIGURE 5.55   Offsetting the vertices.

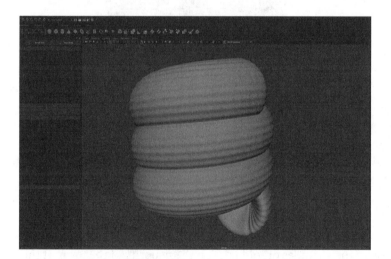

FIGURE 5.56   The final result.

FOLDS AND WRINKLES

This is perhaps one of the hardest geometrical forms to work with, because it involves overlapping lines, which can be extremely visually confusing, and because they require a high density of polygons in certain areas, without having a high density in others. Where do these overlapping lines occur? Many places (Figure 5.57).

As we have seen in previous sections, the overlapping lines and wrinkles occur in the folds of skin (like a hound's jowls), body fat creases in obese animals with high levels of adipose tissue underneath the

FIGURE 5.57 A rooster's wattle, with a great example of wrinkling and folding. (Courtesy of Muhammad Mahdi Karim, CC BY-SA 3.0, https://commons.wikimedia.org/w/index.php?curid=5551774)

skin, and many secreted forms like the shell of an abalone. These folds require a certain finesse in creation and editing and should not be taken lightly. Often they are the final layer of sculpting when working with a high-resolution model.

As with the ridges, we have multiple ways of creating these folding structures, based upon how we intend to model the object and to what capacity the wrinkles or fold take up the majority of the form. If the foundational construction of the geometry is based upon folds, then we *must* begin with a curve-based approach, making the development of the shape contingent upon the shape of the folds.

If, on the other hand, we need to insert fold into an already-existing piece of geometry, such as the fatty folds in a creature's belly or the wrinkles in a face, then we must insert selective detail and edit that detail as best we can to create the folded appearance.

Modeling with Wrinkled Curves

Modeling a surface that consists entirely of wrinkles and folds is not very common; most of the things you will be asked to model will have pieces of the skin or body that are folded, but not the entire thing.

Nevertheless, it's a good exercise in modeling technique to be able to conjure up a whole mess of folds at any time you might be called upon to do it, just so far as you understand the morphology and geometry behind it!

More often than not, the wrinkle-based model will be a piece of another model, like the wattle on a rooster, which is the little red, bumpy thing hanging from its neck for display and mating purposes. Modeling this would happen separately from the rooster main model and would simply be attached or merged into the main mesh.

As in the ridges example above, I am beginning with a simple curve. This profile curve will contain all of the primary shape that wrinkles and folds are based upon. Notice how in Figure 5.58 I have drawn (with a Bezier curve) a wavy, meandering, stream-bed–like curve. The wavy randomness is part of the primary structure. The other part of this primary structure is the fact that the lobes of the curves overlap. This overlapping is what will give us surface-based folding once we create the geometry. In this particular case, we will be using this curve as the path curve in our extrusion, allowing another curve to be the profile.

Now, for the sake of simplicity and demonstration of the principle, I will position an oval as my profile curve (although we could use an open curve just as easily). The oval will flow down the length of the folded path and form overlapping ripples. Simply use the Extrude Surface tool and the result will appear as it does in Figure 5.59, with overlapping folds that

FIGURE 5.58   A wrinkle-making curve, where the folds overlap.

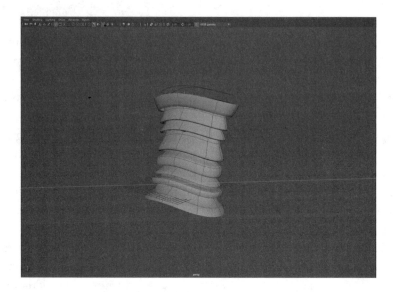

FIGURE 5.59 An extrusion of the wrinkle-making curve from Figure 5.58, creating a wrinkled and folded surface.

resemble loose, hanging skin. Using similar techniques, you can build any wrinkled, folded, surface necessary for an extraneous piece of skin, flap, or otherwise.

Inserting Wrinkles and Folds

One of the most common problems for organic modeling is the insertion of multiple fat rolls or other wrinkled skin features into an existing simple model. This is difficult for a couple of reasons; primarily, it requires a much higher amount of polygons and edge loops concentrated in the area that requires the wrinkles or folds, which can create the need for inserting detail with edge loops across an entire model, or somehow concentrating the detail in the needed area.

In Figure 5.60 I have a low-polygon model, but I want to put some fat wrinkles in the abdomen/belly, for artistic purposes. The problem is that in order to create the overlapping curve shape, as we saw in Figure 5.59, I will need far more edge loops in the belly area. One solution is to add multiple cross-section edge loops and edit from there, as you can see in Figure 5.61.

The problem with this approach is that the edge loops add the same amount of detail to the area all across the body, and not just in one specific

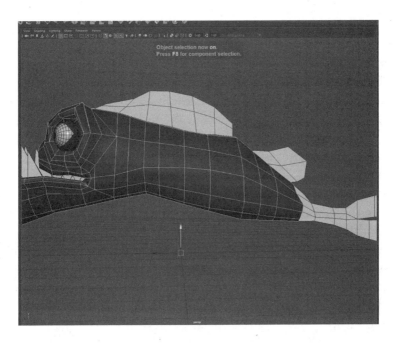

FIGURE 5.60   I want to insert some belly fat folds into this character.

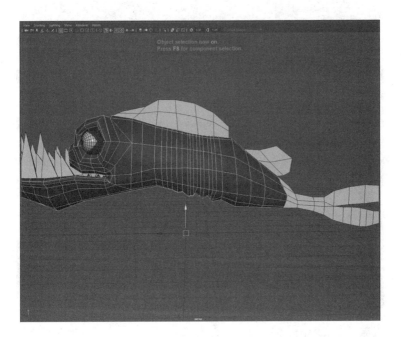

FIGURE 5.61   The insertion of edge loops works, but it creates geometry on top of the character as well.

spot! What I really want to do is to add a series of belly fat rolls in only the belly area, and not anywhere else.

In this case, I will need to break the continuity of my edge-looped model, in the area affected. This will make subsequent modeling changes much more difficult, so this is seen as strictly a "finishing" modeling move, as a detail, instead of a primary modeling technique. You really want to have the model completed as much as possible before you embark on generating localized features.

You can see in Figure 5.62 that I have selectively added in new half edge loops by using the Edit Mesh > Add Divisions and only adding the divisions in the V, without using the U (which requires the Linear option, as you can see). This adds the divisions locally, without adding them across the entire model. The disadvantage now is that the T-edges remove the possibility of editing the edge loops in that area as entire units across the model. The great advantage is that now I can selectively sculpt, in this case with some simple vertex offsets, the belly fat rolls I wanted to include (Figure 5.63).

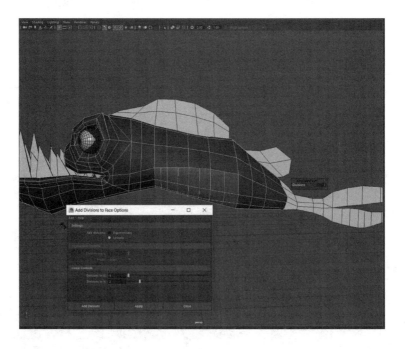

FIGURE 5.62   Inserting divisions into the selected faces.

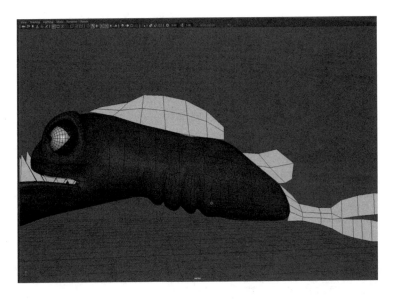

FIGURE 5.63 (See color insert.) Making the same belly fat rolls as before, but only selected areas have increased detail.

CONCLUSION

The material in this section is designed to give you the tools to create the basic structural shapes that formulate all organic shapes. Using these particular techniques and skills to build the particular structures exhibited should give you a fabulous toolset for organic modeling and creating any life-form, real or fantastical, you can imagine. Although they seem simple and easy to reproduce in and of themselves, they will often be a small part of a much bigger structure, or a repeating part of a hierarchical design. These can be seen as the Lego pieces of nature, and the more you familiarize yourself with the techniques and tools the faster you will be able to piece together more complex organisms using them. In Chapters 6 and 7, you will find them in use over and over again.

CHAPTER 6

Modeling Plant Structures

PART 1: THE MAGNOLIA LEAF

Let's begin with the simplest structure: the leaf. The leaf of a magnolia conforms beautifully to our three-point arc curve, as we learned in Chapter 5. In order to better develop our curve, I am using a reference image as an image plane, as you can see in Figure 6.1.

Step 1: Creating the Blade

The first step is to use the reference image to trace out the centerline curve with a two-point Bezier. This curve will be the point of reference for both the central leaf vein and the blades of the leaf, which extend from both sides.

I then use a three-point Bezier curve to trace the outline of the leaf shape on both sides, as you can see in Figure 6.2. There should be two separate curves, one for each side. The end points of these curves should meet along the central spine of the leaf.

The next step is to create the Surface Loft between the two curves, output as a polygon, with the settings as you can see in Figure 6.3.

Once the loft has been completed, we will next create a simple tapered tube surface defining the spine of the leaf. The profile curve in this case is a flattened oval, and the path curve the leaf spine, as indicated in Figure 6.4.

Next you can make some quick edits to the leaf shape, making it appear more dimensional by creating a slight curve across the cross section, so that the profile resembles a flattened M-shape. And you should

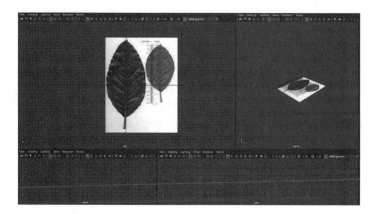

FIGURE 6.1   The visual aid in leaf modeling.

FIGURE 6.2   Building the curves to generate the leaf shape.

be done! Keep in mind that since the number of leaves can be quite high in a tree, this particular model is much higher resolution than you would typically find in a standard tree generator for real time, although it would be constructed in a similar manner. The biggest difference would definitely be in the use of a single polygon plane with a cutout texture map instead of the modeled leaf shape. Leaves on trees occur in large enough amounts and from far enough away (generally speaking) that we can use very low-resolution images with instanced textures and be very efficient!

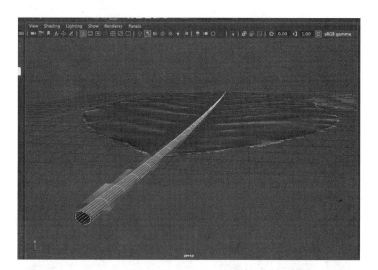

FIGURE 6.3   Extruding the mid-rib of the leaf as a tapered tube.

FIGURE 6.4   Lofting the two curves together creates the exact shape of the leaf as designed.

The Leaf Whorl

Since magnolias have whorled leaf clusters at the end of the secondary branches, the best method of organization is to create the leaf whorl and centerpiece as a group, where they will surround the center seed or flower (which we will model below).

Importing the flower model (see further below for instructions), we will generate the leaf whorl spiral around the end point of the secondary branch. The leaves, as we see in the reference, make a slow spiral up the end of the branch, for three revolutions. We will set up for this by lining up the flower and the leaf model, as seen in Figure 6.5.

Now creating the leaf whorl is as simple as modeling by duplication, in which we will offset the leaf slightly in the Translate Y and the Rotate X, which will give us a mile spiral. I have chosen six duplications (Figure 6.6).

FIGURE 6.5 We have the leaf model and the flower model, lined up and scaled to replicate.

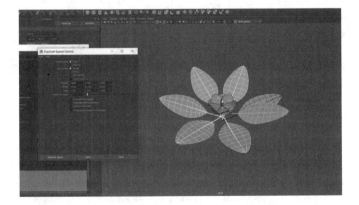

FIGURE 6.6 (See color insert.) Modeling by duplication allows me to create a spiral growth around the central stem.

FIGURE 6.7 Some stems have no flowers, so we make alternate versions for visual randomness.

We can make a few different versions of the leaf whorl if we like; definitely we will need one with the fertilized seed pod, since the magnolia often has both in view, even when flowering (Figure 6.7).

PART 2: THE TRUNK

In order to create the primary profile for the trunk extrusion, I start by creating a NURBS Primitive Circle with 12 sections. This will give me enough Control Vertices to create the shape of the base (Figure 6.8).

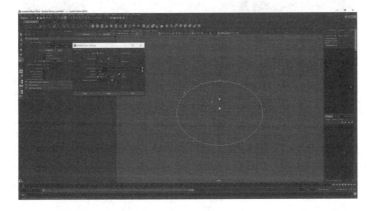

FIGURE 6.8 The circle will give us a starting point for our tree trunk.

The next step I take is to import a reference image as an image plane, taken from a tree trunk cross section, which is easy to find with a simple search online. It helps if you can find a similar species to the one you're intending to create. For the sake of this tutorial, I located a similar shape to the magnolia tree species that I want to create. Placing the image plane in the y-axis, I can then simply move the points of the Primitive Circle to roughly approximate the shape of the base! We don't need for it to be exact, since every tree's cross section is unique. Make sure that when you move the point of the circle to match the reference cross section that you do it only in the world x- and z-axes, leaving the circle two-dimensional (Figures 6.9 and 6.10).

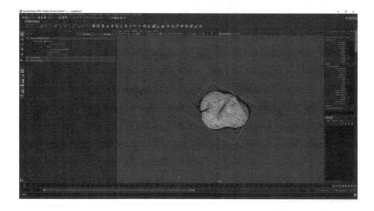

FIGURE 6.9   Importing the trunk cross-section image plane, from the image of a sawed-down tree.

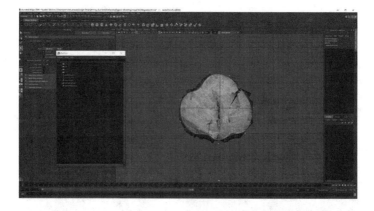

FIGURE 6.10 (See color insert.)   I match the vertices of our circle to the shape of the trunk.

The next step is to create the path curve that the profile curve will be extruded along. I will create a 14-point linear NURBS curve, from the relative center of the profile trunk curve to the end of the length, as you can see in Figure 6.11. Due to the randomness of growth patterns, I throw a few mild kinks into the 14-point curve to give the trunk shape some level of visual interest when the extrusion is made.

I then will use the Extrude Along Curve, choosing first the Trunk Profile curve, and second the Path Curve, selecting the Extrude Option box. As you can see in Figure 6.12, I add values in the Rotation and Scale parameter boxes. Rotation adds a twist to the Extrusion, which gives it a

FIGURE 6.11 The length of the tree trunk, with a few kinks for random appearance.

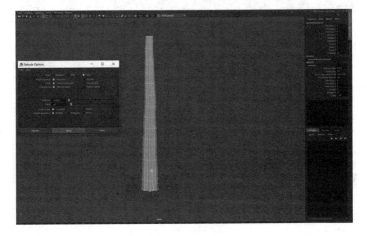

FIGURE 6.12 Extrusion of the trunk curve.

slight amount of visual interest. Scale, as we learned in the previous section, adds a tapering of the thickness of the Extruded Surface. As you can see in Figure 6.12, the trunk shape has a significant taper and some slight irregularities that give it a slightly crooked appearance. This crookedness will highly depend on the species of tree. In some trees, like most tall pine species, the trunk is almost completely straight. Some trees have extremely crooked growth patterns. In the case of my magnolia tree here, I am going to give a small amount of irregularity similar to the reference images.

Also, for construction purposes, we must convert the output geometry to polygons. In this case I have used the Modify > Convert > NURBS to Polygons option, using Quads with General and one edge loop per span of the NURBS surface, which are all illustrated in Figure 6.13. This will create a polygonal version to take on exactly the same amount of subdivisions as the original NURBS surface has. This will create a single polygonal mesh that has a single edge loop for each control vertex in the NURBS surface.

A problem here with our generated surface is the fact that the Scale, or Taper value, is uniform from base to tip! If we look carefully at an actual example of the tree, we can see that the taper is exponential, which means that the tapering value increases as we go from base to tip. In order to add this feature to our trunk, we must use a nonlinear deformer to model the exponential taper into the length of the trunk.

By using the Flare Non-Linear Deformer, I am able to quickly take advantage of the parameters of the beginning diameter and the ending

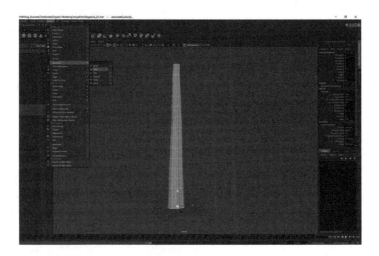

FIGURE 6.13   Choosing the taper deformer to enhance the shape.

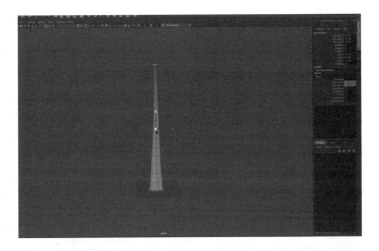

FIGURE 6.14   The exaggerated, nonlinear taper of the tree trunk.

diameter (separated into *x*- and *z*-axes), also adjusting the "curve," or exponential amount of change from the base to the end. Figure 6.14 shows the values I used for my Exponential Taper, as you can see in the Channel Box Editor on the right-hand side. This tapers the end of the tree trunk more rapidly toward the end of the extrusion.

PART 3: THE ROOTS

One of the defining characteristics of the root structure of trees is the significant lateral spreading and the heavy amount of meandering paths. The roots extend from the bottom of the trunk and spread out and down into the earth. The good news is that the roots of the tree are rarely visible, so the detail does not need to be as heavy as the rest (unless for some reason the roots will need to be seen prominently).

In order to generate the polygonal cap for the roots extraction, we must first convert the extrude surface created in the previous step to polygons! I use the Modify > Convert > NURBS to polygons with the following options:

1. Quads

2. General (type of conversion)

3. Per Span # of Isoparms = 1 (both U and V)

This is an absolutely necessary step in order to create the branching structures for our roots and upper branches! The extrusion surface is created as NURBS, so we won't be able to branch from the main trunk without this conversion.

Next, I will simply use the Mesh > Fill Hole Tool. This will create "caps" of connected polygonal faces on both the top and bottom of the model (Figure 6.15). These caps will not be quads, since it will simply create as many polygons as it needs to create the face for the ends. It will have as many sides as the amount of vertices that you used to create the basic trunk shape.

Now that we have created the caps, we need to give ourselves some radial faces in order to extrude the roots. The first operation to prepare ourselves for this is to use Poke Face. Poke is an operation that creates a vertex in the center of the selected face and subsequently triangulates the rest in a semiradial pattern around the center vertex. After this operation is complete, I will use the multicut tool to cut an inner radial edge loop (a technique previously covered in Chapter 5), the result of which is seen in Figure 6.16. Now we can insert as many edge loops as we like between the inner loop and the outer rim! We won't need to create any more faces, however, but simply use the ones we have to create the extrusions.

You can see in Figure 6.17 that I have created multiple curves for the roots. These curves take on the shape of the roots as they spread outward and downward. Once again, the roots are not a feature of a tree that is prominently displayed; rather they dig below the ground plane and are usually only visible if the tree has been uprooted and needs to be seen from that perspective. So I make these roots' curves approximate at best. I begin with a single root path

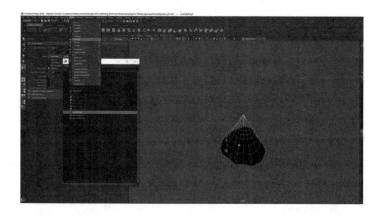

FIGURE 6.15　The base of our tree, without a cap. Any extrusion from a circular curve is basically a tube.

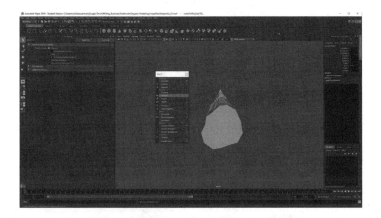

FIGURE 6.16   Using fill hole to generate a cap for our trunk.

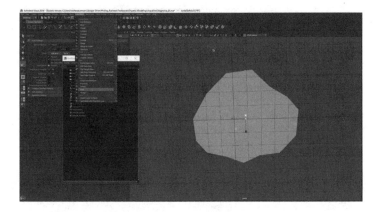

FIGURE 6.17   The cap preparing for the Poke Face.

curve and then duplicate that curve several times, making minor tweaks to the position and the shape of each one to add in an element of randomness and heterogeneous appearance (Figure 6.18).

Using the Tapered Tube Extrusion technique we used in Chapter 5, we can simply extrude the faces of the base (in this case i used two at a time, but you could do each individual face if you chose) along the path curves of the root, as seen in Figure 6.19. The Scale (or Taper) value is set to 1 in order to have the roots reach a point at the end. This technique of extruding a tapered tube is almost universal in the branching structure, roots or otherwise, and is an essential tool in modeling plants like our tree (Figure 6.20).

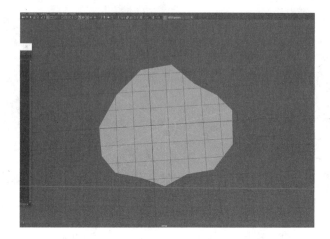

FIGURE 6.18   Poking the face and creating the inner edge loop.

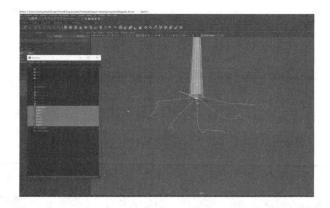

FIGURE 6.19   Laying out the meandering root curves.

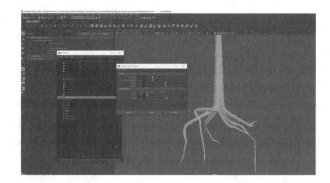

FIGURE 6.20   Extruding faces along the root curves to create the multibranched root structure.

PART 4: THE UPPER BRANCHES

The upper branches of a tree can take on many morphologies, especially in the crookedness, angle, number of subbranches, and the leafing structures. In our magnolia tree, there are several primary branches from the main trunk, followed by secondary branches, which terminate in a whorl (circular) leafing pattern around the flower and subsequent seed (Figure 6.21).

FIGURE 6.21 The branching structure of the magnolia tree at the base.

Primary Branches

The first thing we need to do is to pay careful attention to the primary branching shape. Figure 6.21 is a close-up of a reference tree. What we see is the first primary branches, which are often the biggest, extending from the tree. You can also see that the shape is very bulky, fattening the center of the tree, usually due to the heavier and older growth of the bark around the area. In order to generate this branching shape, we have several options. We can simply choose a single face and extrude that, but the squareness and lack of curvature in the extruded segment would make it look very unnatural. However, this is possible for very low-resolution models.

The next option, and the most time-consuming, would be to create a full radial edge loop area and extrude the limb from the edge loop ring on the outer rim. Once this radial area has been built we can then extrude the outer rim as we would any other polygon, creating the branch from a rounded area on the trunk. This is the best solution in terms of shape and appearance; however, it's not the best in terms of efficiency and time value. One of the problems with hand-modeling something like a tree is that the process can be extremely time-consuming! We all want to model faster and more efficiently (Figures 6.22 and 6.23).

There is a middle version compromise that we can take, which still gives us a rounded appearance but doesn't make us take the time to build the

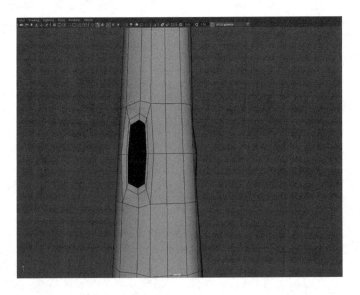

FIGURE 6.22 The rounded branch section. This is the true shape of the natural branching mechanism.

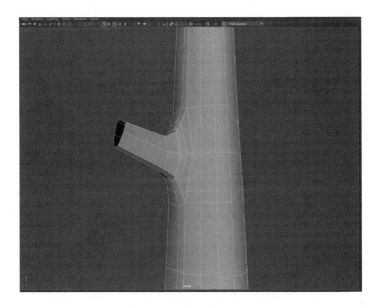

FIGURE 6.23   Pulling the rounded branch out from the base.

full radial structure. The trick is to find four quads together and shape the vertices in a rounded manner, as we can see in Figure 6.24.

Then a curve can be drawn in this case with the Pencil Curve tool, which will draw a random style of curve as if you are using a pencil. I use this to increase the waviness of the result. Place the curve, extending from the four quads you intend to extrude, and use the Extrude tool, with options to increase the divisions to at least 15 or 16 (here I use 20), and add a Taper of 0.1 or 0, and if you want a bit of twist (depending on your tree type). This will create an extended branch from the selected four quads that has a rounded base but without the radial edge looping (Figures 6.25 and 6.26).

For maximum results, I tend to use the radial edge looping method on the lower branches, which are more prominently viewed, and the quicker technique on the upper branches.

Secondary Branches

The secondary branches come off of the primary branch, and these terminate in the leaf whorls with flowers. These are naturally much shorter, more slender, more numerous, and lighter than the primary branches. Also, due to their high volume, much of their shapes will be obscured by the foliage. For this reason, when modeling the secondary branches we can take some simple shortcuts to limit the modeling overhead and

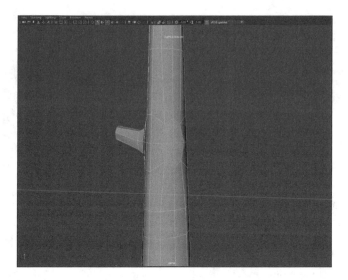

FIGURE 6.24 A quick shortcut to the radial extrusion method: rounding four quads and extruding them produces a similar shape.

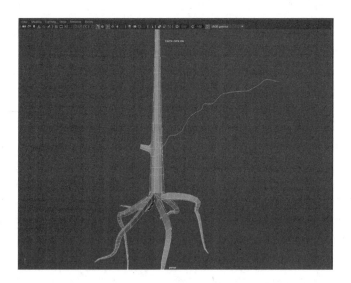

FIGURE 6.25 Choosing the rounded quad area and the path curve for extrusion.

speed things up. Although these shapes are definitely "rounded," if we are seeing things from a semi-obscured distance, they won't really be necessary to created rounded branching structures. In fact many auto-tree-building software kits don't even use geometry at all for these branches; rather they use cutout textures (Figure 6.27).

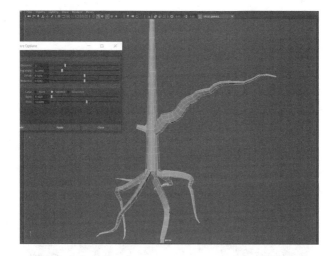

FIGURE 6.26   The resulting extrusion, with a slight twist and a tapering form.

FIGURE 6.27   The secondary branches and the leaf terminations of a magnolia tree.

The best method of generating these secondary branches is to pick a random set of branch faces on the extended secondary branch, mostly on the upper parts of the branch (facing the sun, of course, since trees rarely send their branches downward!) (Figure 6.28).

Next we will create a series of extrusions of the face, scaling the extrusions locally with each iteration and slightly offsetting them from the previous extrusion. Once you have done this five or six times, you will have crooked, tapering branches extending from the primary branch, as you can see in Figure 6.29. We do this all at once as a global operation, so we

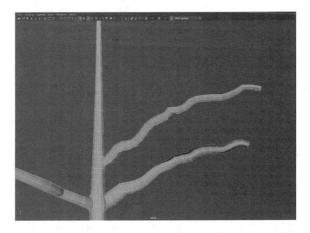

FIGURE 6.28 Multiple branches can be made from single quad selections randomly chosen on a branch.

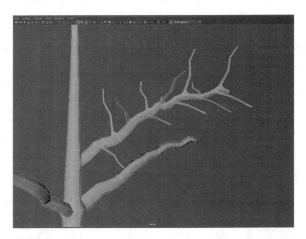

FIGURE 6.29 Quick, feasible secondary branching all done at the same time through multiple extrusions.

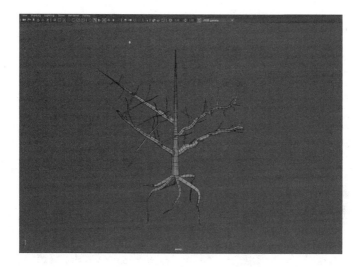

FIGURE 6.30 Several more secondary branches done on each primary branch. Secondary branches need less detail than primary, so we can get away with single-face extrusions.

can quickly populate an entire primary branch with a series of secondary branches. You could opt for the extrude using a curve for each secondary branch, but that would be five times slower than this method, and the results would not be significantly better (Figure 6.30).

PART 5: THE FLOWER

As you can see from Figure 6.31, the flower is a radial structure with two layers surrounding a central stem. The petals of the flower are cupped teardrop shapes, which curl upward slightly.

The first step is to create a NURBS Primitive Circle and edit the control vertices to create a teardrop shape, as you can see in Figure 6.32.

Next, we will create a planar surface, which will fill in the circle with a NURBS surface, which we will then in turn convert to polygons (Figure 6.33).

Next we will create the cupped shape, which we will create with a simple Bend Non-Linear Deformer to tip up the top of the petal (Figure 6.34).

Next we will group the bend deformer with the petal polygon and set the pivot to slightly in front of the petal model. This allows us to make small adjustments to the shape of the petals we duplicate. The pivot in front of the petal represents the centerpiece of the flower, which the petals will revolve around (Figure 6.35).

FIGURE 6.31   The magnolia leaf. (Courtesy of DavetheMage, CC BY 3.0, https://commons.wikimedia.org/w/index.php?curid=9406594)

FIGURE 6.32   Editing a simple circle to form the teardrop shape of the leaf.

Next we will do a simple model by duplication and duplicate our petal four times with a rotational offset of 75 degrees, which will make a radial pattern (Figure 6.36).

The next step is to duplicate the lower layer and rotate it slightly, moving it above the lower layer and create an elongated sphere to indicate the centerpiece of the flower (Figure 6.37).

FIGURE 6.33 A planar, or flat, surface derived from the curve. This is only possible if the curve is absolutely flat.

FIGURE 6.34 A simple bend can form the cupped shape of the petal and give it a 3D appearance.

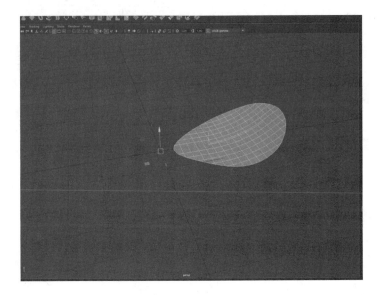

FIGURE 6.35   Moving the pivot to the outside of the petal termination will allow us to duplicate it around a hub.

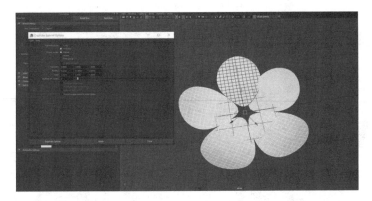

FIGURE 6.36   The radial petal configuration made by duplication of the initial petal.

POPULATING THE LEAVES

Unfortunately, in a hand-modeled world the process of sticking leaves on trees is a lengthy, boring, and inefficient process. We will discuss the merits of procedural modeling in this section's conclusion, but for now let's just pretend those options don't exist! How do we get these leaves onto the branches we've created? Basically, we will have to position them individually onto each secondary branch termination. While this seems arduous,

FIGURE 6.37 Duplicating and adjusting the second layer of petals gives us the entire flower structure if we add in the elongated sphere (bolus) shape of the central form.

long, and difficult, it's not incredibly tough to put together with the proper planning. Keep in mind that all of these things could easily be automated, which would be a great subject for another book, but the focus of this book is all about the creation of organic objects and geometry.

The first thing to do is to create the proper grouping and subsequently edit the pivot point of that group so that we can easily snap it into place with accuracy, saving us time and energy.

Using the Vertex Snap tools, I can easily snap the base of each whorl to the end of each secondary branch, which will populate the secondary branches easily. I use a few tricks to create randomness and variation. The flower petals are randomly hidden in various whorls, to give it visual interest, and the leaf whorl is nonuniformly scaled slightly as well as rotated differently for each branch end, including some individual leaves that will tilt toward the direction of the sun (Figure 6.38).

PROCEDURAL TREE MODELING

As you can see from this chapter, the modeling of an entire plant is not necessarily difficult; however, it is extremely time-consuming. The variation in the branches, the placement of the leaf clusters, and the need for individual tweaks to specific elements can take many, many hours to complete.

FIGURE 6.38 Population of leaves and flowers at the termination of each secondary branch. This would take forever if done by hand, but procedural tree makers do it through code in seconds.

Imagine the creation of an entire environment for a game or film! It would take months.

The solution to the creation of a complex plant environment quickly and easily is the procedural generation of these structures, based on algorithms and mathematical principles. As we have seen, the branching and basic geometrical structure of a tree or other kind of plant can be converted into a logical and mathematical formula, which in turn can be fed variables that turn out a level of randomness and range of species. This allows a tremendous amount of variation in the resulting geometry with one single equation. It also allows for population of the models across areas based on variables that would allow for creation of these models and variables based on other inputs, such as a texture map or time for animations.

Many programs have procedural modules for creating trees, bushes, and other plant growth (such as grasses). These environment creators don't do anything magical, but they create branching structures through algorithms and populate the leaves and flowers or fruits in an automated manner. The variables that can lead to this structural automation are things like forms of branching a leaf growth. For instance, choosing the branching form can lead to different species morphology. A pine tree has a single trunk, fairly straight, and the secondary branches have a specific angle, which are fairly straight in their upward growth, which has a variable height. A magnolia tree, such as we have worked on here, has multiple main branches (in some species), with slightly crooked primary branches, exhibiting a spiral leaf whorl surrounding a flower or seed pod. These differences can all be programmed into the algorithm and exposed as a set of options for a user to input!

As an organic modeler in post-2017, you will probably not be asked to hand-model a tree. But this material is important nonetheless, on the off chance you *are* responsible for creating a treelike structure in a character model. (The Ents in *The Lord of the Rings* and Groot from *Guardians of the Galaxy* are two examples from recent memory.) It also is excellent practice for things like branching, multiple extrusion techniques (secondary branches), and modeling through duplication. Creating this kind of structure can give you a general sense of construction and growth in the sense of geometry, as well as modeling by assembly.

CHAPTER 7

Organic Modeling Workflow

As we briefly went over in Chapter 4, "Organic Modeling Techniques," here we will take on the process of layout, preparation, and low-level modeling of a fully formed vertebrate. For this exercise I have chosen man's best friend, the dog! Specifically, a greyhound, since they have a long, lean, and fairly clean physiology. The very first stage of organic modeling is to get and align your reference images. Figure 7.1 clearly illustrates the image plane layout in Maya, in which I have imported a side view (which is the length of the spine for our standard quadruped vertebrate) and the top view, which provides the cross-section shape. These will be our initial guidelines for the first stage of modeling. I have chosen to put the feet exactly on the Y-0 point, so that the model is more easily rigged for real-time or video rendering, with the point of contact for the feet at the ground.

The next specific step is to create and position a simple cube. This cube should be centered on the main portion of the spine, from the cervical vertebrae (the head comes later) to the end of the tail length. The cube must be halved, by creating a division along the length or z-axis, and the half on the negative side deleted.

The next step is to duplicate the existing half of the cube as an Instance with a –1 value in the x-axis for our symmetrical modeling workflow. This ensures that anything done to the half on the positive side will be mirrored on the negative side (Figure 7.2).

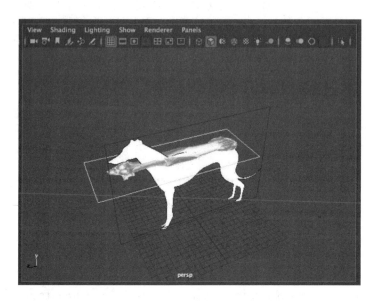

FIGURE 7.1 The image planes for modeling, lined up along the length of the spine to provide the best reference.

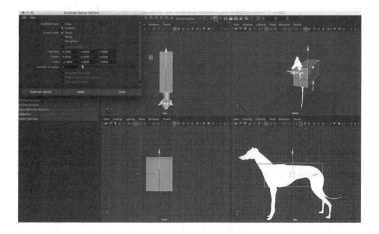

FIGURE 7.2 Creating the half cube along the length of the spine and duplicating it with a mirrored instance to set up our symmetrical modeling.

Now we will fill in the length of the spine with enough edge loops to properly edit the torso. This is done with some level of intuition and experience, but the nice thing about working in the edge loop methodology is that entire areas of detail can easily be added or removed at will. We only need to insert enough edge loops to get the desired shape of the length of the torso (Figure 7.3).

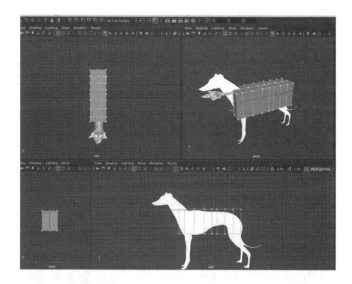

FIGURE 7.3   Adding the edge loops along the length of the spine so that we can create the proper shaping.

Now that we've inserted the edge loops, the next step is to cleanly alter the shape along the length of the spine to resemble the profile shape of our creature. Here I am *only* moving these vertices in the *y*-axis. This ensures clean, flowing edge loop lines and parameterization (Figure 7.4).

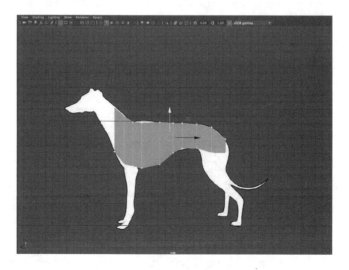

FIGURE 7.4   Shaping the model in the perpendicular-to-spine axis.

The next step is to do the same in the Top-Down view, which will add the next level of detail to our modeling (Figures 7.5 and 7.6).

Now we create the ride of the spine and the bowing of the belly by using our tried-and-true parabolic curve to give us a guideline in shaping the tubelike structure of the spinal length. The best way to do this is

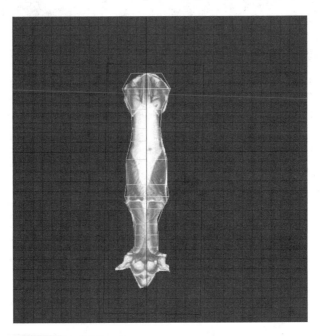

FIGURE 7.5 Adjusting the model from the top down, along the length of the spine.

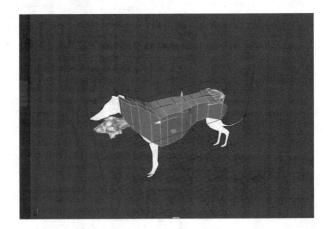

FIGURE 7.6 Now we have a cutout 3D shape that conforms to the basic appearance in two dimensions.

to move the vertices on the outside of the centerline inward on the global *y*-axis. This will begin to develop the cross-section shape along the spine, making the curve-like profile as discussed previously (Figure 7.7).

The next step in our process is to pull up on the lower vertices (defining the belly) and down on the upper vertices, which defines the primary ridge of the spine (Figures 7.8 and 7.9).

FIGURE 7.7   Now we begin to taper and contour the shape to make it rounded.

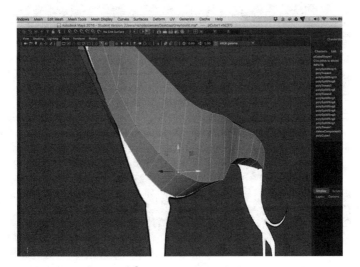

FIGURE 7.8   Pinching the vertices inward at the bottom makes the torso taper from top to belly.

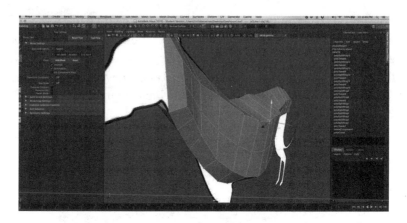

FIGURE 7.9 Adding an edge loop in and tweaking the upper vertices along the length of the spine will begin to give us some better contours.

Now we should insert an edge loop into the center of the body, which will define the curve of the cross-section geometry. This allows us to define the "slices" of the creature running down the length of the spine, which gives us the distal taper and contouring perpendicular to the spine (Figure 7.10).

Transforming these vertices selectively along the spine in the x-axis will provide us with the changing of the width of the animal along the

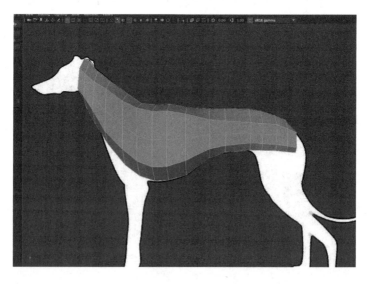

FIGURE 7.10 (See color insert.) The middle edge loop will provide us one more point in the curve of the torso from top to bottom.

spine. These should generally be individually tweaked at this stage in the process, so that we can have total control over the width of the animal along the body (Figures 7.11 and 7.12).

The rounding of the cross section should be carefully considered here, as this will define the curvature of it and any increase in detail from here on in will be exponentially more difficult to control. Any area that you need to adjust here in the cross section should be inserted as an extra edge loop if you find it necessary (Figures 7.13 and 7.14).

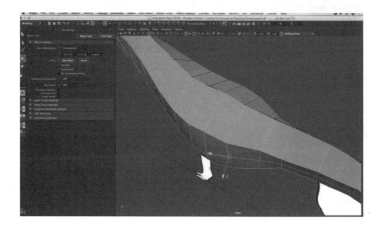

FIGURE 7.11 I pull out the vertices along the mid-curve edge loop to make the elliptical shape.

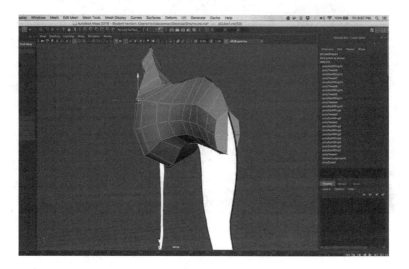

FIGURE 7.12 The resulting curvature of the torso begins to develop.

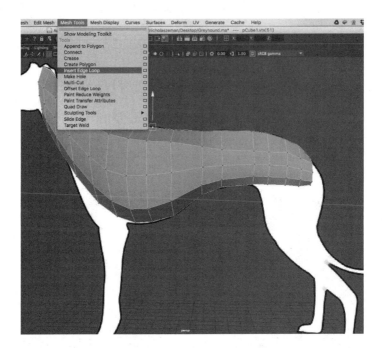

FIGURE 7.13 Inserting edge loops will become necessary to improve the model detail along the length of the spine.

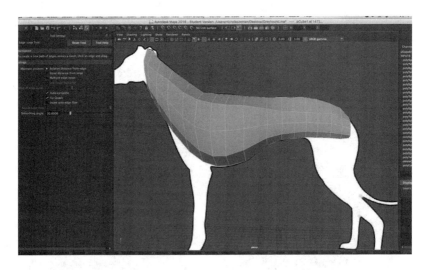

FIGURE 7.14 Building the shape of the belly.

CREATING THE TAIL

In pulling out the tail of the animal, I generally work straight out from the spine and put any necessary bend in it after the fact. Tails can be tricky because they have a wide variety of shapes that taper to a point at the end. In this case I simple extruded the tail faces out with several divisions to the end of the tail in the reference silhouette and ignored the strong curve in the vertebrae until after the initial extrusion was complete, at which point I edited the flow of the edge loops to match the image (Figures 7.15 through 7.17).

An alternative method of generating the tail geometry, and one I generally prefer, is to use the Extrude Along Curve, as discussed in Chapter 5. The first step is to draw a Bezier curve from the side view as in Figure 7.18.

Now, you must shape the underside of the belly to taper into the tail edge loop that we will be using for the extrusion. This is the most difficult part of the process, because the belly of a greyhound, as you can see in Figure 7.18, slopes downward and then upward into the bowel area, while the tail extends only from the upper part of the spinal cord. The best method I have found to accomplish this is to extrude a separate face along the curve of the tail, which we will create to match the topology of the area we will later graft it onto. In Figure 7.19 you can see the extra polygon create for the tail base. The reason that we do this is to allow us to sidestep an issue with the extrusion along a curve of two polygonal faces mirrored to one another (sine we are in symmetrical modeling mode), which would otherwise create a crossing effect of the resulting extrusion.

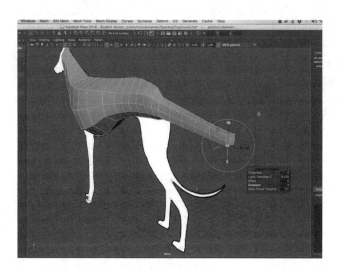

FIGURE 7.15   Pulling out the tail as an extrusion.

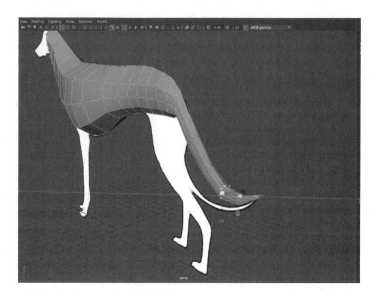

FIGURE 7.16 Editing the edge loops of the extruded tail.

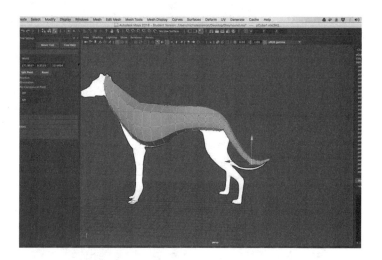

FIGURE 7.17 Working on matching the shape of the tail.

So we use the Create Polygon Tools, snapping to vertices, in order to make a perfect replica of the area we want to extrude for the tail, but as a single face with a single normal, which will allow it to flow down the Bezier curve I have created for the tail path.

Next, we will (in Object Selection mode) right-click the tail-base face and select the actual face subobject (not the object) and then select the

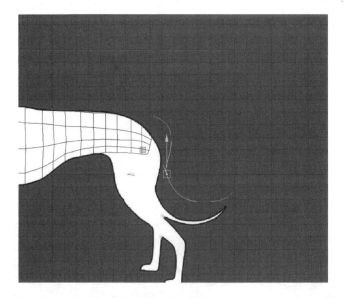

FIGURE 7.18   A better way of making the tail—using an extrusion along a curve.

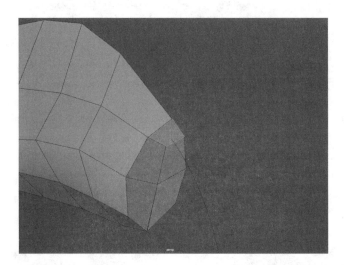

FIGURE 7.19   Choosing the top part of the torso to match the tail shape.

tail path curve. You will then use the Mesh Extrude Action, opening the dialogue box and making sure that Use Selected is set in the Curve Section. This will create the extrusion along the path of any curve you have selected to create a tapered tube, as you saw in Chapter 5, but with a polygonal face instead of a curve. In order to have enough sections to follow the path properly, you must create a higher number of Divisions in the Extrude Options than 1! Here I have used 16 divisions to get enough for the shape, and set Taper to a small value in order to narrow the tail cross section as it follows the path, creating the tapered tube shape. You can play around with the number of Divisions to your liking. My suggestion is to start with the minimal amount and increase it later if necessary.

The base of the tail is set such that it can easily be grafted or merged onto the main body of the creature after we finish with the symmetrical modeling, as it won't be able to be altered symmetrically at this point (Figures 7.20 and 7.21).

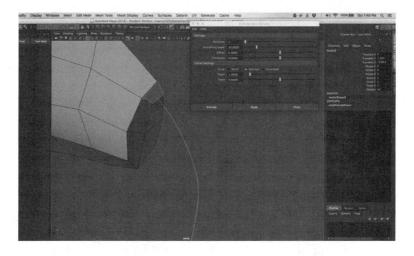

FIGURE 7.20   Pulling of the geometry to make the tail a separate entity.

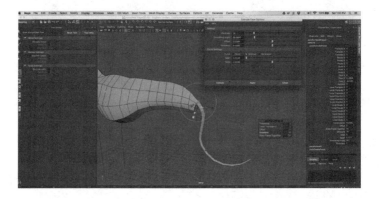

FIGURE 7.21   The tail face extrusion as a separate piece of geometry that we can merge onto the main body later.

EXTRUDING THE LIMBS

Now that we have the basic spinal length of the creature developed in the lowest resolution (minus the head), we can begin to extrude the limbs. One thing that I really like to do before this stage happens is to create some strategy based upon reference images. In Figure 7.22 below, you can see a reference image that clearly depicts the front of the greyhound body in perspective, which gives us a great view of how the forelimbs extrude from the body and come down to the ground.

As you can see in Figure 7.22, the legs clearly come straight down from the powerful chest of the animal, almost perfectly aligned with the y-axis

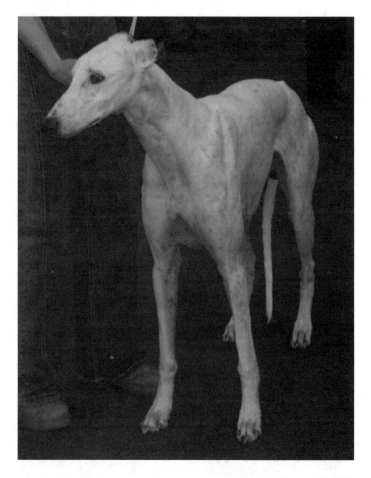

FIGURE 7.22 Another reference image for our limb extrusion. (Courtesy of Wikimedia Commons, CC BY-SA 3.0, https://commons.wikimedia.org/w/index.php?curid=349328)

(as most running quadrupeds do, such as horses, dogs, camels, bison, and goats). For this reason, we must carefully strategize which faces will be extruded as a branch off of the main spinal length model that we currently have. If we don't have a set of faces set up, we must manipulate the model slightly by shifting edge loops in order to create the area manually. As you can see in Figure 7.23, I have selected four quads that will serve as the main shoulder branch base, which will include the main bulk of the mid-body but not the faces adjacent to the spinal ridge or the ridge of the belly.

Now I will create the extrusion, making careful note to keep the extruded faces connected by Keep Faces Together, and pull them out slightly on the x-axis. This creates the base extrusion of the shoulder. If you look at Figure 7.24, it will appear very unnatural looking at first … it's up to us to shape the shoulder area later!

The next step is to then sculpt the shoulder area a little bit, making the area more natural and lifelike. I like to do this before I work on the leg extrusion, because I prefer to work with the most anatomically natural shape as I can to help me envision the end result better. This could be done after the basic leg extrusions; however, I find that it helps to keep the shapes as natural and rounded as possible to assist in the Visual Model being created in your head. This way you can spot irregularities and problems early in your modeling process, before you add so much detail that you can't fix them. In Figure 7.25 I rounded out the shoulder area a bit to give a more natural appearance.

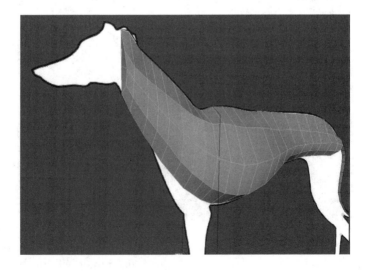

FIGURE 7.23 Choosing the faces for the front leg extrusion.

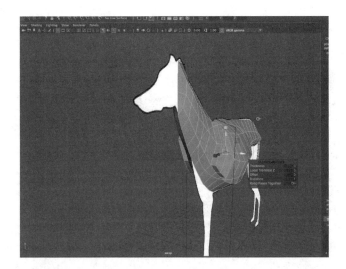

FIGURE 7.24 Pulling the legs outward first.

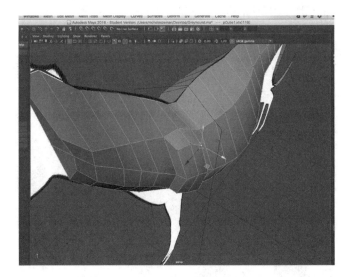

FIGURE 7.25 Rounding out the shoulder area.

The next step is to extrude the bottom faces of the shoulder to the ground plane to begin the leg shaping. Select the bottom faces and extrude them to the ground, scaling them together in the y-axis to flatten the polygons to a solid plane, as illustrated in Figure 7.26.

Next you will insert edge loops at the main junctures of the leg, such as the elbow, heel of the hand, and the top of the foot, as illustrated in Figure 7.27.

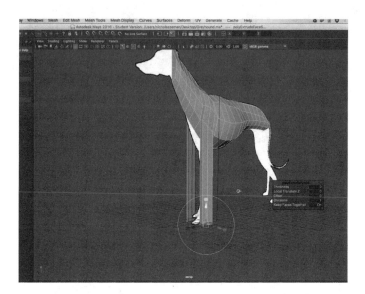

FIGURE 7.26   The extrusion downward of the legs.

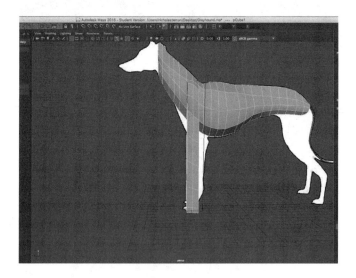

FIGURE 7.27   Adding edge loops to the leg cross section so we can shape the limb.

The next step is vital but tedious, where you will shape the vertices into the leg cross section. The first thing to keep in mind is that you must keep as few edge loops in the leg cross section as possible, only putting the most important one in at first. This is so you can pull and push individual vertices to create a rounded appearance for the leg, which is extremely important to shape right now. One pitfall of this low-poly modeling technique is that the extrusions tend to be highly flat and square at first, creating some work for the modeler to do by individually sculpting the vertices to form a more natural, rounded appearance. As you can see in Figure 7.28, the leg has been rounded in cross section from the original extrusion, making it seem more natural in appearance. This part of the process takes a while to get correct, and indeed you should take your time positioning and shaping the vertices at this lower resolution because it will naturally carry through any iterative resolution increase later.

Next we will focus on contouring the length of the leg bone, making it rounded until it becomes ovoid, by pulling the vertices running the edge loops downward out from the normal angle. During this time I like to scan all of the vertices along the legs and shoulders, making sure I tweak them slightly to create a fluid and even parameterization. This is a good time to roll the model around in perspective, assessing any small incremental changes that might need to happen before we begin to add more edge loops into the equation (Figure 7.29).

The next step is to pull out the paws from the three faces at the base of the leg. This will begin the construction of the forepaw, which extrudes straight forward from what was previously the base of the leg extrusion (Figure 7.30).

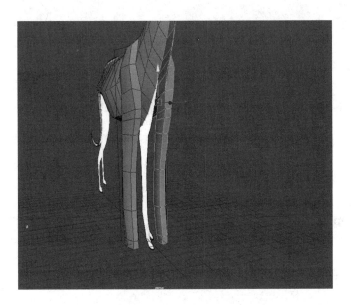

FIGURE 7.28   Rounding the cross section of the leg to be more like an ellipse.

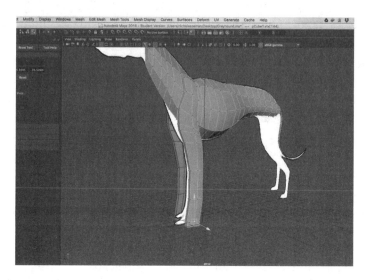

FIGURE 7.29   Slowly forming the shape of the front legs.

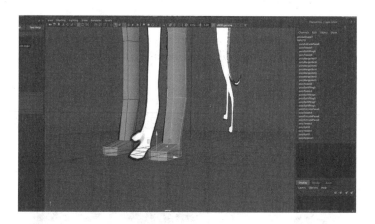

FIGURE 7.30   Extruding the front paws forward.

I have tapered it in the *y*-axis slightly to give a better representation of the slant of the angle between the wrist and the toes as they touch the ground.

Now we will extrude the front heel out from the back of the front paw with the single face, extending it slightly and scaling the face to exhibit some type of taper for us to alter later (Figure 7.31).

Next we will insert the edge loop into the forepaw and create the nice, vaulted shape that the dog paw possesses. Figure 7.32 illustrates the extra

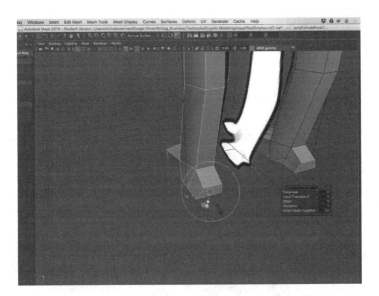

FIGURE 7.31 Pulling out the heel of the front paws.

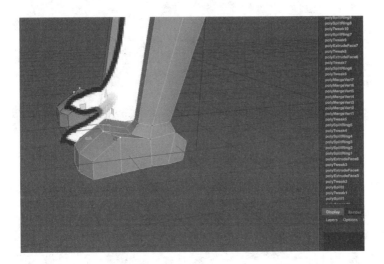

FIGURE 7.32 The basic shaping of the paw.

edge loop and the resulting shape. This shape is really important in setting the low-resolution shape of the paw area, because it will be far more difficult down the road to shape a higher resolution mesh.

The next step is to begin inserting edge loops as cross sections of the front legs, and *only* cross-section edge loops! We want to shape the leg slowly and efficiently, making the divisions only where we need them to shape the taper and flaring of the leg as it appears in our reference material (Figure 7.33).

At this juncture we don't really want to spend too much time sculpting in the finer detail. We still have big-picture work to do!

The next stage of development in our model is to create the back legs by extruding all of the faces that make up the hip-bone structure. We will select the top faces that connect the center as well with the back legs, since from behind they make a horseshoe shape and the hip's bone structure actually extends outward from the body (Figure 7.34).

Next we will extrude the bottom faces downward to the ground plane in order to make the full length of the leg. In the case of a canine leg,

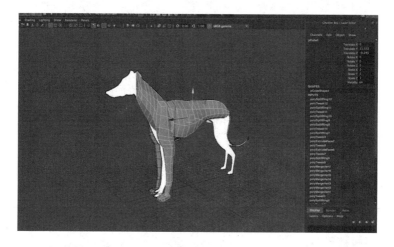

FIGURE 7.33   Continuing to edit the front leg shape.

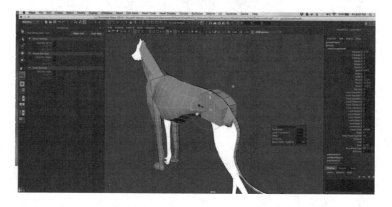

FIGURE 7.34   Extruding the hind legs outward first to form the hips.

the faces will be back slightly at an angle, which will give us the beginning shape of the length of the leg, which we will fill in afterward and shape with edge loops (Figure 7.35).

Next we will sculpt the hip in the x- and y-axes, slowly tweaking the vertices one by one until we achieve a round appearance. There really is no shortcut to this step; you literally have to move each vertex individually and round out the hard corners of the extruded faces. This is also extremely important to do now, before you add in multiple new edge loops that will make it near impossible to manipulate the model successfully afterward. One thing to constantly keep in mind is the simple arc that we have been using all over our organic modeling technique. Organic surfaces use this simple arc in all manner of locations, especially rounded areas such as the hips and the muscles of the body. If you can shape the vertices into an arc along two or more axes, you will achieve a much more natural shape. It's also one of the pitfalls of novice modelers to leave these areas far too square after making the extrusion. Remember to follow the cross-section shape all the way down the leg and make it as oval as possible (Figures 7.36 and 7.37).

Once the hips have been rounded and satisfyingly shaped to reflect the physiology of the animal, the next step is to add in the cross-section edge loops of the leg. Be careful to only add in five or six at first, which will represent the major joints and changes of angle along the length of the leg.

FIGURE 7.35 (See color insert.) Pulling the legs down with another extrusion to the ground plane.

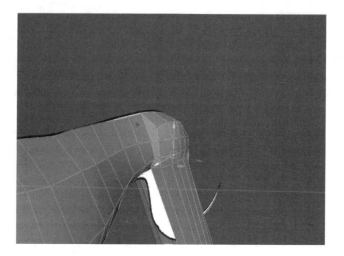

FIGURE 7.36 Rounding the shape of the hip.

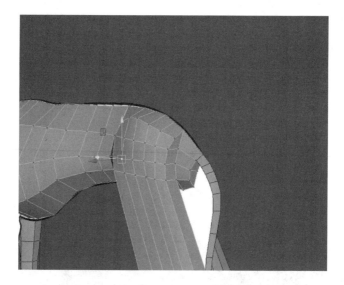

FIGURE 7.37 Vertex-by-vertex editing is tedious, but necessary. It's best to do this in the early stages of modeling.

This is important because the next step is to begin to shape the taper and flaring of the leg between the joints and to get the neutral bend in the leg correct. A dog's hind leg is similar to ours, with a hip socket and a knee at the top, *but* the major difference is that the foot is extremely elongated, with the ball making contact to the ground. The heel is the "reverse angle" joint that many people naturally assume is some kind of joint that we humans don't have. In reality they have the same bone structure as we do, just different placement.

When inserting these edge loops we want to be very careful here to angle them correctly. The normal, or perpendicular angle to the edge loop, should be aiming at the next edge loop going down the leg. We want to avoid having edge loops with normals that match world positioning, which is what would happen if we never angled them at all (Figure 7.38).

Next we will need to extrude the paw forward, just as we did with the front. The rear paw has a very similar shape, so we can just copy what we did in the front paw with the basic shaping. We extrude the main face forward, then add in an edge loop in the center to lift the middle part upward like a vaulted ceiling (Figure 7.39).

There are times when you are modeling at this initial, low-polygon stage that you have too much detail in certain areas that is slowing you down by forcing you to contend with vertices that don't need to be there. In the case of the hind leg, it appears that there were too many cross-section edge loops in the hind legs, which is now becoming difficult to work with when they get bunched up together in the lower hind-leg structure. As soon as I find myself in this situation, I always scan the structure of the polygons to determine exactly where I can strip out some edge loops without drastically altering the model. Remember that in this low-polygon stage we really want the bare minimum of edge loops. In Figure 7.40 I have highlighted two edge

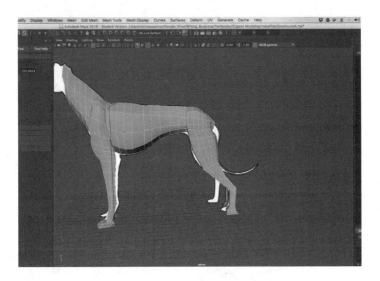

FIGURE 7.38   Inserting the leg edge loops and forming the shape, bit by bit.

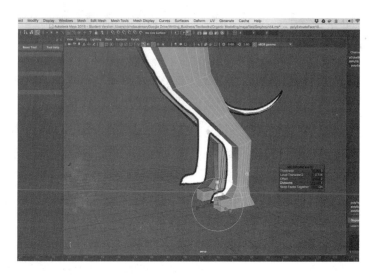

FIGURE 7.39   Modeling the back paws.

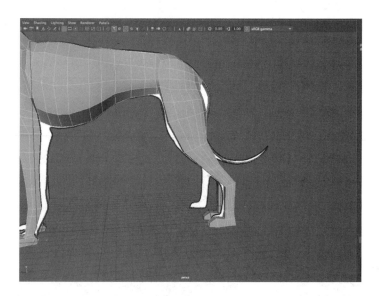

FIGURE 7.40   These two edge loops are unnecessary, so we can remove them completely and reduce our overhead.

loops that aren't really giving me any extra dimensionality or curvature in the hind-leg area. Once I have selected them, I will choose Mesh > Delete Edge/Vertex from the pull-down menu. You must use this option for edge loops or it will leave the vertices intact! We want to delete both the edge and the vertex (Figures 7.40 through 7.42).

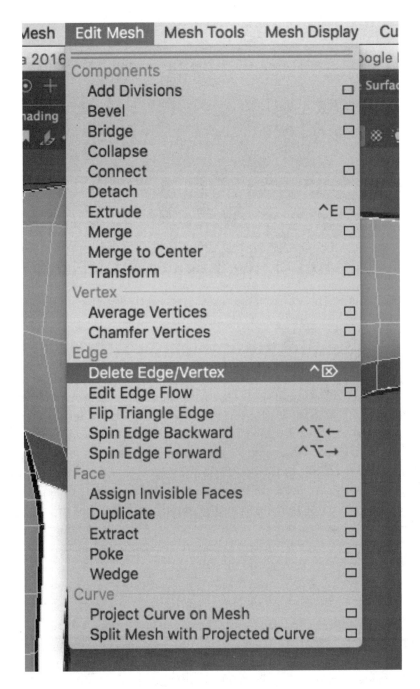

FIGURE 7.41   Using Delete Edge/Vertex will totally remove the edge loop selected without leaving any artifact geometry.

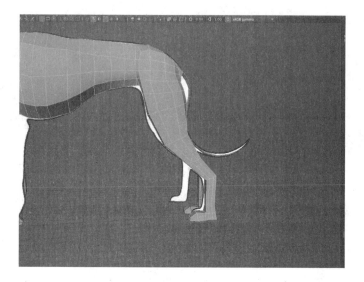

FIGURE 7.42 (See color insert.) The resulting shape has the same contours with fewer vertices.

MODELING THE HEAD

The head of any animal, as most modelers will tell you, is usually at least as detailed as the rest of the body. In many cases, depending on the level of detail you intend to show, it will be up to three times more dense in terms of polygons than the rest of the body. For this reason, the head is modeled last in the basic modeling steps. In this case, I am skipping over the second level of detailing on the body in order to preserve time and keep the process moving. The head of a human is going to be far more difficult, due to the added level of complexity of the mouth structure, but the dog has a profoundly humanlike face, minus the snout. The eyes of a dog are very expressive, and therefore no small amount of detail must be created when placing them on our greyhound model.

Step 1: Detailed Reference Images

In Figures 7.43 and 7.44 I have added some detailed reference images of the greyhound head as image planes. These will give me the added guidance I will need to shape and sculpt the head into a realistic scale and dimension.

Since we modeled our spinal tube first, from cervical spine to the tip of the tail, we now have to create the shape of the skull by extruding the pieces at the termination forward, to create the first few divisions, ending right *before* the extension of the jaw and snout! This is important because

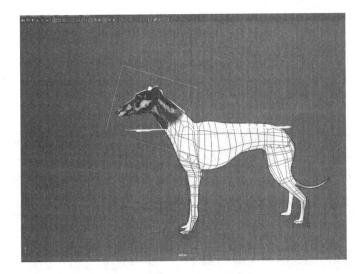

FIGURE 7.43 Using a higher resolution head reference image is important for higher detail areas.

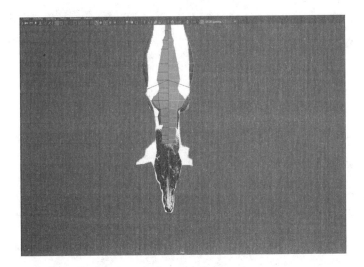

FIGURE 7.44 The top of the head reference image plane.

we want the split to be at the point of rotation of the jaw. The one caveat to the extrusion of the end pieces here is that they will create hidden "inner" faces, which must be deleted with every extrusion, or after the editing has been done and the extrusions are complete.

The next few steps we will be extruding the jaw and snout forward, slowing and carefully shaping them with the most basic of tweaks to the vertices in a very low resolution. The snout and the jaw, as we can see in Figures 7.45 through 7.48, are independent entities, and they can be independently shaped late by inserting extra edge loops where needed. Each piece extruded and tapered will be detailed later, after the rest of the facial structures have been modeled.

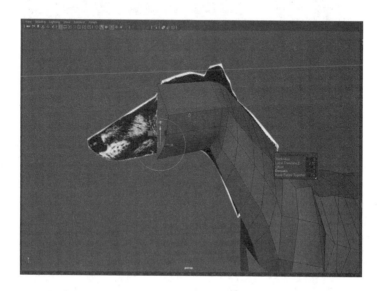

FIGURE 7.45   Extruding the geometry of the head till the snout begins.

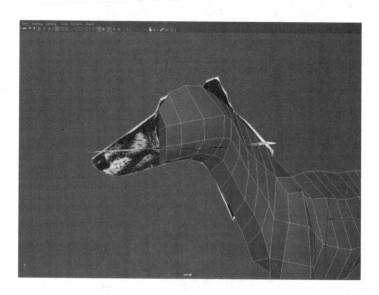

FIGURE 7.46   Inserting edge loops for further editing.

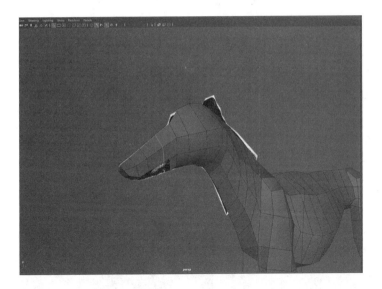

FIGURE 7.47   Pulling the top snout outward and shaping it.

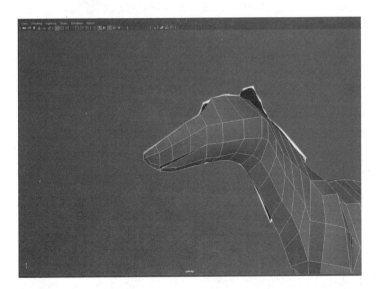

FIGURE 7.48   Pulling out the jaw with an extrusion.

The structure of a dog's face is vastly different than the structure of a human face, not just because of the long snout and the jaw, but also because of the placement of the eyes. Human eye direction is directly aligned with our forward vector (direction perpendicular to the ground), and so the eye sockets face straight forward. The dog eye sockets are slightly recessed into

FIGURE 7.49 The front and foreshortened view of the greyhound. This is a particularly difficult perspective to model from. (Courtesy of Vincent Eisfeld, CC BY-SA 4.0, https://commons.wikimedia.org/w/index.php?curid=41049216)

the skull and do not face straight forward; however, when looking at the foreshortened view, as you can see in Figure 7.49, it appears as if they do. You can also see in Figure 7.49, the eyes and eyelids are far less elaborate and folded than a human's eyelids. The good news is that we don't have nearly as much work to do in sculpting them.

Creating the Eye Socket

Now here is where the practical application of radial edge looping can clearly be seen. Radial edge looping is the only way we can get a proper structure for the eye inside of the head geometry. The first step is to insert the edge loops selectively to increase the detail around the brow ridge, eye socket, and adjacent areas. In this case, we absolutely do not want to add the edge loops all the way through the entire model but instead terminate the extra geometry before it extends past the neck. You can use the multicut tool to set up the areas with partial edge loops, which terminate wherever you want. Figure 7.50 illustrates the insertion of a partial edge loop so that we can begin to define the focus of the eye.

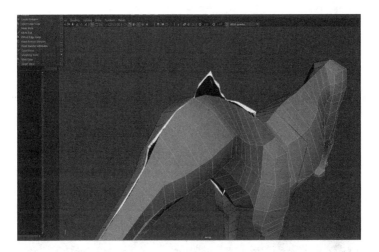

FIGURE 7.50   Adding a partial edge loop for extra detail in the eye socket area.

In order to create the radial geometry for the eye socket, we must first select a pole vertex to build the area. One of the important things to know about this pole vertex is that it should be approximately where the eyeball would be if looking at the eye straight down the vector. This will be the center of the eye socket. Figures 7.51 and 7.52 show the selected pole vertex.

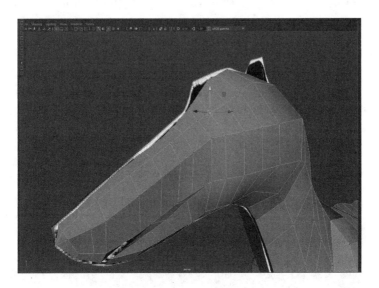

FIGURE 7.51   Choosing the pole for the radial edge loop structure that will generate the eye socket.

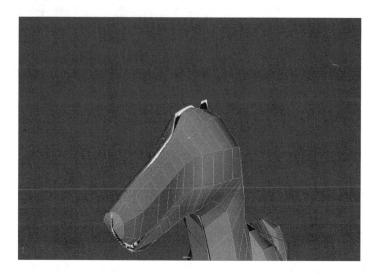

FIGURE 7.52   The front view check to see if this is a good place for an eyeball!

As we learned in Chapter 6, you can create the inner radial edge loop by using the multicut tool. This should be very tight to the pole vertex, as you can see in Figure 7.53.

Now we insert the radial edge loops around the center, slowly shaping the area by carefully tweaking the vertices around the pole to form the shape of the eye socket (Figure 7.54). This is one of the most tedious parts

FIGURE 7.53   Beginning the radial structure.

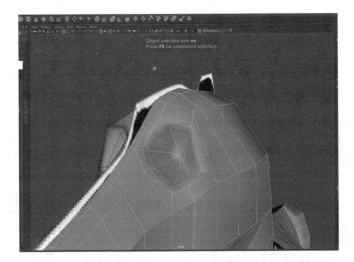

FIGURE 7.54   Building the eye socket with simple vertex transforms and inserting radial edge loops.

of the model; because there is no global method of positioning the vertices in the proper place, it's left to the modeler to create the basic appearance of the skull and eye socket. One very useful trick to sculpting this area, as you can see in Figure 7.55, is to create a simple sphere representing the eyeball, which you can position and use as a 3D reference to slowly and carefully tweak the positions of the vertices around it.

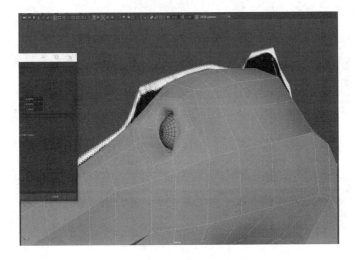

FIGURE 7.55   Adding a new edge loop on the outside of the eye socks by using Insert Edge Loop.

The next steps are long and will require a lot of patience as you slowly sculpt, with minute vertex tweaks, the area surrounding that eyeball reference. You can see the results of these tweaks in Figures 7.56 through 7.58. Try to pay attention to the brow ridge and look at the model from as many dimensions as you can.

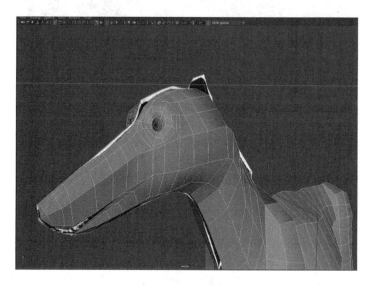

FIGURE 7.56   A few more edge loops in the eye socket provide better detail.

FIGURE 7.57   Adding an edge loop in the head will usually add it across the body, which we want to avoid.

FIGURE 7.58 The semicompleted head structure from perspective. Always check your eye placement from several perspectives while modeling.

Building the Ears

At this point the head should start to be much more detailed than the body. This is entirely normal for any organic mammal model, because the head has so much detail in it. Since the ears are such a prominent feature of a dog, we should pay some attention to them next. Ears in humans are a very radial structure, but the dog has a much more triangular shape, with the radial part only being the actual hole that enters into the head. The ears of a dog are also extrusions from the skull, which can be pulled out from the faces behind the eyebrow ridge. Figure 7.59 illustrates the two polygon faces as I extrude them away from the head. These faces will be scaled as a tapering structure, keeping the first extrusion close to the skull. The next extrusion will be much the same, tapered close to a rounded point and skewed slightly off from the previous vector, so that the whole structure looks like a thick, triangular hemisphere pulling off of the skull, as you can see in Figure 7.60.

Now we must create the cupping of the inner ear, by creating a half-radial edge loop with the multicut tool, cutting the contiguous edges in the inner ear (Figure 7.61). This will allow us to create that basic cupped shape by pulling those inner vertices and faces inward with another inner extrusion, as you can see in Figure 7.62. As you extrude the cup area inside, it will form the inner scoop naturally. The inside of the ears are not usually

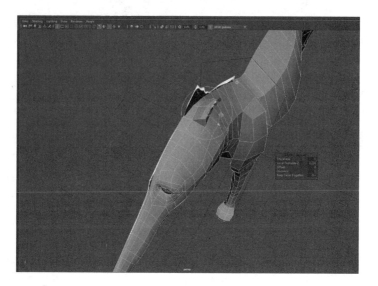

FIGURE 7.59   Extruding the ear base.

FIGURE 7.60   Continuing with the ear extrusion and shape.

something we see in great detail, so pay more attention to the overall shape than the inside area.

After shaping the ears, there is certainly much more detail work to do on the head by making minor tweaks and sculpting, but the prominent foundational features and appearance of the greyhound head, with skull, snout, jaw, eyes, and ears, are there to improve as you wish (Figure 7.63).

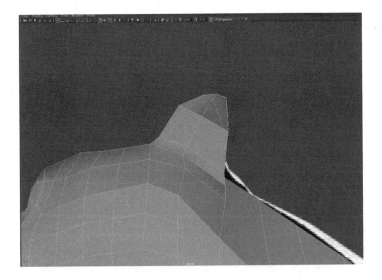

FIGURE 7.61   Inserting the semi-radial edge loop for the inner ear.

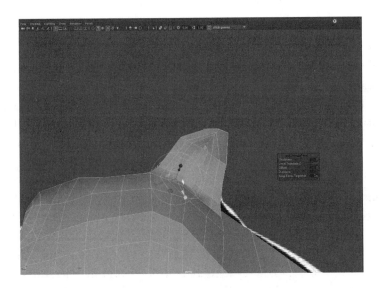

FIGURE 7.62   Using the Extrude I can now shape the inner cup of the dog ear.

DETAILING THE BODY

Inserting Edge Loops

Now that the basic structure of the head has been created and saved, we go back to the main body to do some more work! Of course, for an extremely low-resolution mobile-based game we *could* just clean it up and go, but we

FIGURE 7.63 (See color insert.) The ear from a perspective.

might want some normal maps or just a high-resolution version for the cinematic scenes. Either way, the important thing here is to selectively add detail where we need it, inserting edge loops in the areas we want to fill out or created a more rounded appearance. The first place I can prominently see that needs to be rounded is the rib cage and belly area. The edge loops as currently laid out do not have enough points in the cross section to create a proper torso shape. Therefore I will simply add in some edge loops on either side of the spinal center, which will give us the horseshoe shape discussed in the Animal Physiology of the spine previously. Figure 7.64 shows the inserted edge loops. Notice the broken edge loop by the neck, which is an artifact of adding the extra detail to the head without adding it to the entire body. This can be joined now, using the multicut tool. The intention is always to separate the increased detail of the head from the body, but when there is an opportunity to merge the flow of the geometry, it's always best to do so. These edge loops can now be edited to raise upward, flattening out the back as it spreads away from the spine center. This is a perfect example of a global tweak that greatly improves the flow of the geometry. I can also add these in the belly, below the torso, to round out that area as well, as you can see in Figure 7.65.

These are just two of many, many adjustments and edits that you can make to the overall shaping of the model, which will result in a much smoother and more realistic appearance. The paws and legs here are not

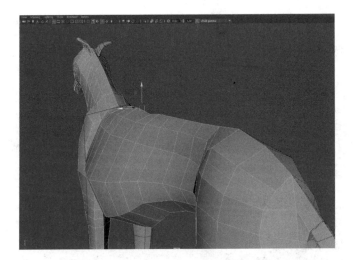

FIGURE 7.64 I add the edge loop on the outside of the spinal ridge to form the horseshoe shape.

FIGURE 7.65 Rounding out the entire form with vertex editing.

complete, but for the sake of brevity I am leaving the finer points of their modeling out of the material.

Working with Smoothing

Polygonal smoothing, as we have seen previously, is the doubling of vertices and the attempt to round out otherwise hard edges. On a global scale, it can do a decent job, but be wary of just hitting the Smooth button

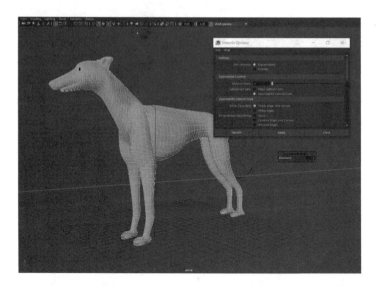

FIGURE 7.66   The smoothed version.

and thinking you are finished! Often the smooth will create strange or unusual results, depending on the geometry you feed it. Figure 7.66 is a basic smooth, run on the entire model. A slightly better idea is to double the faces and work with the sculpting tools to fine-tune the mesh yourself, where you can only change the areas that need adjusting.

Mirroring and Completion

The model, as it currently stands, is still in two halves, one mirroring the other. We want to keep this setup as long as possible, so that we don't double the amount of work for ourselves. But there will finally come a time when you must merge the two halves together. In this case, we will use the mirror geometry tool, which will create a mirror image of your polygonal mesh and attach it by merging the vertices along the seams. Note that if you have any vertices along that center line that aren't exactly on top of one another, they will not properly merge together. Figure 7.67 shows the merge before it happens (it's better to do this with the lower resolution version, before you do any smoothing). Figure 7.68 shows the mirror geometry box with the mirrored geometry completed. Now we can attach the tail, using the Merge Vertices tools to "weld" the tail piece to the flank of the spine. Once the spine is attached, it should be a matter of deleting the history and running any version of smooth that you want to increase the polygon count to prepare it for your sculpting and deformative tweaking.

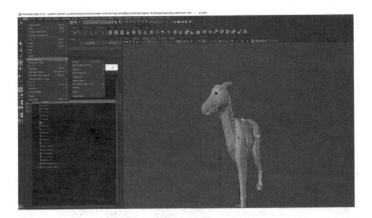

FIGURE 7.67 Deleting the instanced half and preparing for the mirroring of the geometry.

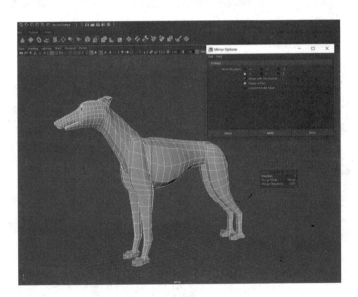

FIGURE 7.68 The completed, low-resolution model.

Options for increasing geometry are variable:

1. *Simple Smooth*: This, as discussed, will increase polygons exponentially and attempt to round out any hard angle in the flow (Figure 7.69).

2. *Add Divisions*: Adding divisions will double the poly count but not attempt any smoothing (Figure 7.70).

FIGURE 7.69 A full poly smooth version.

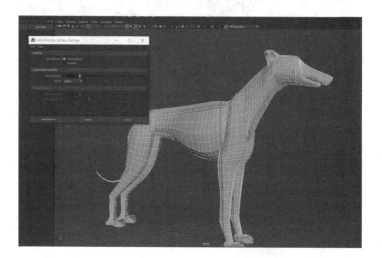

FIGURE 7.70 A version with divisions added to double the polygons while retaining the original shape.

3. *Add Divisions, Smooth*: Once the divisions have been added, you can run a smooth on the result. This will quadruple the amount of polygons but the smooth will be far less dramatic and will retain your original lines much more conservatively. This is the best options for high-res sculpting (Figure 7.71).

FIGURE 7.71 A smooth operator on the doubled version; provides a less "mushy" result.

FINE-TUNE MODELING WITH DEFORMERS

In order to tweak the overall shape of certain areas of your model, it may be necessary to use various deformation techniques that will assist you in proportionally editing the geometry in certain targeted areas. This allows you to tweak and edit large areas in certain ways, such as pinching or bulging parts while leaving other parts alone. Some of the most commonly needed adjustments to any organic model are often the taper and flare of areas, which would be very hard to do using sculpting or individual vertex adjustments. Once the model has been completed and the geometry has been exponentially increased to allow for higher detailed adjustments, simple vertex offsets won't be available. The tools to edit the model at this point should be based on some sort of proportional influence, such as the deformation-based modeling tools can offer.

In this case the lattice is an excellent way to independently tweak areas of the higher resolution model using a small set of vertices. It allows me to make some fairly minor tweaks to a few lattice points and affect the model smoothly and with local control (Figure 7.72).

The lattice has variable levels of divisions, as you can see in Figure 7.73, where you are able to subdivide the lattice in three dimensions, but only *before* you start to add lattice tweaks. Once you offset the lattice points you can no longer increase or decrease the level of divisions. The lattice can be used in

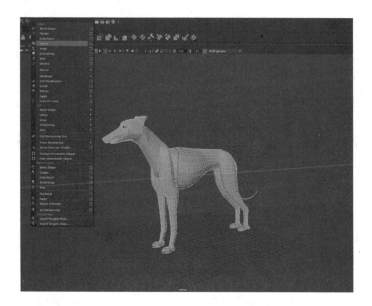

FIGURE 7.72 (See color insert.) Creating a lattice to tweak the model.

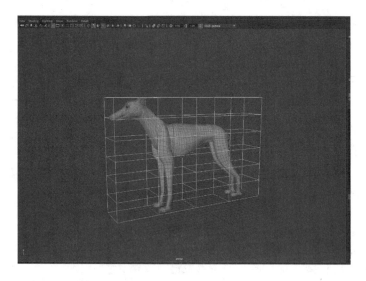

FIGURE 7.73 A lattice can be applied to the entire model at once.

a locally selected number of vertices, or it can be applied to the entire mesh. My suggestion is to select an area and apply the lattice to that area instead of applying it to the entire object, because this will help to avoid unnecessary movement in vertices far away from the intended edits (Figure 7.74). Figures 7.75 and 7.76 illustrate the selected area of influence and how the

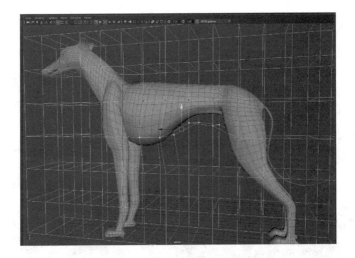

FIGURE 7.74   I use the lattice points to make minute changes to specific areas.

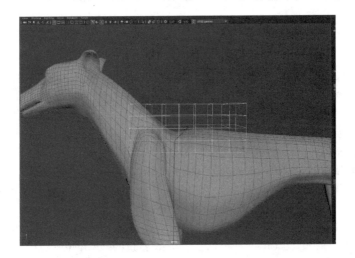

FIGURE 7.75   Applying a lattice to one specific part. In this case I want to remove the strange bump in between the shoulders.

lattice can be targeted to a specific location. In this case there is an annoying bump below the neck that I want to edit, and I will apply the deformation of the lattice to only that area, which helps me target a little better.

Sculpting

Although there are tools built specifically for the sculpting and fine-tuning of very heavily detailed geometry, Maya itself has some simple

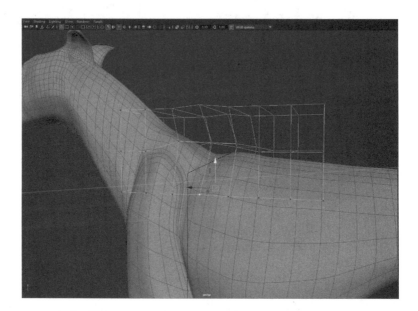

FIGURE 7.76   Offsetting the lattice point to change the shape of the base of the neck.

sculpting tools that can greatly ease the work of individual vertex editing when the model has begun to get too dense. This works by editing areas of the model based on normals (the outward and inward vectors of a surface). These sculpt tools can provide results where other modeling tools can't, such as my upper shoulder indention in the greyhound model, which was an artifact of the smoothing process. Using the sculpt tool I can pull the vertices away from their current normal, lifting the bump out of the skin as if I were working with clay. There are also many, many other brush tools that allow a greater amount of movements of the vertices based on various algorithms; however, the two most often used are Sculpt (normal-based movement) and Smooth, which mellows out the differences in normals between a soft area of the model. Both of these tools can be very useful in making minor and major changes to a high-density polygonal surface that would otherwise be impossible. Tools like the Sculpt tool make modeling a much more organic process, allowing the artist to feel more like a sculptor of clay than an architect. But the primary model, as we have seen, can't really be "sculpted" from nothing. The base model, on which we have spent the focus of this section, must be constructed, edited, and adjusted at a ground resolution

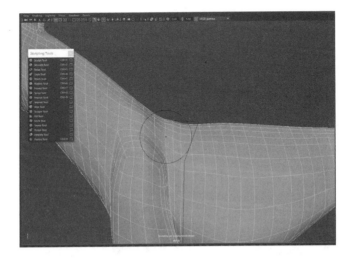

FIGURE 7.77 Applying a brush-based deformer to the geometry can get me some better results than a lattice.

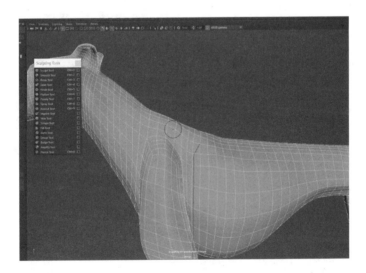

FIGURE 7.78 Working out that shoulder bump with the simple Sculpt tool.

level by hand before it can become properly structured enough to be sculpted with final detail. This is the secret to the process of organic modeling. In order to get creative and detailed with brush-based tools, you must generate a base-level model that is anatomically proportioned and constructed (Figures 7.77 and 7.78)!

CHAPTER 8

Modeling Organic Structures with Nonorganic Techniques

INTRODUCTION

Many, many creatures that you might be asked to model are not in need of a seamless, skinned polygonal structure. There are many examples of hard-bodied organisms, such as insects, arthropods, crustaceans, and mollusks. These are animals that have a hard, exterior shell (exoskeleton) separated into segments. These segments, from an external perspective, can be seen as more "assembled" than sculpted.

If we let the form follow the function in terms of modeling practice, we can imagine that the organic modeling methodology, as described in Chapter 4, is not entirely necessary. In fact, it is quite unsuited to the hard-shelled animal structures as a whole because of the need to create multiple, jointed pieces, which may have drastically different shapes.

Each segment can be seen as a model unto itself, or at least each series of shapes, and we can expand our modeling minds to use nonorganic techniques for certain types of structures.

THE ASSEMBLY LINE

Using the assembly line methodology, we can break up any hard-bodied entity into the appropriate pieces. This is very similar to how a car body is put together; we identify and build each shape to fit together with the connecting shapes.

Figures 8.1 and 8.2, respectively, show the pieces of automobile parts and a common beetle, divided into its various pieces. If you see some similarity, then you are correct! The assembly of an insect, a worm, or a lobster all have very similar structures. Therefore, when modeling them, we might take similar approaches.

Blueprinting

Blueprinting refers to the layout and planning of the pieces in your creature or automobile. It can be achieved by examining a model, by either reference image or actual anatomical drawings. Or if you want to really get up close and personal you can go out and find a dead/dried specimen to poke around with in your free time. Keep in mind that we are *only* concerned with the external structures of the animal and not the internal organs and connective tissues. Those will not be visible.

Blueprinting includes making a list, or visual dictionary (with drawings, just like Figure 8.2 and our beetle). This will help you figure out what needs to be constructed and what needs to have adjacent,

FIGURE 8.1 Pieces of a car body, laid outside of a factory. In the same way, many exoskeleton creatures are assembled in pieces. (Courtesy of Tony Harrison from Farnborough, UK—Auto Italia Spring Car Day, Brooklands, May 2010 IMG_9092Uploaded by AlbertHerring, CC BY-SA 2.0, https://commons. wikimedia.org/w/index.php?curid=29228477)

Taf. 50.

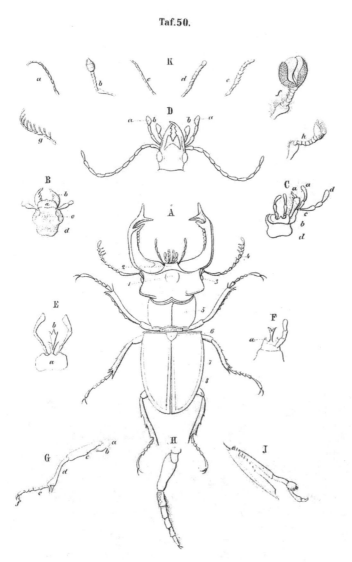

FIGURE 8.2 The assembly of an arthropod or insect. (Courtesy of Wikimedia Commons, https://commons.wikimedia.org/w/index.php?curid=1189647)

form-fitting edges. Creating a list of these pieces will help you organize the construction of the pieces in a fast, efficient manner.

The nice thing about our nonorganic modeling methodology is that we don't have to stick to any one modeling method for the entire creature; we can use whatever technique works for the segment at hand, provided we keep in mind that the segments must fit together properly in the end! Think of this as a 3D puzzle game using Legos. Each piece can be independently modeled, but if certain parts don't match edges and shapes they won't be able to snap together in the end.

Primary Pieces (Unique Shapes)

Most creatures in the category of hard-bodied animals have one or two pieces that are completely unique and only occur once, such as the head and the torso/carapace section, which the legs extend from (if there are any legs).

A carapace or torso piece can be modeled as two separate pieces that fit together or as a solid cube that is edited to take on the shape of the intended result.

Segmented Pieces

These are shapes that are created by pieces overlapping other pieces, commonly found in the abdomen and body of insects, arthropods, and worms. Each piece is a repetition of the former, with slightly different dimensions and shapes, which fit together perfectly. These should always be modeled together, one after the other, and placed in descending order (Figure 8.3).

FIGURE 8.3 (See color insert.)   A closeup of a bee's abdomen, which clearly illustrates the segmented construction. (Courtesy of USGS Native Bee Inventory and Monitoring Laboratory, Beltsville, USA,—Andrena-nuda,-female,-abdomen_ 2012-08-03-17.01.27-ZS-PMax, https://commons.wikimedia.org/w/index.php? curid=24746483)

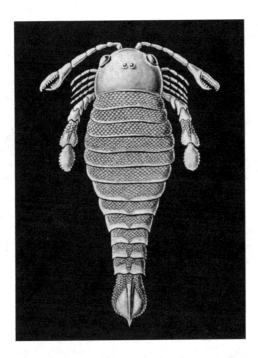

FIGURE 8.4 An extinct, segmented sea scorpion. (Courtesy of Wikimedia Commons, https://commons.wikimedia.org/w/index.php? curid=49516469)

Limbs are also segmented items, extending as they do in specific jointed segments from the center of the body. These too, can be modeled independently, and indeed if you see Figure 8.4 of our bee in flight, you can clearly see that the legs have unique shapes for each segment! Depending on how detailed this will be rendered, the legs can take a rather rough shape, since insect legs are generally too small for the naked eye to discern at a distance. But if you need the creature to be seen in close-up, you will need to study the shaping of the legs in detail to recreate them.

MODELING WITH SEGMENTS

To create a segmented animal, we must first begin with the shape of the cross section of the segment. In Figure 8.5, I created a simple horseshoe shape with a Bezier curve. This will serve as the primary segment curve, and we will use it to completely build the majority of our trilobite animal.

I duplicate the curve and move it back, slightly scaling it downward, and then lofting these two curves together as a polygon. Figure 8.6 shows the result of this loft.

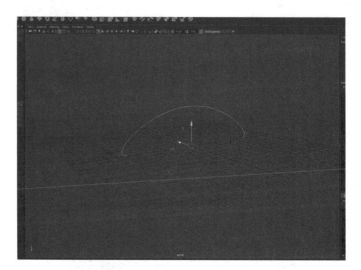

FIGURE 8.5   The curve that will be the basis of the entire structure. The slight pinching at the bottom will give the slight appearance of depth in the surface.

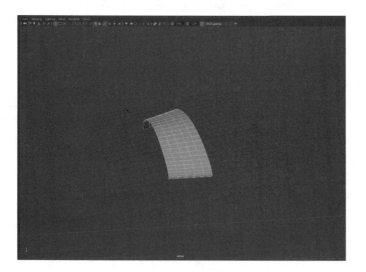

FIGURE 8.6   The lofted surface.

Using our modeling by duplication method, as previously discussed, we can scale, rotate, and offset this curve multiple times to create the wireframe of our creature (Figure 8.7).

Lofting all of these curves together creates an interesting shape, as in Figure 8.8, but the surface is not segmented. We can make it look partially

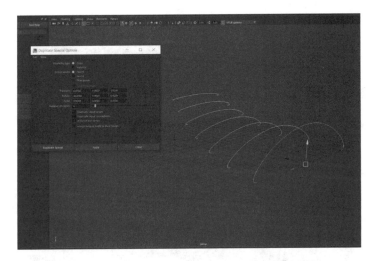

FIGURE 8.7 Modeling by duplication makes the same curve, copied and offset, a perfect tool for creating the body of a segmented animal.

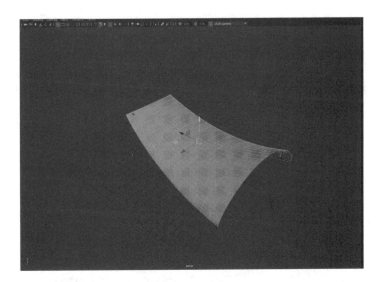

FIGURE 8.8 All of the curves lofted as a single surface.

segmented through model manipulation, as in Figure 8.9, but this is not the best way of approaching this.

The best way to create the segments we want is to actually create each one independently of the previous. By duplicating the curves and offsetting them properly, we can create one segment per pair of

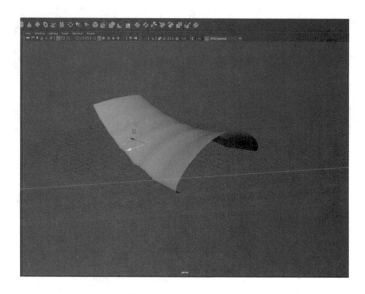

FIGURE 8.9   Indentions to the surface to produce the illusion of segments.

cross-section curves, resulting in the complete segmented shape as seen in Figures 8.10 and 8.11.

Building the rounded head of our trilobite should be easy; all we have to do now is to duplicate the curves, once again, and rotate them into the rounded, curved shape and the resulting surface is seen in Figures 8.12 and 8.13.

FIGURE 8.10   Instead of lofting a single surface, the curves are used to loft multiple surfaces.

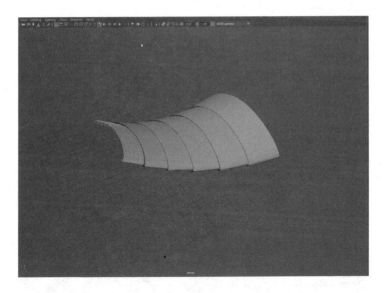

FIGURE 8.11 (See color insert.) Each segment slightly fits into the previous.

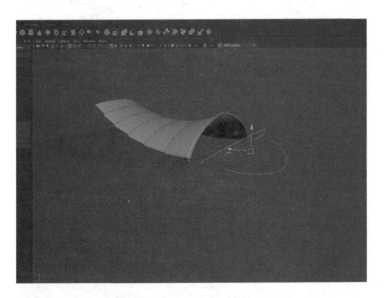

FIGURE 8.12 The same curve is used to produce the head piece.

We can build the tail in a similar manner (Figure 8.14) by duplicating the curves and expanding them horizontally, then lofting them as a separate segment, as you can see in Figure 8.15.

We can then build the belly by creating another curve, shaped to the length and height of our segments. This curve does *not* have to be perfectly

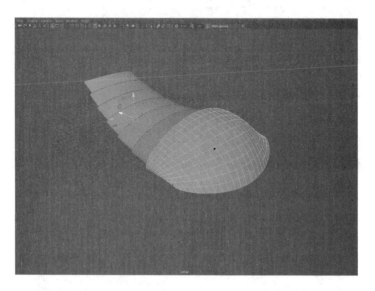

FIGURE 8.13 Once again, a loft between curves is used.

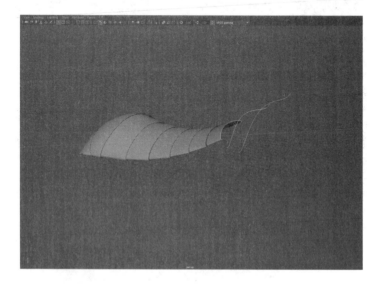

FIGURE 8.14 The tail piece uses the same curves, but flared out to produce a whale-like appearance.

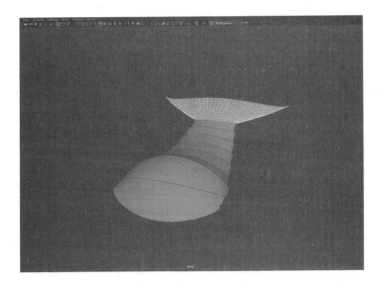

FIGURE 8.15   The lofted tail.

fitted to anything, since this is a segmented animal, and as long as the resulting surface fits into the other without interpenetrating, it will be viewed as accurate. Figures 8.16 through 8.18 should show you the basic gist of the belly creation.

FIGURE 8.16   Building the belly curve.

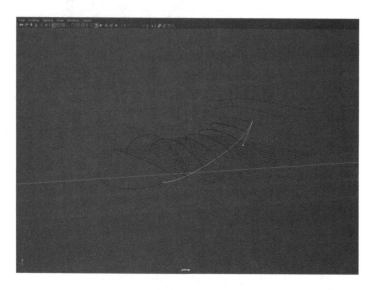

FIGURE 8.17   Adjusting the curve in the cross section to match the upward sweep.

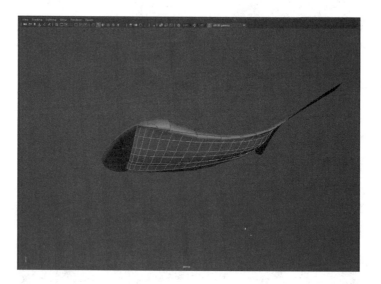

FIGURE 8.18   The bottom of the belly lofted between two belly curves.

Creating the limbs of a segmented animal like an insect, the tapered tube, or flared tube in this case, by way of extrusion, is a good way to generate the geometry. The shapes of the segmented tubes can be created by the profile curve, extended along either a distance or a specific path curve.

Repeating this action will create the subsequent joints in a multisegmented arm or leg (Figures 8.19 through 8.22).

Figure 8.22 is an illustration of a small flair, by extruding all faces of the head carapace, spiking them by making multiple extrusions.

FIGURE 8.19   Another view of the belly, which has been lofted from the profile curves along the length of the upper segments.

FIGURE 8.20   Creating the arm with a cross section and a path curve.

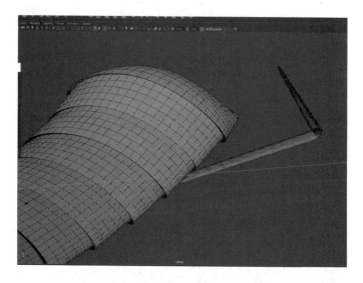

FIGURE 8.21   Extruded arm segments.

FIGURE 8.22 (See color insert.)   Some fancy spiking for our trilobite.

The basics of the segmented forms can be seen here by easily using a single curve to generate simple flowing lines through duplication and offsets. Modeling segmented forms can be a lot easier than other animals because each piece can be separately created and edited and there is no need for a seamless skin with muscular structures deforming it from underneath.

Index